Numerical Linear Algebra and the Applications

Numerical Linear Algebra and the Applications

Editors

Khalide Jbilou
Marilena Mitrouli

MDPI • Basel • Beijing • Wuhan • Barcelona • Belgrade • Manchester • Tokyo • Cluj • Tianjin

Editors
Khalide Jbilou
Université du Littoral Côte d'Opale
France

Marilena Mitrouli
National and Kapodistrian University of Athens
Greece

Editorial Office
MDPI
St. Alban-Anlage 66
4052 Basel, Switzerland

This is a reprint of articles from the Special Issue published online in the open access journal *Mathematics* (ISSN 2227-7390) (available at: https://www.mdpi.com/journal/mathematics/special_issues/numelinear_algebra).

For citation purposes, cite each article independently as indicated on the article page online and as indicated below:

LastName, A.A.; LastName, B.B.; LastName, C.C. Article Title. *Journal Name* **Year**, *Volume Number*, Page Range.

ISBN 978-3-0365-2165-7 (Hbk)
ISBN 978-3-0365-2166-4 (PDF)

Contents

About the Editors

Khalide Jbilou

is a professor of mathematics in the mathematics laboratory LMPA of the University Littoral Côte d'Opale (ULCO). He obtained his PhD in numerical analysis at the University of Lille and completed his habilitation thesis at ULCO in 1999. His research topics are scientific computing, matrix and tensor computation, ill-posed problems, extrapolation, radial basis functions for some PDEs, and model reduction methods, with applications to image processing, control theory and other domains. He has more than 110 publications in international journals, and he is a member of the editorial boards of five international journals. He also edited, as a managing guest editor (or guest editor), more than 10 special issues of high-quality international scientific journals. He has supervised about 16 PhD students and participated in many doctoral thesis and habilitation committees. He has also organized many international conferences on numerical analysis and scientific computing with applications. He is the leader of the approximation and matrix computation group at the applied mathematics laboratory at the University of Littoral Côte d'Opale in Calais. He is currently working on tensors with applications in deep learning and machine learning for large problems focusing on the development of model reduction procedures.

Marilena Mitrouli

received her Ph.D. in Numerical Issues and Computational Problems in Algebraic Control Theory from the Department of Electrical Electronic and Information Engineering, City University, London, in 1991 (supervisor: Professor Nicos Karcanias). She has been a Professor in the Department of Mathematics, University of Athens, Athens, Greece, since 2018. Her research interests are numerical analysis, numerical linear algebra, the study of the growth problem in Hadamard and weighing matrices, the determinants of orthogonal matrices, rank, nullity and the null space of special matrices (Sylvester matrices, generalized Sylvester matrices, and block Toeplitz matrices), extrapolation methods for functions of matrices, matrix theory, canonical forms of matrices (Smith normal form and Jordan form), matrix pencils, and numerical methods for the computation of the greatest common divisor (GCD) and least common multiple (LCM) of polynomials.

She has published 97 papers in international journals, 21 in refereed conference proceedings and 16 in other conference proceedings. To date, there have been 817 citations of her research papers. She has given several lectures in Greek and foreign universities and institutions. She has participated in more than 50 international conferences. She has co-organized two international conferences and four international colloquiums. She has acted as a guest editor for three international journals. She has also acted as a referee for various journals such as the following (as well as various conferences): *Mathematics of Computation, Journal of Computational and Applied Mathematics, Linear Algebra and Its Applications, Computers and Mathematics with Its Applications, Journal of Applied Statistics, IEEE Transactions on Automatic Control*, and *Kybernetica*.

She has taught several undergraduate courses including Numerical Analysis, Numerical Linear Algebra, Computer Graphics, Matrix Theory with Applications, and Informatics, as well as various postgraduate courses such as Numerical Linear Algebra, Computational Mathematics, Applied Linear Algebra, and Linear and Nonlinear Control Theory. She has written two books in Greek and one in Ukrainian. She has supervised four PhD and 23 MSc Students. She was also the external supervisor of one PhD student. She is the President of the ERASMUS Committee of the Mathematics Department of the University of Athens. She has also exchanged ERASMUS visits with other European Universities. She has organized three International Erasmus Days in her department.

Preface to "Numerical Linear Algebra and the Applications"

This Special Issue named Numerical Linear Algebra with Applications is celebrating the **98th** birthday of the Greek mathematician Mr. Constantin M. Petridi, wishing him a long and happy life. The aim of this issue in the journal *Mathematics* was to invite some colleagues to submit their new and high-quality work related to numerical linear algebra and applications in different and modern fields such as machine learning and others.

This Special Issue was edited by Professors Marilena Mitrouli from the National and Kapodistrian University of Athens in Greece and Jbilou from the University of Littoral d'Opale in France.

As this Special Issue was dedicated to Mr. Constantin M. Petridi, we also present, here, a short CV written by Mr. Constantin M. Petridi himself.

CV of Mr. Constantin M. Petridi

Born 1923, Athens, Greece.
Father: Milton C. Petridi, heir to an internationally known tobacco company founded in 1848 in Constantinople (now Istanbul).
Mother: Nina C. Petridi, born Fauqier, stemming from a British colony, Corfu, Greece.
1952 Married Lisa Skouze, daughter of Dimitri Skouzes and Athina Skouze. Have one son, Milton C.Petridi. 1955–1972 I was consul for Sweden at Kavala, Greece, the location of my family's tobacco business. Languages: Fluent in English, French, German, and Swedish.

My Mathematical Life

After graduating from Athens College, Athens, Greece, I studied Mathematics at Stockholm University, graduating with an M.Sc.

My professors were

- Fritz Carlson, also the Director of the Leffler Institute (Mathematics),
- Harald Cramer (Probability Theory and Theoretical Statistics),
- Oscar Klein (Theoretical Mechanics).

1947–1949: I was an Assistant to both chairs of Mathematics at the Royal Technical University of Stockholm. My best friend, at that time, was fellow student Tord Ganelius.

1948: A Swedish business of my father, who knew the world renowned Hungarian Mathematician Prof. Marcel Riesz, invited the latter to examine my mathematical background and research interests. The result: Marcel Riesz invited me to become his student at Lund University, Sweden.

For better or for worse, I cannot say, I decided to remain in Stockholm.

End of 1948: I gave a manuscript to Prof. Carlson, titled *Mathematical Structures defined by Identities.* Carlson sent it to Prof. Trygve Nagell, Oslo University, as a greater expert on such matters. In reply, Nagell, in a long letter, said that my "Basic ideas undoubtedly opened new perspectives for Mathematics". He suggested, for example, that I axiomatize trigonometry (Fourier coefficient formulas).

Early 1949: I returned to Greece to take up the business of my father, who, in the meantime, had died.

A several-decades-long "Mathematical" interruption followed. I continued, however, my mathematical research, whenever I had time, and read mathematical reviews for recent developments.

1982: I left the tobacco business to devote myself, completely again, to mathematics.

1996: My old friend Tord Galenius, who, by then, was a permanent secretary of the Swedish Academy of Sciences (Crafoord Prizes), introduced me to Prof. Torsten Ekedahl, University of Stockholm. I had Q4 papers, on which I had written that the number I_n of irreducible identities (algebras) was equal to

$$I_n = \sum_{k=1}^{\left[\frac{n+1}{2}\right]-1} (-1)^{k-1} \binom{n-k+1}{k} S_{n-k}^2,$$

where $S_i :=$ are the Catalan numbers $\frac{1}{i+1}\binom{2i}{i}$.

Ekedahl praised my findings, telling me to send him the LaTeX manuscript, after my return to Greece. Unfortunately, my hopes were dashed, as Ekedahl died some time later, aged 54. The Mathematical Community acclaimed his achievements, including Jean-Pierre Serre.

2001: I started to publish my hitherto-discovered mathematical findings as ArXiv preprints. Peter Krikelis, Assistant, Athens University, wrote them in LaTeX form. The number of downloads (reads) was great.

My interest in mathematics started early in childhood, which I think is due to the **unexpected results it yields and its elegance**. I remember, for example, how awe-stricken I was, when reading, as a child, that the discriminant in a formula of the Fibonacci numbers is an integer.

Besides the above, I am, however, also interested in the work of other mathematicians, looking up in Wikipedia, etc., their published results.

In conclusion, as many of my papers are on number theory, I quote one of the giants of the past: Carl Fridrich Gauss: *Mathematics is the Queen of Sciences and Number Theory is the Queen of Mathematics.*

Khalide Jbilou, Marilena Mitrouli
Editors

mathematics

Article

Solving High-Dimensional Problems in Statistical Modelling: A Comparative Study †

Stamatis Choudalakis ‡, Marilena Mitrouli ‡, Athanasios Polychronou ‡ and Paraskevi Roupa *,‡

Department of Mathematics, National and Kapodistrian University of Athens, Panepistimiopolis, 15784 Athens, Greece; stchoud@math.uoa.gr (S.C.); mmitroul@math.uoa.gr (M.M.); apolychronou@math.uoa.gr (A.P.)
* Correspondence: parask_roupa@math.uoa.gr
† This paper is dedicated to Mr. Constantin M. Petridi.
‡ These authors contributed equally to this work.

Abstract: In this work, we present numerical methods appropriate for parameter estimation in high-dimensional statistical modelling. The solution of these problems is not unique and a crucial question arises regarding the way that a solution can be found. A common choice is to keep the corresponding solution with the minimum norm. There are cases in which this solution is not adequate and regularisation techniques have to be considered. We classify specific cases for which regularisation is required or not. We present a thorough comparison among existing methods for both estimating the coefficients of the model which corresponds to design matrices with correlated covariates and for variable selection for supersaturated designs. An extensive analysis for the properties of design matrices with correlated covariates is given. Numerical results for simulated and real data are presented.

Keywords: high-dimensional; minimum norm solution; regularisation; Tikhonov; ℓ_p-ℓ_q; variable selection

Citation: Choudalakis, S.; Mitrouli, M.; Polychronou, A.; Roupa, P. Solving High-Dimensional Problems in Statistical Modelling: A Comparative Study. *Mathematics* **2021**, *9*, 1806. https://doi.org/10.3390/math9151806

Academic Editor: Nickolai Kosmatov

Received: 3 June 2021
Accepted: 26 July 2021
Published: 30 July 2021

1. Introduction

Many fields of science, and especially health studies, require the solution of problems in which the number of characteristics is larger than the sample size. These problems are referred to as high-dimensional problems. In the present paper, we focus on solving high-dimensional problems in statistical modelling.

We consider the linear regression model

$$y = X\boldsymbol{\beta} + \boldsymbol{\epsilon}, \tag{1}$$

where $X = [\,\mathbf{1} \;\; \boldsymbol{x}_1 \;\; \cdots \;\; \boldsymbol{x}_d\,]$ is the design matrix of order $n \times (d+1)$, which is supposed to be high-dimensional, i.e., $n < d$. The columns $\boldsymbol{x}_i \sim N(\mathbf{0}_n, \sigma_i^2 I_n)$, $i = 1, 2, \ldots, d$, are the correlated covariates of the model and all the elements of the first column of the design matrix are equal to 1 in correspondence with the mean effect. The response vector $\boldsymbol{y}$ has length n, $\boldsymbol{\epsilon} = (\epsilon_1, \epsilon_2, \ldots, \epsilon_n)^T$ is the n-vector of independent and identically distributed (i.i.d.) random errors, where $\epsilon_i \sim N(0, \sigma^2)$ for all $i = 1, 2, \ldots, n$.

In the present study we focus on the following two points.

1. Estimation of the regression parameter $\boldsymbol{\beta} \in \mathbb{R}^{d+1}$.
   From numerical linear algebra point of view, the statistical model (1) can be considered as an underdetermined system. This kind of system has infinitely many solutions. The first way to determine the desired vector $\boldsymbol{\beta}$ is to keep the solution with the minimum norm. This solution is referred to as minimum norm solution (MNS), [1] (p. 264). Another way of solving these problems is based on regularisation techniques. Specifically, these methods allow us to solve a different problem which

has a unique solution and thus to estimate the desired vector $\boldsymbol{\beta}$. One of the most popular regularisation methods is Tikhonov regularization, [2]. Another regularization technique which is used is the ℓ_p-ℓ_q regularization, [3,4].
It is of major importance to decide whether problem (1) can be solved directly in the least squares sense or regularisation is required. Therefore, we describe a way of choosing the appropriate method for solving (1) for design matrices with correlated covariates. For these matrices we study extensively their properties. We prove that as the correlation of the covariates increases, the generalised condition number of the design matrix increases as well and thus the design matrix becomes ill-conditioned.

2. To ascertain the most important factors of the statistical model.
Variable selection is a major issue in solving high-dimensional problems. By means of variable selection we refer to the specification of the important variables (active factors) in the linear regression model, i.e., the variables which play a crucial role in the model. The rest of the variables (inactive factors) can be omitted.
We deal with the variable selection in supersaturated designs (SSDs) which are fractional factorial designs in which the run size is less than the number of all the main effects. In this class of designs, the columns of X, except the first column, have elements ± 1. The symbols 1 and -1 are usually utilised to denote the high and low level of each factor, respectively. The correlation of SSDs is usually small, i.e., $r \leq 0.5$. The analysis of SSDs is a main issue in Statistics. Many methods for analysing these designs have been proposed. In [5], a Dantzig selector was introduced. Recently, a sure independence screening method has been applied in a model selection method in SSDs [6], and a support vector machine recursive feature elimination method for feature selection [7]. In our study, as we want to retain sparsity in variable selection, we adopt the ℓ_p-ℓ_q regularisation and the SVD principal regression method, [8], in order to determine the most important factors of the statistical model.

In the regression model (1), there is no error setting in the design matrix X which defines the model. It is always considered an unperturbed matrix X with covariates from normal distribution with well determined rank. However, we assume i.i.d. random error $\boldsymbol{\epsilon} = (\epsilon_1, \epsilon_2, \ldots, \epsilon_n)^T$, $\epsilon_i \sim N(0, \sigma^2)$ for all $i = 1, 2, \ldots, n$, incorporated in the model as given from relation (1). Thus, we are having well-posed problems on the set of the data according to the work in [9].

The paper is organised as follows. In Section 2, we briefly present some methods for solving high-dimensional problems. We initially display the MNS and in the sequel we present two regularisation methods. Specifically, Tikhonov regularisation and a general regularisation technique, ℓ_p-ℓ_q regularisation method, are discussed. The described methods are used in estimating the regression parameter $\boldsymbol{\beta}$ of (1) for design matrices with correlated covariates and the results are given in Section 3. These methods can be applied to ill-posed problems as well. Variable selection for SSDs can be found in Section 4. We end up this work with several concluding remarks in Section 5.

2. Methods Overview

In this section, we present some methods for solving high-dimensional problems.

2.1. Minimum Norm Solution

The system (1), which is an underdetermined system, does not have a unique solution. In fact, this underdetermined system has infinitely many solutions, and we are seeking a solution such that its norm is minimised, i.e., the minimum norm solution (MNS) $\underset{\boldsymbol{\beta} \in \mathbb{R}^{d+1}}{\operatorname{argmin}} \|\boldsymbol{y} - X\boldsymbol{\beta}\|_2^2$, [1] (p. 264). A necessary and sufficient condition for the existence of MNS is given in the following theorem.

Theorem 1. *Let $X \in \mathbb{R}^{n\times(d+1)}$ be a high-dimensional matrix, i.e., $n < d$, with $rank(X) = n$, and $\boldsymbol{\beta}^*$ be a solution of the underdetermined system $X\boldsymbol{\beta} = \boldsymbol{y}$. Then, $\boldsymbol{\beta}^*$ is a MNS if and only if $\boldsymbol{\beta}^* \in Range(X^T)$.*

Proof. As $\boldsymbol{\beta}^*$ is a solution of the underdetermined system $X\boldsymbol{\beta} = \boldsymbol{y}$, we have

$$X\boldsymbol{\beta}^* = \boldsymbol{y} \Leftrightarrow (\boldsymbol{\beta}^*)^T X^T = \boldsymbol{y}^T. \tag{2}$$

Let us consider the QR factorisation of X^T, i.e.,

$$X^T = QR = Q\begin{bmatrix} R_1 \\ 0_{d+1-n,n} \end{bmatrix},$$

where $Q \in \mathbb{R}^{(d+1)\times(d+1)}$ is orthogonal and $R_1 \in \mathbb{R}^{n\times n}$ is upper triangular. Therefore, (2) can be rewritten as

$$(\boldsymbol{\beta}^*)^T QR = \boldsymbol{y}^T \Leftrightarrow (Q^T\boldsymbol{\beta}^*)^T R = \boldsymbol{y}^T. \tag{3}$$

If we set

$$z = Q^T\boldsymbol{\beta}^*, \tag{4}$$

then

$$(3) \Leftrightarrow z^T R = \boldsymbol{y}^T \Leftrightarrow R^T z = \boldsymbol{y}.$$

Moreover, we have

$$(4) \Leftrightarrow Q^{-1}\boldsymbol{\beta}^* = z \Leftrightarrow \boldsymbol{\beta}^* = Qz \Leftrightarrow \boldsymbol{\beta}^* \in Range(Q) \Leftrightarrow \boldsymbol{\beta}^* \in Range(X^T).$$

□

Taking into account the result of the above theorem, we obtain the formula for the MNS $\boldsymbol{\beta}^*$, which is given by

$$\boldsymbol{\beta}^* = X^T(XX^T)^{-1}\boldsymbol{y}. \tag{5}$$

Formula (5) cannot be used directly for calculating the vector $\boldsymbol{\beta}$, as it is not a stable computation. Therefore, we state the Algorithm 1 for a stable way of calculating the MNS through the singular value decomposition (SVD) of the design matrix X, [1] (p. 265). The operation count for this algorithm is dominated by the computation of the SVD, which requires a cost of $\mathcal{O}(nd^2)$ flops.

Algorithm 1: Computation of MNS via *SVD*.

Inputs: Design matrix $X \in \mathbb{R}^{n\times(d+1)}$, $n < d$, $rank(X) = n$
Response vector $\boldsymbol{y} \in \mathbb{R}^n$
Output: MNS solution $\boldsymbol{\beta}^*$
– Compute the *SVD* of X, i.e., $X = USV^T = \sum_{i=1}^{n} s_i \boldsymbol{u}_i \boldsymbol{v}_i^T$
– Compute the solution $\boldsymbol{\beta}^* = \sum_{i=1}^{n} \frac{\boldsymbol{u}_i^T \boldsymbol{y}}{s_i} \boldsymbol{v}_i$

2.2. The Discrete Picard Condition

It is crucial to identify when problem (1) can be directly solved with a satisfactory MNS solution or different ways of handling the solution must be employed. In [10], a criterion for deciding whether a least squares problem can have a satisfactory direct solution or not is proposed. This criterion employs the SVD of the design matrix X and the discrete Picard condition as defined in [11,12]. Let $X = USV^T = \sum_{i=1}^{n} s_i \boldsymbol{u}_i \boldsymbol{v}_i^T$ be the SVD of X, where s_i are the singular values of X with corresponding left singular vectors $\boldsymbol{u}_i$ and right singular vectors v_i, $i = 1, 2, \ldots, n$. The discrete Picard condition ensures that the solution can be approximated by a regularised solution [13].

Definition 1 (The discrete Picard condition). *The discrete Picard condition (DPC) requires that the ratio* $\frac{|c_i|}{s_i}$ *decreases to zero as* $i \to n$, *i.e.,*

$$\frac{|c_i|}{s_i} \to 0, \quad \text{as } i \to n,$$

where $c_i = u_i^T y$. *The DPC implies that the constants* $|c_i|$ *tend to zero faster than the singular values tend to zero.*

Example 1. *Let us now consider design matrices of order* 50×101, *their columns have same variance* σ^2 *and same correlation structure* r. *In particular, we test two design matrices* X *with* $(r, \sigma^2) = (0.9, 0.25)$ *and* $(r, \sigma^2) = (0.999, 1)$. *In Figure 1, we display the ratios* $\frac{|c_i|}{s_i}$ *and* $\frac{|\hat{c}_i|}{s_i}$, *which correspond to the noise-free and the noisy problem,* $c_i = u_i^T y$, $\hat{c}_i = u_i^T \hat{y}$, $i = 1, 2, \ldots, n$, $\hat{y} = y + \epsilon$. *If the graphs are close enough the MNS is satisfactory; otherwise, regularisation techniques are necessary for deriving a good approximation of the desired vector* β. *As we can see in Figure 1, the values of the depicted ratios are very close in the design matrix with* $r = 0.9$ *case whereas in the highly correlated matrix with* $r = 0.999$ *case the ratios differ. This implies that a regularisation method is necessary for the second case.*

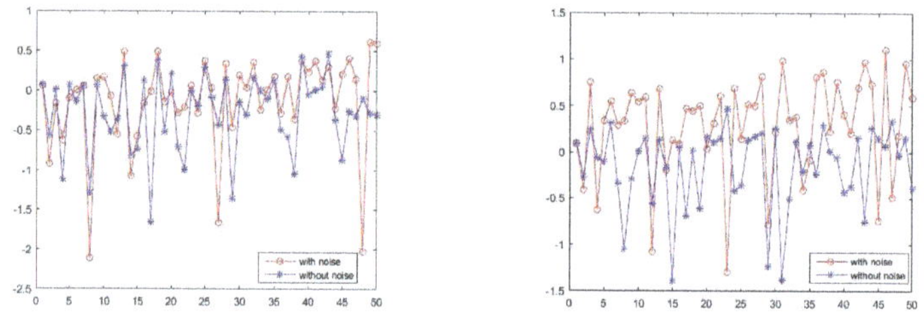

Figure 1. The ratios $|c_i|/s_i$ and $|\hat{c}_i|/s_i$ for the design matrices of order 50×101 for $(r, \sigma^2) = (0.9, 0.25)$ (**left**) and $(r, \sigma^2) = (0.999, 1)$ (**right**).

2.3. Regularisation Techniques

There are cases where the MNS β^* cannot achieve a good approximation of the desired unknown solution β. As in the linear regression model as described in (1) the design matrix X is always unperturbed, and thus its rank can be a priori known, we can adopt regularisation techniques. In the present section, we present two regularisation methods. In particular, we present the popular Tikhonov regularisation [2] and the ℓ_p-ℓ_q regularisation which has recently received considerable attention [3,4]. Both of these techniques replace the initial problem with another one which is close to the original.

2.3.1. Tikhonov Regularisation

A regularisation method that is widely used is Tikhonov regularisation. The standard form of Tikhonov regularization, which corresponds in linear regression model (1), is given by

$$\min_{\beta \in \mathbb{R}^{d+1}} \{\|y - X\beta\|_2^2 + \lambda^2 \|\beta\|_2^2\}, \tag{6}$$

where λ is the regularisation parameter. The solution of the penalised least-squares problem (6) is given by the formula

$$\beta_\lambda = (X^T X + \lambda^2 I_{d+1})^{-1} X^T y = X^T (X X^T + \lambda^2 I_n)^{-1} y,$$

as it holds the identity $(X^TX + \lambda^2 I_{d+1})^{-1}X^T = X^T(XX^T + \lambda^2 I_n)^{-1}$. Indeed, we have $X^T(XX^T + \lambda^2 I_n) = (X^TX + \lambda^2 I_{d+1})X^T \Rightarrow (X^TX + \lambda^2 I_{d+1})^{-1}X^T = X^T(XX^T + \lambda^2 I_n)^{-1}$.

As we can see, Tikhonov regularisation depends on the regularization parameter λ. An appropriate method for selecting λ leads to the derivation of a satisfactory approximation $\boldsymbol{\beta}_\lambda$ of the desired regression parameter $\boldsymbol{\beta}$. The error $\boldsymbol{\epsilon}$ in the input data for the statistical model that we study follows the standard norm distribution, i.e., $\boldsymbol{\epsilon} \sim N(\mathbf{0}_n, \sigma^2 I_n)$. Therefore, the norm of the error is known, and it is given by $\|\boldsymbol{\epsilon}\|_2 = \sqrt{n-1}\sigma$. In the case of known error norm, the appropriate method for the selection of the regularisation parameter is the discrepancy principle, which is reported in Algorithm 2 [14] (p. 283). Following also the analysis presented in [9], and due to the uniqueness of λ for most reasonable values of $\boldsymbol{\epsilon}$ (see, for example, in [15]), we adopt this method for our study.

Algorithm 2: Discrepancy principle.

Inputs: Design matrix $X \in \mathbb{R}^{n\times(d+1)}$, $n < d$, $rank(X) = n$
Response vector $\boldsymbol{y} \in \mathbb{R}^n$
Error norm $\|\boldsymbol{\epsilon}\|_2 = \sqrt{n-1}\sigma$
Output: Regularisation parameter λ
– Compute the SVD of X, i.e., $X = USV^T$
– Set $\boldsymbol{c} = U^T\boldsymbol{y}$
– Choose $\lambda > 0$ such that $\lambda^4\boldsymbol{c}^T(S + \lambda^2 I)^{-2}\boldsymbol{c} = \|\boldsymbol{\epsilon}\|^2$, over a given grid of λ.

2.3.2. ℓ_p-ℓ_q Regularisation

A more general regularisation technique is the so-called ℓ_p-ℓ_q regularisation [3]. The main idea of this approach is based on the replacement of the minimisation problem $\|\boldsymbol{y} - X\boldsymbol{\beta}\|_2$ by an ℓ_p-ℓ_q minimisation problem of the form

$$\min_{\boldsymbol{\beta}\in\mathbb{R}^{d+1}} \{\frac{1}{p}\|\boldsymbol{y} - X\boldsymbol{\beta}\|_p^p + \mu\frac{1}{q}\|\boldsymbol{\beta}\|_q^q\}, \quad (7)$$

where $\mu > 0$ is the regularisation parameter and $0 < p, q \leq 2$. The solution of the minimisation problem (7) is given by

$$\hat{\boldsymbol{\beta}}_\mu = \underset{\boldsymbol{\beta}\in\mathbb{R}^{d+1}}{\operatorname{argmin}}\{\frac{1}{p}\|\boldsymbol{y} - X\boldsymbol{\beta}\|_p^p + \mu\frac{1}{q}\|\boldsymbol{\beta}\|_q^q\}. \quad (8)$$

Remark 1. *In case of $p = q = 2$, the regularised minimisation problem (7) reduces to Tikhonov regularisation.*

Concerning the selection of the regularisation parameter, we choose the optimal value of μ, i.e., the value that minimises the error norm $\|\hat{\boldsymbol{\beta}}_\mu - \boldsymbol{\beta}\|_2$ over a given grid of values for μ. Concerning the computational cost, the implementation of the ℓ_p-ℓ_q regularisation requires $\mathcal{O}(nd)$ flops.

3. Design Matrix with Correlated Covariates

In high-dimensional applications, the design matrix $X = \begin{bmatrix} \mathbf{1} & \boldsymbol{x}_1 & \cdots & \boldsymbol{x}_d \end{bmatrix}$ has correlated covariates $\boldsymbol{x}_i \sim N(\mathbf{0}_n, \sigma_i^2 I_n)$, $i = 1, \ldots, d$, where σ_i^2 is the variance of $\boldsymbol{x}_i$ and the correlation structure is given from the relation

$$r_{ij} = cor(\boldsymbol{x}_i, \boldsymbol{x}_j) = \frac{\boldsymbol{x}_i{}^T\boldsymbol{x}_j}{\|\boldsymbol{x}_i\|\|\boldsymbol{x}_j\|}, \; i, j = 1, \ldots, d, \; i \neq j,$$

with $-1 \leq r_{ij} \leq 1$.

Next, we present a thorough investigation of the properties that characterize these matrices.

3.1. Correlated Covariates with Same Variance and Correlation

We initially consider design matrices with correlated covariates which have same variance σ^2 and same correlation r. In the following theorem, we formulate and prove in detail the types for the singular values of the design matrix X. In [16], this case of design matrix is considered and there exists a brief description of the eigenvalues of the matrix $X^T X$.

Theorem 2. *Let* $X = \begin{bmatrix} \mathbf{1} & \boldsymbol{x}_1 & \cdots & \boldsymbol{x}_d \end{bmatrix} \in \mathbb{R}^{n \times (d+1)}$ *be a high-dimensional design matrix of full rank whose columns* $\boldsymbol{x}_i \sim N(\mathbf{0}_n, \sigma^2 I_n)$, $i = 1, 2, \ldots, d$, *with correlation structure* r. *The singular values of the matrix* X *are*

$$s_1 = \sqrt{n}, \; s_2 = \cdots = s_{n-1} = \sigma\sqrt{(n-1)(1-r)}, \; s_n = \sigma\sqrt{(n-1)[(d-1)r+1]}.$$

Proof. The n singular values of X are the square roots of the n non-zero eigenvalues of $X^T X$. Therefore, we compute the matrix $X^T X$, i.e.,

$$X^T X = \begin{bmatrix} 1 & \ldots & 1 \\ x_{11} & \ldots & x_{n1} \\ \vdots & \ddots & \vdots \\ x_{1d} & \ldots & x_{nd} \end{bmatrix} \begin{bmatrix} 1 & x_{11} & \ldots & x_{1d} \\ \vdots & \vdots & \ddots & \vdots \\ 1 & x_{n1} & \ldots & x_{nd} \end{bmatrix}$$

$$= \begin{bmatrix} \sum_{j=1}^{n} 1 & \sum_{j=1}^{n} x_{j1} & \ldots & \sum_{j=1}^{n} x_{jd} \\ \sum_{j=1}^{n} x_{j1} & & & \\ \vdots & & \hat{X}^T \hat{X} & \\ \sum_{j=1}^{n} x_{jd} & & & \end{bmatrix} = \begin{bmatrix} n & 0 & \ldots & 0 \\ 0 & & & \\ \vdots & & \hat{X}^T \hat{X} & \\ 0 & & & \end{bmatrix},$$

where $\hat{X} = \begin{bmatrix} \boldsymbol{x}_1 & \cdots & \boldsymbol{x}_d \end{bmatrix}$ and $\sum_{j=1}^{n} x_{ji} = 0, \forall\, i = 1, \ldots, d$, due to the construction of the design matrix X according to the normal distribution. Therefore, the matrix $X^T X$ has one eigenvalue equal to n.

Moreover, we can express the variance σ^2 of each covariate $\boldsymbol{x}_i = \begin{bmatrix} x_{1i} & x_{2i} & \cdots & x_{ni} \end{bmatrix}^T$ in terms of vector norms as follows:

$$\sigma^2 = \frac{1}{n-1} \sum_{j=1}^{n} (x_{ji} - \bar{\boldsymbol{x}}_i)^2 = \frac{1}{n-1} \|\boldsymbol{x}_i - \bar{\boldsymbol{x}}_i\|^2,$$

where $\bar{\boldsymbol{x}}_i$ denotes the mean value of each $\boldsymbol{x}_i$. As the mean value of each $\boldsymbol{x}_i$ is zero, we have

$$\sigma^2 = \frac{1}{n-1} \|\boldsymbol{x}_i\|^2 \Rightarrow \|\boldsymbol{x}_i\|^2 = (n-1)\sigma^2, \;\; \forall\, i = 1, \ldots, d. \tag{9}$$

The submatrix $\hat{X}^T \hat{X}$ of $X^T X$ can be written as

$$\hat{X}^T\hat{X} = \begin{bmatrix} \|x_1\|^2 & r\|x_1\|\|x_2\| & \dots & r\|x_1\|\|x_d\| \\ r\|x_1\|\|x_2\| & \|x_2\|^2 & \dots & r\|x_2\|\|x_d\| \\ \vdots & \vdots & \ddots & \vdots \\ r\|x_d\|\|x_1\| & r\|x_d\|\|x_2\| & \dots & \|x_d\|^2 \end{bmatrix}$$

$$\stackrel{(9)}{=} \begin{bmatrix} (n-1)\sigma^2 & r(n-1)\sigma^2 & \dots & r(n-1)\sigma^2 \\ r(n-1)\sigma^2 & (n-1)\sigma^2 & \dots & r(n-1)\sigma^2 \\ \vdots & \vdots & \ddots & \vdots \\ r(n-1)\sigma^2 & r(n-1)\sigma^2 & \dots & (n-1)\sigma^2 \end{bmatrix}$$

$$= (n-1)\sigma^2 \begin{bmatrix} 1 & r & \dots & r \\ r & 1 & \dots & r \\ \vdots & \vdots & \ddots & \vdots \\ r & r & \dots & 1 \end{bmatrix} = (n-1)\sigma^2[(1-r)I + rJ],$$

where J is the $d \times d$ matrix with all elements equal to 1. The non-zero eigenvalues of $\hat{X}^T\hat{X}$ are $\lambda_1 = (n-1)\sigma^2(1-r)$ with algebraic multiplicity $n-2$ and $\lambda_2 = (n-1)\sigma^2[(d-1)r+1]$ with algebraic multiplicity 1. Therefore, the singular values of X are $s_1 = \sqrt{n}$, $s_2 = \cdots = s_{n-1} = \sigma\sqrt{(n-1)(1-r)}$, $s_n = \sigma\sqrt{(n-1)[(d-1)r+1]}$. □

Let us denote by $\kappa(X)$ the generalised condition number of X, i.e., $\kappa(X) = \|X\|_2 \cdot \|X^{+}\|_2$, where $X^{+} = X^T(XX^T)^{-1}$ is the pseudoinverse of X, [1] (p. 246). It is known that the generalised condition number can be expressed in terms of the maximum s_{max} and the minimum s_{min} singular value of X as $\kappa(X) = \frac{s_{max}}{s_{min}}$, [1] (p. 216).

In Theorem 3, we express the generalised condition number of X in terms of the correlation structure r.

Theorem 3. *Let $X = \begin{bmatrix} \mathbf{1} & x_1 & \cdots & x_d \end{bmatrix} \in \mathbb{R}^{n\times(d+1)}$ be a high-dimensional design matrix of full rank whose columns $x_i \sim N(\mathbf{0}_n, \sigma^2 I_n)$, $i = 1,2,\dots,d$, with correlation structure r. The generalised condition number of X is given by*

1. $\kappa(X) = \sqrt{\frac{n}{(n-1)\sigma^2(1-r)}}$, *if* $r \le \frac{1}{d-1}\left(\frac{n}{(n-1)\sigma^2} - 1\right)$,
2. $\kappa(X) = \sqrt{\frac{(d-1)r+1}{1-r}}$, *if* $\left(r > \frac{1}{d-1}\left(\frac{n}{(n-1)\sigma^2} - 1\right) \text{ and } \sigma^2 < \frac{n}{n-1}\right)$ *or* $\left(r > 1 - \frac{n}{(n-1)\sigma^2} \text{ and } \sigma^2 > \frac{n}{n-1}\right)$,
3. $\kappa(X) = \sqrt{\frac{(n-1)\sigma^2((d-1)r+1)}{n}}$, *if* $r < 1 - \frac{n}{(n-1)\sigma^2}$.

Proof. It is obvious that $s_n = \sigma\sqrt{(n-1)[(d-1)r+1]} > s_i$, $i = 2,\dots,n-1$ holds. Therefore, we have to distinguish three cases. The first case is $s_1 \ge s_n$, the second case is $s_i < s_1 < s_n$ and the last one is $s_1 < s_i$.

First case: If $s_1 \ge s_n$, then $\kappa(X) = \frac{s_1}{s_i} = \sqrt{\frac{n}{(n-1)\sigma^2(1-r)}}$. The restriction $s_1 \ge s_n$ can be rewritten as follows:

$$
\begin{aligned}
& n \geq (n-1)\sigma^2((d-1)r+1) \\
\Leftrightarrow \quad & \frac{n}{(n-1)\sigma^2} \geq (d-1)r+1 \\
\Leftrightarrow \quad & \frac{n}{(n-1)\sigma^2} - 1 \geq (d-1)r \\
\Leftrightarrow \quad & r \leq \frac{1}{d-1}\left(\frac{n}{(n-1)\sigma^2} - 1\right).
\end{aligned}
$$

Second case: If $s_i < s_1 < s_n$, then $\kappa(X) = \frac{s_n}{s_i} = \sqrt{\frac{(d-1)r+1}{1-r}}$. The restriction $s_i < s_1 < s_n$ can be reformulated as follows:

$$
\begin{aligned}
& (n-1)\sigma^2(1-r) < n < (n-1)\sigma^2(dr+1-r) \\
\Leftrightarrow \quad & \begin{cases} 1-r < \dfrac{n}{(n-1)\sigma^2} \\ (d-1)r > \dfrac{n}{(n-1)\sigma^2} - 1 \end{cases} \quad \Leftrightarrow \begin{cases} r > 1 - \dfrac{n}{(n-1)\sigma^2} \\ r > \dfrac{1}{d-1}\left(\dfrac{n}{(n-1)\sigma^2} - 1\right) \end{cases}.
\end{aligned}
$$

Moreover, we make the check

$$
\begin{aligned}
& \frac{1}{d-1}\left(\frac{n}{(n-1)\sigma^2} - 1\right) < 1 - \frac{n}{(n-1)\sigma^2} \\
\Leftrightarrow \quad & n - (n-1)\sigma^2 < (d-1)(n-1)\sigma^2 - n(d-1) \\
\Leftrightarrow \quad & (n-1)\sigma^2(1+d-1) > n + nd - n \\
\Leftrightarrow \quad & \sigma^2 > \frac{n}{n-1}.
\end{aligned}
$$

Therefore, we conclude that the generalised condition number $\kappa(X)$ is equal to $\sqrt{\frac{(d-1)r+1}{1-r}}$ if the following relation holds.

$$
\begin{aligned}
r > \frac{1}{d-1}\left(\frac{n}{(n-1)\sigma^2} - 1\right) \quad & \text{and} \quad \sigma^2 < \frac{n}{n-1} \quad \text{or} \\
r > 1 - \frac{n}{(n-1)\sigma^2} \quad & \text{and} \quad \sigma^2 > \frac{n}{n-1}
\end{aligned}
$$

Third case: If $s_1 \leq s_i$, then $\kappa(X) = \frac{s_n}{s_1} = \sqrt{\frac{(n-1)\sigma^2((d-1)r+1)}{n}}$. This restriction is equivalently written as

$$
n < (n-1)\sigma^2(1-r) \Leftrightarrow \frac{n}{(n-1)\sigma^2} < 1 - r \Leftrightarrow r < 1 - \frac{n}{(n-1)\sigma^2}.
$$

□

Taking into consideration the derived formulae for the generalised condition number of the design matrix X, we see that if $r \approx 1$ the generalised condition number $\kappa(X)$ becomes large. A detailed example is presented next.

Example 2. *In this example, we plot the generalised condition number of X as a function of the correlation r. We consider* $n = 50$, $d = 100$ *and* $\sigma^2 = 2$. *In Figure 2, we display* $\kappa(X)$ *for correlation* $r \longrightarrow 1$. *As we see in Figure 2, as correlation r tends to 1, the generalised condition number* $\kappa(X)$ *increases rapidly.*

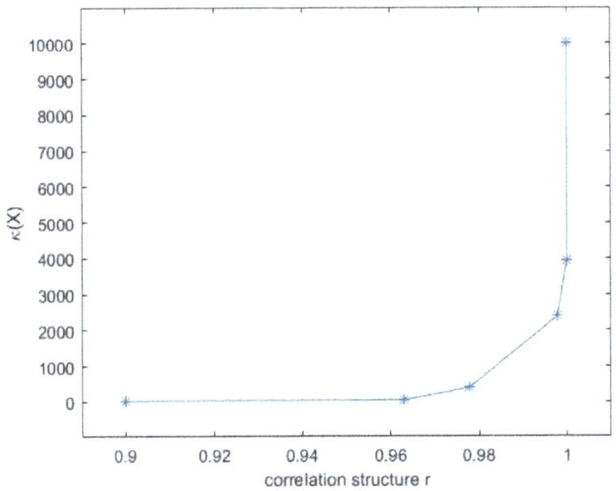

Figure 2. The generalised condition number of X as a function of the correlation r.

3.2. Highly Correlated Covariates with Different Variance and Correlation

Next, we consider a general and more usual case in which the covariates $\boldsymbol{x}_i \sim N(\mathbf{0}_n, \sigma_i^2 I_n)$ of the design matrix X have different variance σ_i^2 and correlation r_{ij}, $i, j = 1, \ldots, d$. Based on the results presented in [17] for the eigenvalues of the matrix $X^T X$, we record analytic formulae for the singular values of X in the following theorem.

Theorem 4. *Let* $X = \begin{bmatrix} \mathbf{1} & \boldsymbol{x}_1 & \cdots & \boldsymbol{x}_d \end{bmatrix} \in \mathbb{R}^{n\times(d+1)}$ *be a high-dimensional design matrix of full rank whose columns* $\boldsymbol{x}_i \sim N(\mathbf{0}_n, \sigma_i^2 I_n)$, $i = 1, 2, \ldots, d$, *with highly correlation structure* r_{ij}. *The singular values of the matrix* X *are*

$$s_1 = \sqrt{n}, \ s_2 = \sqrt{(n-1)\sum_{j=1}^{d} \sigma_i^2 + \mathcal{O}(\delta)}, \ s_3 = \cdots = s_n = \sqrt{\mathcal{O}(\delta)},$$

assuming that $1 - r_{ij} = \mathcal{O}(\delta)$ *as* $\delta \to 0$.

As we record in Section 3.1, the generalised condition number is equal to the ratio $\frac{s_{max}}{s_{min}}$ and in the present case $s_{min} = \mathcal{O}(\delta)$ considering that $1 - r_{ij} = \mathcal{O}(\delta)$, i.e., highly correlated covariates. Therefore, the value of $\kappa(X)$ is large and this affects the solution of the corresponding problem.

Remark 2. *As the correlation r increases the generalised condition number $\kappa(X)$ increases as well. From Theorems 2 and 4 we deduce that the case of highly correlated covariates leads to possible instability and thus regularisation is recommended. This result is confirmed from Table 1 which is presented in Section 3.3.*

3.3. Numerical Implementation

The implementation of the simulation study presented in this section and in Section 4 has been done by using the Julia Programming Language.

Given the high-dimensional design matrix X of order $n \times (d+1)$, the response vector $\boldsymbol{y}$ of order n and the n-vector $\boldsymbol{\epsilon} = (\epsilon_1, \epsilon_2, \ldots, \epsilon_n)^T$ of i.i.d. random errors, $\epsilon_j \sim N(0,1)$, $j = 1, 2, \ldots, n$, we estimate the vector $\boldsymbol{\beta}$ by using the methods which are described in Section 2. We consider design matrices X with correlated covariates and we distinguish the two aforementioned cases. The results for the first case, i.e., the covariates of the design matrices having same correlation r and same variance σ^2, are recorded in Tables 1 and 2. The results for the second case are displayed in Table 3.

The implemented simulation scheme is the following. For each design matrix X, a random vector $\boldsymbol{\beta}$ is generated and $\boldsymbol{y} = X\boldsymbol{\beta}$ denotes the noise free response vector. Then,

100 iterations are performed, in each one the response vector is perturbed by noise ϵ^i resulting in a noisy response vector $\hat{y} = y + \epsilon^i, i = 1, 2, \ldots, 100$. Eventually, the regression parameter $\hat{\beta}$ is computed by using both the MNS given by Algorithm 1 and the regularisation techniques. The quality of the generated approximation solution $\hat{\beta}$ is assessed by the mean square error (MSE) between β and $\hat{\beta}$ which is given by the formula

$$MSE(\hat{\beta}) = E[\|\hat{\beta} - \beta\|_2^2].$$

In Algorithm 3, we summarise the simulation scheme.

Algorithm 3: Simulation scheme.

Input: Design matrix $X \in \mathbb{R}^{n\times(d+1)}$
Result: $MSE(\hat{\beta})$
$\beta = randn(n);$
$y = X\beta;$
for $i \leftarrow 1$ **to** 100 **do**
  $\hat{y} = y + \epsilon^i;$
  $\beta^* = MNS(\hat{y});$
  $\beta_\lambda = Tikhonov(\hat{y});$
  $\hat{\beta}_\mu = \ell_p\text{-}\ell_q(\hat{y})$
end

In Tables 1–3, we present the results of estimating the regression parameter β for different orders of the design matrices X. In the two first columns of the tables, the correlation r and the variance σ^2 of the covariates are recorded, respectively. In Table 3, we record the interval in which lies the correlation and the variance. In the third column, the adopted methods are written. Specifically, we record MNS, Tikhonov regularisation and ℓ_p-ℓ_q regularisation technique for different pairs of (p, q). The fourth column contains the used grid of values for the regularisation parameter λ or μ for Tikhonov or ℓ_p-ℓ_q regularisation, respectively. In the last column the $MSE(\hat{\beta})$ of the derived approximation solutions $\hat{\beta}$ are recorded.

Table 1. Results for $X_{5\times21}$.

r	σ^2	Method	λ/μ	MSE ($\hat{\beta}$)
0.5	0.25	MNS		1.3063×10^{-1}
		Tikhonov	[1, 10]	8.3874×10^{-1}
		$\ell_{1.8}$-$\ell_{1.8}$	$[10^{-7}, 10^{-2}]$	1.1949×10^{-1}
0.5	1.0	MNS		1.3093×10^{-1}
		Tikhonov	[1, 10]	8.0127×10^{-1}
		$\ell_{1.8}$-$\ell_{1.8}$	$[10^{-7}, 10^{-2}]$	1.2216×10^{-1}
0.9	0.25	MNS		5.5782×10^{-1}
		Tikhonov	[1, 10]	9.4101×10^{-1}
		$\ell_{1.8}$-$\ell_{1.8}$	[0.1, 10]	1.2571×10^{-1}
0.9	1.0	MNS		6.2096×10^{-1}
		Tikhonov	[1, 10]	8.5836×10^{-1}
		$\ell_{1.8}$-$\ell_{1.8}$	[0.1, 10]	6.0884×10^{-1}
0.999	0.25	MNS		4.4474
		Tikhonov	[1, 10]	1.774
		$\ell_{0.1}$-ℓ_2	$[10^{-7}, 10^{-2}]$	7.3793×10^{-1}
0.999	1.0	MNS		2.0129
		Tikhonov	[1, 10]	1.0456
		$\ell_{1.2}$-$\ell_{1.2}$	[0.1, 10]	6.8626×10^{-1}

Table 2. Results for $X_{50\times 101}$.

r	σ^2	Method	λ/μ	MSE ($\hat{\beta}$)
0.9	0.25	MNS		4.5894×10^{-1}
		Tikhonov	[1, 10]	7.0511×10^{-1}
		ℓ_2-$\ell_{0.1}$	$[10^{-7}, 10^{-2}]$	4.5093×10^{-1}
0.9	1.0	MNS		4.8802×10^{-1}
		Tikhonov	[1, 10]	6.0754×10^{-1}
		ℓ_2-$\ell_{0.1}$	$[10^{-7}, 10^{-2}]$	4.8614×10^{-1}
0.999	0.25	MNS		3.5306
		Tikhonov	[1, 10]	1.0022
		ℓ_2-$\ell_{0.1}$	[0.1, 10]	8.3247×10^{-1}
0.999	1.0	MNS		1.1970
		Tikhonov	[1, 10]	9.6625×10^{-1}
		$\ell_{1.8}$-$\ell_{1.8}$	[0.1, 10]	7.4754×10^{-1}

Table 3. Results for $X_{25\times 51}$.

r	σ^2	Method	λ/μ	MSE ($\hat{\beta}$)
[0.27, 0.91]	[0.19, 1.17]	MNS		2.1252×10^{-1}
		Tikhonov	[1, 10]	6.2245×10^{-1}
		$\ell_{1.8}$-$\ell_{1.8}$	[0.1, 10]	9.3163×10^{-2}
[−0.32, 0.85]	[0.13, 2.32]	MNS		1.6819×10^{-1}
		Tikhonov	[1, 10]	5.9699×10^{-1}
		$\ell_{1.8}$-$\ell_{1.8}$	[0.1, 10]	1.2632×10^{-1}
[0.06, 0.91]	[0.42, 1.93]	MNS		1.1623×10^{-1}
		Tikhonov	[1, 10]	5.8305×10^{-1}
		$\ell_{1.8}$-$\ell_{1.8}$	[0.1, 10]	1.0371×10^{-1}

As we can see in these tables, in the case of highly correlated design matrices, the regularisation is necessary for deriving a good approximation of the desired vector β. On the other hand, if the correlation of the design matrix is not high, MNS can achieve a fair estimation and a regularisation method does not improve the results, as it is verified by the $MSE(\hat{\beta})$. Therefore, according to the presented results, for matrices with moderate correlated covariates, regularisation is redundant, as MNS yields adequate results. However, as the correlation between the covariates rises, the regularisation is essential.

Note that in case of design matrices with same variance and correlation $r = 0.999$ (Tables 1 and 2) the regularisation techniques, Tikhonov and ℓ_p-ℓ_q, can achieve comparable results. The choice of the pair of parameters (p, q) and the values of the required regularisation parameter play an important role for the efficient implementation of both methods.

4. Variable Selection in SSDs

In this section, we are interested in selecting the active factors of SSDs by using the methods which are described in Section 2. In our comparison, we also include SVD principal regression method which is used in SSDs, and it was proposed in [8]. We briefly refer to this method as SVD regression. The main computational cost of this approach is the evaluation of the SVD.

We measure the effectiveness of these methods through the Type I and Type II error rates. In particular, Type I error measures the cost of declaring an inactive factor to be active and Type II measures the cost of declaring an active effect to be inactive. In our numerical experiments, we consider 500 different realisations of the error ϵ and in the presented tables we record the mean value of Type I, II error rates.

It is worth mentioning that both the MNS and Tikhonov regularisation give that all the factors are active, i.e., Type I = 1, Type II = 0, for all the tested SSDs. Therefore, these methods are not suitable for variable selection and we do not include them in the following presented tables.

Example 3 (An illustrative example). *In this example, we shall exhibit in detail the performance of each method for a particular problem. For this purpose, we adopt the illustrative example presented in [8], with design matrix*

$$X = \begin{bmatrix} + & - & - & - & - & - & - & - & - & - \\ + & + & + & + & + & + & + & - & - & - \\ + & + & + & + & - & - & - & + & + & + \\ - & + & - & - & + & + & - & + & + & - \\ - & - & + & - & + & - & + & + & - & + \\ - & - & - & + & - & + & + & - & + & + \end{bmatrix} = \begin{bmatrix} x_1 & x_2 & \dots & x_{10} \end{bmatrix}.$$

Then a first column $\mathbf{x}_0$ with all entries equal to 1 is added to the matrix, which corresponds to the average mean. The simulated data are generated by the model

$$y = 5x_0 + 4x_2 + 3x_5 + \epsilon,$$

where $\epsilon \sim N(\mathbf{0}_6, I_6)$. A response vector y obtained by using this model is

$$y = \begin{bmatrix} -1.54 & 12.02 & 6.82 & 12.44 & 4.62 & -1.21 \end{bmatrix}^T.$$

The exact regression parameter β and the predicted coefficients by each method are demonstrated below.

$$\beta = \begin{bmatrix} 5 & 0 & 4 & 0 & 0 & 3 & 0 & 0 & 0 & 0 & 0 \end{bmatrix}^T,$$
$$\hat{\beta}_{MNS} = \begin{bmatrix} 5.525 & 0.1208 & 2.4508 & 1.1475 & 0.1758 & 2.0842 & 1.1125 & -0.1908 & 1.2175 & 0.2458 & -1.0575 \end{bmatrix}^T,$$
$$\hat{\beta}_{Tik} = \begin{bmatrix} 4.7237 & 0.1114 & 2.2592 & 1.0578 & 0.1621 & 1.9212 & 1.0255 & -0.1759 & 1.1223 & 0.2266 & -0.9748 \end{bmatrix}^T,$$
$$\hat{\beta}_{\ell_2\ell_{0.1}} = \begin{bmatrix} 5.5214 & 0.0 & 3.9482 & 0.0 & 0.0 & 2.8458 & 0.0 & 0.0 & 0.0 & 0.0 & 0.0 \end{bmatrix}^T,$$
$$\hat{\beta}_{SVD} = \begin{bmatrix} 5.5245 & 0.0 & 3.901 & 0.0 & 0.0 & 2.801 & 0.0 & 0.0 & 0.0 & 0.0 & 0.0 \end{bmatrix}^T.$$

As we can see from the generated approximation solutions $\hat{\beta}$, the MNS and Tikhonov regularised solution cannot specify the active factors of the model and completely spoil the sparsity. On the other hand, the ℓ_p-ℓ_q regularisation method and the SVD regression can determine appropriately the active factors of the model.

Example 4 (Williams' data). *We consider the well-known Williams' dataset (rubber age data) which is reported in Table 4. It is a classical dataset of SSDs and it is tested in several works, such as in [8]. As it is written in [8], as the columns 13 and 16 in the original design matrix are identical, the column 13 is removed for executing our numerical experiments. For this dataset we consider two cases, the real case and 3 synthetic cases.*

We initially deal with the real case where the design matrix X and the response vector y are given, without the initial knowledge of the desired vector β. In literature, it is reported that the active factor is x_{15}. In this case, according to our numerical experiments, the SVD regression and the ℓ_p-ℓ_q regularisation method for $p = 0.8$, $q = 0.1$ indicate that the factor x_{15} is important. In particular, the proposed models, i.e., the coefficients β_i are given in Table 5.

The second case corresponds to 3 synthetic cases, see in [8] and references therein, which are given below. For these simulated cases, we record the results in Table 6. In particular, we compute Type I and II error rates for the described methods. We apply the ℓ_p-ℓ_q regularisation method for $\mu = 5$ and the SVD regression for the significance level $a = 0.05$. As we notice in this table, both the ℓ_p-ℓ_q regularisation and the SVD regression can select sufficiently the important factors, as we see from the corresponding Type I, II error rates. The first model has the particularity that it includes the interaction of the factors

x_5, x_9 which does not usually appear in SSDs analysis. The first model is a challenging case for all the methods.

Model 1: $y \sim N(15x_1 + 8x_5 - 6x_9 + 3x_5x_9, I_{14})$
Model 2: $y \sim N(8x_1 + 5x_{12}, I_{14})$
Model 3: $y \sim N(10x_1 + 9x_2 + 2x_3, I_{14})$

Table 4. The Williams' data—rubber age data.

1	2	3	4	5	6	7	8	9	10	11	12	13	14	15	16	17	18	19	20	21	22	23	y
+	+	+	-	-	-	+	+	+	+	+	-	-	-	+	+	-	-	+	-	-	-	+	133
+	-	-	-	-	-	+	+	+	-	-	-	+	+	+	-	+	-	-	+	+	-	-	62
+	+	-	+	+	-	-	-	-	+	-	+	+	+	+	+	-	-	-	-	+	+	-	45
+	+	-	+	-	+	-	-	-	+	+	-	-	+	+	-	+	+	+	-	-	-	-	52
-	-	+	+	+	+	-	+	+	-	-	-	-	+	+	+	-	-	+	-	+	+	+	56
-	-	+	+	+	+	+	-	+	+	+	-	+	+	-	+	+	+	+	+	+	-	-	47
-	-	-	-	+	-	-	+	-	+	-	+	+	-	+	+	+	+	+	+	-	-	+	88
-	+	+	-	-	+	-	+	-	+	-	-	-	-	-	-	-	+	-	+	+	+	-	193
-	-	-	-	-	+	+	-	-	-	+	+	-	+	-	+	+	-	-	-	-	+	+	32
+	+	+	+	-	+	+	+	-	-	-	+	+	+	-	+	-	+	-	+	-	-	+	53
-	+	-	+	+	-	-	+	+	-	+	-	+	-	-	-	+	+	-	-	-	+	+	276
+	-	-	-	+	+	+	-	+	+	+	+	-	-	+	-	-	+	-	+	+	+	+	145
+	+	+	+	+	-	+	-	+	-	-	+	-	-	-	-	+	-	+	+	-	+	-	130
-	-	+	-	-	-	-	-	-	-	+	+	+	-	-	-	-	-	+	-	+	-	-	127

Table 5. The selected model for William's data (real case).

Method	Intercept	x_{15}
$\ell_{0.8}$-$\ell_{0.1}$	6.11	−1.13
SVD Regression	102.7857	−36.0341

Table 6. Results for William's Data (synthetic cases).

Model	Method	Type I	Type II
Model 1	$\ell_{1.8}$-$\ell_{0.8}$	0.23	0.56
	SVD Regression	0.15	0.74
Model 2	$\ell_{2.0}$-$\ell_{0.1}$	0.00	0.00
	SVD Regression	0.05	0.00
Model 3	$\ell_{2.0}$-$\ell_{0.1}$	0.00	0.27
	SVD Regression	0.07	0.33

Example 5 (A 3-circulant SSD). *In this example, we consider one more SSD, which is also used in [18], and it is recorded in Table 7. We test the behaviour of the methods for variable selection by considering three models which can be found in [19] and are given below.*

Model 1: $y \sim N(10x_1, I_8)$
Model 2: $y \sim N(-15x_1 + 8x_5 - 2x_9, I_8)$
Model 3: $y \sim N(-15x_1 + 12x_5 - 8x_9 + 6x_{13} - 2x_{17}, I_8)$

The results are presented in Table 8. For the three used models, we apply the ℓ_p-ℓ_q regularisation method for $\mu = 5, 5.5, 0.5$ respectively and the SVD regression for $a = 0.25$. According to the presented numerical results, we see that both the ℓ_p-ℓ_q regularisation and the SVD regression can achieve satisfactory Type I and II error rates for the Model 1. On the other hand, for the Model 2 the SVD regression fails to specify the active factors whereas the ℓ_p-ℓ_q regularisation method achieves better Type II error. However, neither of the methods produce fair results for the Model 3. The coefficients of this model are not sufficiently close and this fact affects the behaviour of the methods.

Table 7. A 3-circulant SSD.

1	2	3	4	5	6	7	8	9	10	11	12	13	14	15	16	17	18	19	20	21
-	-	-	-	-	-	-	+	+	-	-	-	+	-	+	+	+	-	+	+	+
+	+	+	-	-	-	-	-	-	-	+	+	-	-	-	+	-	+	+	+	-
+	+	-	+	+	+	-	-	-	-	-	-	-	+	+	-	-	-	+	-	+
+	-	+	+	+	-	+	+	+	-	-	-	-	-	-	-	+	+	-	-	-
-	-	-	+	-	+	+	+	-	+	+	+	-	-	-	-	-	-	-	+	+
-	+	+	-	-	-	+	-	+	+	+	-	+	+	+	-	-	-	-	-	-
-	-	-	-	+	+	-	-	-	+	-	+	+	+	-	+	+	+	-	-	-
+	+	+	+	+	+	+	+	+	+	+	+	+	+	+	+	+	+	+	+	+

Table 8. Results for 3-circulant SSD.

Model	Method	Type I	Type II
Model 1	$\ell_{2.0}$-$\ell_{0.1}$	0.00	0.00
	SVD Regression	0.08	0.00
Model 2	$\ell_{0.6}$-$\ell_{1.3}$	0.39	0.13
	SVD Regression	0.08	0.67
Model 3	$\ell_{1.8}$-$\ell_{0.8}$	0.39	0.45
	SVD Regression	0.17	0.80

Example 6. *In this example we consider a real data set presented in [20] that deals with moss bags of Rhynchostegium riparioides which were exposed to different water concentrations of* 11 *trace elements under laboratory conditions. The design matrix X can be found in Table 1 in [20]. We consider the main effects, the second- and third-order interactions of influent factors. Therefore, we have a* 67×232 *SSD and we can select the important factors applying the* ℓ_p-ℓ_q *regularisation for* $\mu = 0.75$ *and the SVD regression for significance level* $a = 0.05$.

From Table 9, we see that both ℓ_2-$\ell_{0.1}$ and SVD regression methods identify the main effect Zn as active factor. The second order interactions Cd/Mn, As/Pb and Mn/Ni are also identified as active. These results are in agreement with [20].

Table 9. Important elements and interactions.

Method	Main Effects	Second-Order Interactions	Third-Order Interactions
ℓ_2-$\ell_{0.1}$	Fe, Zn	Al/Hg, As/Pb, Cd/Mn, Mn/Ni	Al/As/Mn, Al/Cr/Zn, As/Cd/Fe, As/Cd/Mn, Cr/Mn/Zn, Cu/Hg/Mn Fe/Hg/Ni, Fe/ Ni/Pb
SVD Regression	Zn	As/Pb, Cd/Mn, Fe/Mn, Fe/Zn, Mn/Ni, Pb/Zn	

5. Conclusions

In the present work, we analysed the properties of design matrices with correlated covariates. Specifically, we derived and proved formulae for the singular values of these matrices and we studied the connection of the generalised condition number with the correlation structure. Moreover, we described some available methods for solving high-dimensional problems. We checked the behaviour of the MNS and the necessity of applying regularisation techniques in estimating the regression parameter β in the linear regression model. We concluded that in solving high-dimensional statistical problems the following remarks must be taken into consideration.

1. Regularisation should be applied only if the given data set satisfies the discrete Picard condition. In this case, the choice of the regularisation parameter can be uniquely chosen by applying the discrepancy principle method.
2. The regression parameter $\boldsymbol{\beta} \in \mathbb{R}^{d+1}$ can be satisfactory estimated by the MNS if the design matrix is not highly correlated but in case of highly correlated data matrices we have to adopt regularisation techniques. The quality of the derived estimation $\hat{\boldsymbol{\beta}}$ of $\boldsymbol{\beta}$ is assessed by the computation of $MSE(\hat{\boldsymbol{\beta}})$.
3. In variable selection, where sparse solutions are needed, SVD regression or ℓ_p-ℓ_q regularisation can be used. When only few factors of the experiment are needed to be specified (maybe only the most important), SVD regression may be preferable since it avoids regularisation and the troublesome procedure of defining the regularisation parameter. The quality of the variable selection which is proposed by the estimation methods is assessed by the evaluation of Type I and II error rates.

In conclusion, the proposed scheme for the selection of the appropriate method for the solution of high-dimensional statistical problems is summarised in the following logical diagram, see Figure 3.

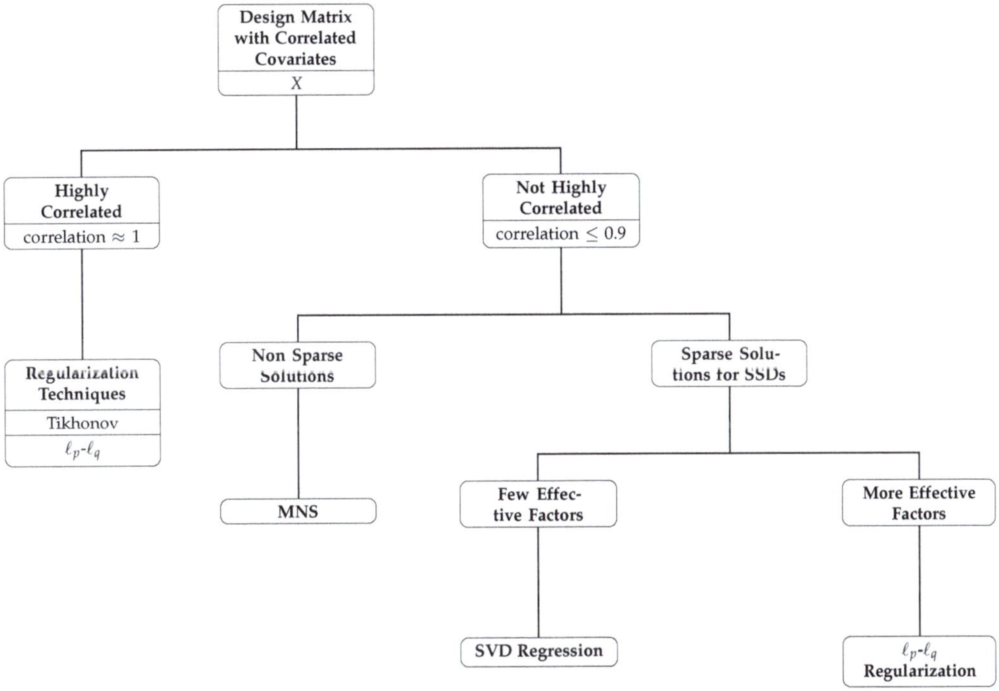

Figure 3. Logical diagram for choosing the appropriate method for the solution of high-dimensional statistical problems.

Author Contributions: Conceptualization, M.M.; methodology, M.M. and P.R.; software, S.C., A.P., P.R.; validation, M.M. and P.R.; formal analysis, S.C., A.P., P.R.; investigation, M.M.; data curation, S.C., A.P., P.R.; writing—original draft preparation, S.C., M.M., A.P., P.R.; writing—review and editing, S.C., M.M., A.P., P.R.; supervision, M.M.; project administration, M.M. All authors have read and agreed to the published version of the manuscript.

Funding: This research received no external funding.

Institutional Review Board Statement: Not applicable.

Informed Consent Statement: Not applicable.

Acknowledgments: The authors are grateful to the reviewers of this paper whose valuable remarks improved this work.

Conflicts of Interest: The authors declare no conflict of interest.

References

1. Datta, B.N. *Numerical Linear Algebra and Applications*, 2nd ed.; SIAM: Philadelphia, PA, USA, 2010.
2. Tikhonov, A.N. On the solution of ill-posed problems and the method of regularization. *Dokl. Akad. Nauk SSSR* **1963**, *151*, 501–504.
3. Huang, G.; Lanza, A.; Morigi, S.; Reichel, L.; Sgallari, F. Majorization-minimization generalized Krylov subspace methods for ℓ_p-ℓ_q optimization applied to image restoration. *BIT Numer. Math.* **2017**, *57*, 351–378. [CrossRef]
4. Buccini, A.; Reichel, L. An ℓ_2-ℓ_q regularization method for large discrete ill-posed problems. *J. Sci. Comput.* **2019**, *78*, 1526–1549. [CrossRef]
5. Candes, E.; Tao, T. The Dantzig Selector: Statistical Estimation When p is much larger than n. *Ann. Stat.* **2007**, *35*, 2313–2351.
6. Drosou, K.; Koukouvinos, C. Sure independence screening for analyzing supersaturated designs. *Commun. Stat. Simul. Comput.* **2019**, *48*, 1979–1995. [CrossRef]
7. Drosou, K.; Koukouvinos, C. A new variable selection method based on SVM for analyzing supersaturated designs. *J. Qual. Technol.* **2019**, *51*, 21–36. [CrossRef]
8. Georgiou, S.D. Modelling by supersaturated designs. *Comput. Stat. Data Anal.* **2008**, *53*, 428–435. [CrossRef]
9. Yagola, A.G.; Leonov, A.S.; Titarenko, V.N. Data errors and an error estimation for ill-posed problems. *Inverse Probl. Eng.* **2002**, *10*, 117–129. [CrossRef]
10. Winkler, J.R.; Mitrouli, M. Condition estimation for regression and feature selection. *J. Comput. Appl. Math.* **2020**, *373*, 112212. [CrossRef]
11. Hansen, P.C. The discrete picard condition for discrete ill-posed problems. *BIT* **1990**, *30*, 658–672. [CrossRef]
12. Hansen, P.C. *Rank-Deficient and Discrete Ill-Posed Problems*; SIAM: Philadelphia, PA, USA, 1998.
13. Hansen, P.C. The L-curve and its use in the numerical treatment of inverse problems. In *Computational Inverse Problems in Electrocardiology, Advances in Computational Bioengineering 4*; WIT Press: Southampton, UK, 2000; pp. 119–142.
14. Golub, G.H.; Meurant, G. *Matrices, Moments and Quadrature with Applications*; Princeton University Press: Princeton, NJ, USA, 2010.
15. Engl, H.W.; Hanke, M.; Neubauer, A. *Regularization of Inverse Problems*; Kluwer: Dordrecht, The Netherlands, 1996.
16. Koukouvinos, C.; Lappa, A.; Mitrouli, M.; Roupa, P.; Turek, O. Numerical methods for estimating the tuning parameter in penalized least squares problems. *Commun. Stat. Simul. Comput.* **2019**, 1–22. [CrossRef]
17. Koukouvinos, C.; Jbilou, K.; Mitrouli, M.; Turek, O. An eigenvalue approach for estimating the generalized cross validation function for correlated matrices. *Electron. J. Linear Algebra* **2019**, *35*, 482–496. [CrossRef]
18. Liu, Y.; Dean, A. k-Circulant supersaturated designs. *Technometrics* **2004**, *46*, 32–43. [CrossRef]
19. Li, R.; Lin, D.K.J. Analysis Methods for Supersaturated Design: Some Comparisons. *J. Data Sci.* **2003**, *1*, 249–260. [CrossRef]
20. Cesa, M.; Campisi, B.; Bizzotto, A.; Ferraro, C.; Fumagalli, F.; Nimis, P.L. A Factor Influence Study of Trace Element Bioaccumulation in Moss Bags. *Arch. Environ. Contam. Toxicol.* **2008**, *55*, 386–396. [CrossRef] [PubMed]

Σ mathematics

Article
Eigenvalue Estimates via Pseudospectra †

Georgios Katsouleas *,‡, Vasiliki Panagakou ‡ and Panayiotis Psarrakos ‡

Department of Mathematics, Zografou Campus, National Technical University of Athens, 15773 Athens, Greece; vpanagakou@mail.ntua.gr (V.P.); ppsarr@math.ntua.gr (P.P.)
* Correspondence: g_katsouleas@mail.ntua.gr
† This paper is dedicated to Mr. Constantin M. Petridi.
‡ These authors contributed equally to this work.

Abstract: In this note, given a matrix $A \in \mathbb{C}^{n \times n}$ (or a general matrix polynomial $P(z)$, $z \in \mathbb{C}$) and an arbitrary scalar $\lambda_0 \in \mathbb{C}$, we show how to define a sequence $\{\mu_k\}_{k \in \mathbb{N}}$ which converges to some element of its spectrum. The scalar λ_0 serves as initial term ($\mu_0 = \lambda_0$), while additional terms are constructed through a recursive procedure, exploiting the fact that each term μ_k of this sequence is in fact a point lying on the boundary curve of some pseudospectral set of A (or $P(z)$). Then, the next term in the sequence is detected in the direction which is normal to this curve at the point μ_k. Repeating the construction for additional initial points, it is possible to approximate peripheral eigenvalues, localize the spectrum and even obtain spectral enclosures. Hence, as a by-product of our method, a computationally cheap procedure for approximate pseudospectra computations emerges. An advantage of the proposed approach is that it does not make any assumptions on the location of the spectrum. The fact that all computations are performed on some dynamically chosen locations on the complex plane which converge to the eigenvalues, rather than on a large number of predefined points on a rigid grid, can be used to accelerate conventional grid algorithms. Parallel implementation of the method or use in conjunction with randomization techniques can lead to further computational savings when applied to large-scale matrices.

Keywords: pseudospectra; eigenvalues; matrix polynomial; perturbation; Perron root; large-scale matrices; approximation algorithm

Citation: Katsouleas, G.; Panagakou, V.; Psarrakos, P. Eigenvalue Estimates via Pseudospectra. *Mathematics* **2021**, *9*, 1729. https://doi.org/10.3390/math9151729

Academic Editors: Khalide Jbilou and Marilena Mitrouli

Received: 30 May 2021
Accepted: 18 July 2021
Published: 22 July 2021

Publisher's Note: MDPI stays neutral with regard to jurisdictional claims in published maps and institutional affiliations.

1. Introduction

The theory of pseudospectra originates in numerical analysis and can be traced back to Landau [1], Varah [2], Wilkinson [3], Demmel [4], and Trefethen [5], motivated by the need to obtain insights into systems evolving in ways that the eigenvalues alone could not explain. This is especially true in problems where the underlying matrices or linear operators are non-normal or exhibit in some sense large deviations from normality. A better understanding of such systems can be gained through the concept of pseudospectrum, which, for a matrix $A \in \mathbb{C}^{n \times n}$ and a positive parameter $\epsilon > 0$, was introduced as the subset of the complex plane that is bounded by the ϵ^{-1}–level set of the norm of the resolvent $\|(\mu I - A)^{-1}\|$. A second definition stated in terms of perturbations characterizes the elements of this set as eigenvalues of some perturbation $A + E$ with $\|E\| \leq \epsilon$. In this sense, the notion of pseudospectrum provides information that goes beyond eigenvalues, while retaining the advantage of being a natural extension of the spectral set. In fact, for different values of magnitude ϵ, pseudospectrum provides a global perspective on the effects of perturbations; this is in stark contrast to the concept of condition number, where only the worst-case scenario is considered.

On one hand, pseudospectrum may be used as a visualization tool to reveal information regarding the matrix itself and the sensitivity of its eigenvalues. Applications within numerical analysis include convergence of nonsymmetric matrix iterations [6], backward error analysis of eigenvalue algorithms [7], and stability of spectral methods [8]. On the other hand, it is a versatile tool that has been used to obtain quantitative bounds on the transient behavior of differential equations in finite time, which may deviate from the long-term asymptotic behavior [9]. Important results involving pseudospetra have been also been obtained in the context of spectral theory and spectral properties of banded Toeplitz matrices [10,11]. Although emphasis has been placed on the standard eigenproblem, attention has also been drawn to matrix pencils [12] and more general matrix polynomials [13,14] arising in vibrating systems, control theory, etc. For a comprehensive overview of this research field and its applications, the interested reader may refer to [15].

In this note, we propose an application of pseudospectral sets as a mean to obtain eigenvalue estimates in the vicinity of some complex scalar. In particular, given a matrix (or a general matrix polynomial) and a scalar $\lambda_0 \in \mathbb{C}$, we construct a sequence $\{\mu_k\}_{k\in\mathbb{N}}$ that converges to some element of its spectrum. The scalar λ_0 serves as initial term ($\mu_0 = \lambda_0$), while additional terms are constructed through an iterative procedure, exploiting the fact that each term μ_k of this sequence is in fact a point lying on the boundary curve of some pseudospectral set. Then, the next term in the sequence is detected in the perpendicular direction to the tangent line at the point μ_k. Repeating the construction for a tuple of initial points encircling the spectrum, several peripheral eigenvalues are approximated. Since the pseudospectrum may be disconnected, this procedure allows the identification of individual connected components and, as a by-product, a convenient and numerically efficient procedure for approximate pseudospectrum computation emerges. Moreover, this approach is clearly amenable to parallelization or randomization and can lead to significant computational savings when applied to probems involving large–scale matrices.

Our paper is organized as follows. In Section 2, we provide the necessary theoretical background on the method and provide examples for the constant matrix case. As confirmed by numerical experiments, the method can provide a sufficiently accurate pseudospectrum computation at a much-reduced computational cost, especially in cases where the spectrum is convexly independent (i.e., each eigenvalue does not lie in the convex hull of the others) or exhibits large eigenvalue gaps. A second application of the method on Perron-root approximation for non–negative matrices is presented. Then, Section 3 shows how the procedure may be modified to estimate the spectrum of more general matrix polynomials. Numerical experiments showcasing the application of the method on damped mass–spring and gyroscopic systems conclude the paper.

2. Eigenvalues via Pseudospectra

Let the matrix $A \in \mathbb{C}^{n\times n}$ with spectrum $\sigma(A) = \{\mu \in \mathbb{C} : \det(\mu I - A) = 0\}$, where $\det(\cdot)$ denotes the *determinant* of a matrix. With respect to the $\|\cdot\|_2$–norm, the *pseudospectrum* of A is defined by

$$\begin{aligned}\sigma_\epsilon(A) &= \left\{\mu \in \mathbb{C} : \frac{1}{\|(\mu I - A)^{-1}\|_2} \le \epsilon\right\} \\ &= \{\mu \in \mathbb{C} : \mu \in \sigma(A+E) \text{ for some } E \in \mathbb{C}^{n\times n} \text{ with } \|E\| \le \epsilon\} \\ &= \{\mu \in \mathbb{C} : s_{\min}(\mu I - A) \le \epsilon\},\end{aligned}$$

where $s_{\min}(\cdot)$ denotes the smallest *singular value* of a matrix and $\epsilon > 0$ is the maximum norm of admissible perturbations.

For every choice of increasing positive parameters $0 < \epsilon_1 < \epsilon_2 < \epsilon_3 < \dots$, the corresponding closed, strictly nested sequence of pseudospectra

$$\sigma_{\epsilon_1}(A) \subset \sigma_{\epsilon_2}(A) \subset \sigma_{\epsilon_3}(A) \subset \dots$$

is obtained. In fact, the respective boundaries satisfy the inclusions

$$\begin{aligned}\partial\sigma_{\epsilon_1}(A) &\subseteq \{\mu \in \mathbb{C} : s_{\min}(\mu I - A) = \epsilon_1\}\\ \partial\sigma_{\epsilon_2}(A) &\subseteq \{\mu \in \mathbb{C} : s_{\min}(\mu I - A) = \epsilon_2\}\\ \partial\sigma_{\epsilon_3}(A) &\subseteq \{\mu \in \mathbb{C} : s_{\min}(\mu I - A) = \epsilon_3\}\\ \vdots \quad &\quad\quad \vdots\end{aligned}$$

It is also clear that, for any $\lambda \in \sigma(A)$, $s_{\min}(\lambda I - A) = 0$.

Our objective now is to exploit the properties of these sets to detect an eigenvalue of A in the vicinity of a given scalar $\lambda_0 \in \mathbb{C}\backslash\sigma(A)$. This given point of interest may be considered to lie on the boundary of some pseudospectral set, i.e., there exists some non–negative parameter $\hat{\epsilon}_1 > 0$, such that

$$\lambda_0 \in \partial\sigma_{\hat{\epsilon}_1}(A) \subseteq \{\mu \in \mathbb{C} : s_{\min}(\mu I - A) = \hat{\epsilon}_1\}. \tag{1}$$

Indeed, points satisfying the equality $s_{\min}(\mu I - A) = \epsilon$ for some $\epsilon > 0$ and lying in the interior of $\sigma_\epsilon(A)$ are finite in number. Thus, in the generic case, we may think of the inclusion (1) as an equality.

We consider the real–valued function $g_A : \mathbb{C} \to \mathbb{R}_+$ with $g_A(z) = s_{\min}(zI - A)$. In the process of formulating a curve-tracing algorithm for pseudospectrum computation [16], Brühl analyzed $g_A(z)$ and, identifying $\mathbb{C} \equiv \mathbb{R}^2$, noted that its differentiability is explained by the following Theorem in [17]:

Theorem 1. *Let the matrix valued function $P(\chi) : \mathbb{R}^d \to \mathbb{C}^{n\times n}$ be real analytic in a neighborhood of $\chi_0 = \left(x_0^1, \ldots, x_0^d\right)$ and let σ_0 a simple nonzero singular value of $P(\chi_0)$ with u_0, v_0 its associated left and right singular vectors, respectively.*

Then, there exists a neighborhood $\mathcal{N}$ of χ_0 on which a simple nonzero singular value $\sigma(\chi)$ of $P(\chi)$ is defined with corresponding left and right singular vectors $u(\chi)$ and $v(\chi)$, respectively, such that $\sigma(\chi_0) = \sigma_0$, $u(\chi_0) = u_0$, $v(\chi_0) = v_0$ and the functions σ, u, v are real analytic on $\mathcal{N}$. The partial derivatives of $\sigma(\chi)$ are given by

$$\frac{\partial s(\chi_0)}{\partial \chi^j} = \mathrm{Re}\left(u_0^* \frac{\partial P(\chi_0)}{\partial \chi^j} v_0\right), \quad j = 1, \ldots, d.$$

Hence, recalling (1) and assuming $\hat{\epsilon}_1$ is a simple singular value of the matrix $P(\lambda_0) = \lambda_0 I - A$, then

$$\nabla s_{\min}(zI - A)\big|_{z=\lambda_0} = (\mathrm{Re}(v_{\min}^* u_{\min}), \mathrm{Im}(v_{\min}^* u_{\min})) = v_{\min}^* u_{\min},$$

where $u_{\min}$ and $v_{\min}$ denote the left and right singular vectors of $\lambda_0 I - A$ associated to $\hat{\epsilon}_1 = s_{\min}(\lambda_0 I - A)$, respectively [16] (Corollary 2.2).

On the other hand, if λ is an eigenvalue of A near λ_0, it holds $|\lambda - \lambda_0| \leq \hat{\epsilon}_1$. The latter observation follows from the fact that

$$\begin{aligned}\sigma_\epsilon(A) &\supseteq \sigma(A) + D(0,\epsilon)\\ &= \{z \in \mathbb{C} : \mathrm{dist}(z, \sigma(A)) \leq \epsilon\},\end{aligned}$$

where $D(0,\epsilon) = \{z \in \mathbb{C} : |z| \leq \epsilon\}$ and equality holds for normal matrices. So, the scalar

$$\begin{aligned}\mu_1 &= \lambda_0 - \hat{\epsilon}_1 \cdot \frac{\nabla s_{\min}(zI - A)}{|\nabla s_{\min}(zI - A)|}\Bigg|_{z=\lambda_0}\\ &= \lambda_0 - s_{\min}(\lambda_0 I - A) \cdot \frac{v_{\min}(\lambda_0)^* u_{\min}(\lambda_0)}{|v_{\min}(\lambda_0)^* u_{\min}(\lambda_0)|}\end{aligned}$$

can be considered to be an estimate of eigenvalue λ. In particular, $\lambda_0 \in \partial\sigma_{\hat{\epsilon}_1}(A)$ and μ_1 lies in the interior of $\sigma_{\hat{\epsilon}_1}(A)$. Moreover, the sequence

$$\begin{aligned}
\mu_0 &= \lambda_0 \\
\mu_1 &= \mu_0 - s_{\min}(\mu_0 I - A) \cdot \frac{v_{\min}(\mu_0)^* u_{\min}(\mu_0)}{|v_{\min}(\mu_0)^* u_{\min}(\mu_0)|} \\
\mu_2 &= \mu_1 - s_{\min}(\mu_1 I - A) \cdot \frac{v_{\min}(\mu_1)^* u_{\min}(\mu_1)}{|v_{\min}(\mu_1)^* u_{\min}(\mu_1)|} \\
&\vdots \qquad \vdots \\
\mu_k &= \mu_{k-1} - s_{\min}(\mu_{k-1} I - A) \cdot \frac{v_{\min}(\mu_{k-1})^* u_{\min}(\mu_{k-1})}{|v_{\min}(\mu_{k-1})^* u_{\min}(\mu_{k-1})|}
\end{aligned} \tag{2}$$

converges to λ.

The above process requires the computation of the triplet

$$(s_{\min}(\mu_k I - A), u_{\min}(\mu_k), v_{\min}(\mu_k))$$

at every point μ_k; see [18].

Remark. To avoid the computational burden of computing the (left and right) singular vectors, a cheaper alternative would be to consider at each iteration ($k = 0, 1, 2, \ldots$) the canonical octagon with vertices

$$p_{k,j} = \mu_k + e^{\mathbf{i}(j\frac{\pi}{4})} \cdot s_{\min}(\mu_k I - A), \; j = 0, 1, 2, \ldots 7$$

instead and simply compute

$$\theta_{k,j} = s_{\min}\left(p_{k,j} I - A\right), \; j = 0, 1, 2, \ldots 7.$$

In this case, instead of (2), we can set

$$\mu_{k+1} = \mu_k + e^{\mathbf{i}(j_0\frac{\pi}{4})} \cdot \theta_{k,j_0}$$

with j_0 such that

$$\theta_{k,j_0} = \min_{j=0,1,2,\ldots,7} \theta_{k,j} = \min_{j=0,1,2,\ldots,7} \left(s_{\min}\left(p_{k,j} I - A\right)\right).$$

2.1. Numerical Experiments

2.1.1. Pseudospectrum Computation

The approximating sequences in (2) may be utilized to implement a computationally cheap procedure to visualize matrix pseudospectra, at least in cases where the order of the matrix is small or when its spectrum exhibits large eigenvalue gaps. Several related techniques for pseudospectrum computation have appeared in the literature. These fall largely into two categories: grid [14] and path-following algorithms [16,19–21]. Grid algorithms begin by evaluating the function $s_{\min}(zI - A)$ on a predefined grid on the complex plane and lead to a graphical visualization of the boundary $\partial\sigma_\epsilon(A)$ by plotting the ϵ-contours of $s_{\min}(zI - A)$. This approach faces two severe challenges; namely, the requirement of a–priori information on the location of the spectrum to correctly identify a suitable region to discretize, as well as the typically large number of grid points the computations have to be performed upon. path-following algorithms, on the other hand, require an initial step to detect a starting point on the curve $\partial\sigma_\epsilon(A)$ and then proceed to compute additional boundary points for each connected component of $\sigma_\epsilon(A)$. The main drawbacks of this latter approach lie in the difficulty in performing the initial step and the need to correctly identify every connected component of $\sigma_\epsilon(A)$ in order to repeat the procedure and properly trace its boundary. Moreover, cases where pseudospectrum computation is required for a whole tuple of parameters ϵ drastically compromise the efficiency of path-following algorithms.

Our approach is to use the approximating sequences (2) to decrease the number of singular value evaluations and therefore speed up the computation of pseudospectra. The basic steps are outlined as follows:

i. Select a tuple of initial points $\left\{\mu_0^j\right\}_{j=1}^{s} \in \mathbb{C}$ encircling the spectrum; for instance, these can be chosen on the circle $\{z \in \mathbb{C} : |z| = \|A\|\}$.
ii. Construct eigenvalue approximating sequences $\left\{\mu_k^j\right\}_{k=0}^{n_j}$ $(j = 1, \ldots, s)$, as in (2). If $\epsilon_k^j > 0$ $(k = 1, \ldots, n_j)$ are such that $\mu_k^j \in \partial\sigma_{\epsilon_k^j}(A)$, the length n_j of each sequence is determined, so that $s_{\min}(\mu_{n_j}^j I - A) \leq \epsilon_0$ for all $j = 1, \ldots, s$, where ϵ_0 is some prefixed parameter value. In other words, ϵ_0 indicates the tolerance with which the approached by the constructed sequences eigenvalues should be approximated and corresponds to the minimum parameter for which pseudospectra will be computed.
iii. Classify the sequences into distinct clusters, according to the proximity of their final terms. This step may be performed using a k-means clustering algorithm, using a suitable criterion to evaluate the optimal number of groups.
iv. Compute

$$u = \min_{j=1,\ldots,s} \max_{j=1,\ldots,n_j} \epsilon_k^j (> \epsilon_0) \text{ and } \ell = \max_{j=1,\ldots,s} \min_{j=1,\ldots,n_j} \epsilon_k^j (< \epsilon_0).$$

v. If necessary, repeat the procedure for t additional points between the centroids of the detected clusters, constructing additional sequences, so that

$$\min_{j=s+1,\ldots,s+t} \max_{j=1,\ldots,n_j} \epsilon_k^j > u \text{ and } \max_{j=s+1,\ldots,s+t} \min_{j=1,\ldots,n_j} \epsilon_k^j < \ell.$$

vi. Detect boundary points of $\sigma_\epsilon(A)$ for any choice of parameters $\epsilon \in [\ell, u]$ along the polygonal chains formed by the total of $s + t$ constructed sequences of points by interpolation.
vii. Fit closed spline curves passing through the respective sets of boundary points in $\partial\sigma_\epsilon(A)$ for the various choices of $\epsilon \in [\ell, u]$ to obtain sketches of the corresponding pseudospectra $\sigma_\epsilon(A)$.

The proposed method successfully localizes the spectrum, initiating the procedure with a restricted number of points. Then, singular value computations are kept to a minimum by considering points only on the constructed sequences. Pseudospectrum components corresponding to *peripheral* eigenvalues $\lambda \notin \text{co}(\sigma(A)\backslash\{\lambda\})$ not in the convex hull of the other eigenvalues, are thus extremely easy to identify. This approach is also well–suited to cases, where the matrix has *convexly independent* spectrum; i.e., when $\lambda \notin \text{co}(\sigma(A)\backslash\{\lambda\})$, for every $\lambda \in \sigma(A)$. Moreover, it is clearly amenable to parallelization, which could lead to significant computational savings in cases of large matrices.

Application 1. *We consider a random matrix $A \in \mathbb{C}^{6\times 6}$, the sole constraint being that its eigenvalues are distant form each other; the real and imaginary parts of its entries follow the standardized normal distribution scaled by 10^4. For the proposed procedure, we select initial points $\left\{\mu_0^j\right\}_{j=1}^{10} \subset \{z \in \mathbb{C} : |z| = \|A\|_1\}$ and exploit the fact that the corresponding sequences $\left\{\mu_k^j\right\}_{k=0}^{n_j}$ generated as in (2) converge to some element of $\sigma(A)$. The number n_j of terms in each sequence $(j = 1, \ldots 10)$ is determined, so that all values $\left\{s_{\min}(\mu_{n_j}^j I - A)\right\}_{j=1}^{10}$ do not exceed $\epsilon_0 = 0.5$. The sequences are organized into distinct clusters, grouping together those sequences which approximate the same element of $\sigma(A)$. This grouping is performed using a k-means clustering algorithm, where* *the optimal number of clusters is evaluated via the silhouette criterion and using a distance metric based on the sum of absolute differences between points. Since six different groups are identified, clearly all elements of* $\sigma(A)$ *have been sufficiently approximated by at least one of the sequences. For an illustration, refer to Figure 1a; different colors have been used to differentiate between polygonal chains corresponding to distinct clusters. The construction so far required 914 singular value computations. Having calculated all parameter values* ϵ_k^j *such that* $\mu_k^j \in \partial\sigma_{\epsilon_k^j}(A)$ *during the previous procedure, it is possible to interpolate between these known points along the trajectories formed by* $\left\{\mu_k^j\right\}_{k=0}^{n_j}$ *(*$j = 1, \ldots 10$*) to approximate boundary points of* $\partial\sigma_\epsilon(A)$ *for selected values* $\epsilon > \epsilon_0 = 0.5$*. Since all ten trajectories converge to eigenvalues from points encircling* $\sigma(A)$*, to obtain better pseudospectra approximations, it is necessary to repeat the procedure for additional suitably selected points. Hence, for each cluster we consider three additional points; see Figure 1b. In particular, denoting* $c_1, \ldots c_6$ *the centroids of the clusters, for each* j *we consider the three centroids* $\left\{c_{j,k}\right\}_{k=1}^{3}$ *which lie closest to* c_j *and take the convex combinations*

$$p_k^j = \frac{1}{6}\left(5c_j + c_{j,k}\right), \quad k = 1, 2, 3.$$

Then, additional sequences corresponding to these extra points are constructed so that the desired parameter values of ϵ *for which pseudospectra should be computed (in this instance, the triple of* $\epsilon = 1, 5, 10 \in [\ell, u]$*) may be interpolated within these trajectories, as for the ten initial ones. This imposes an extra cost of 1170 additional singular value computations (2084 in total). The resulting approximations of the pseudospectra components identified by the upper left corner trajectories for* $\epsilon = 1, 5, 10$ *are depicted in greater detail in Figure 1c; the relevant eigenvalue is indicated by "*".*

An advantage of this procedure is that it does not require some a–priori knowledge of the initial region Ω on the complex plane where the spectrum is located. In fact, the very nature of this specific example, whose spectrum covers a wide area Ω, would render computations on a suitable grid impractical. Another way in which this method diverges from conventional grid algorithms is in that the computations are performed on a dynamically chosen set of points, iteratively selected as the corresponding trajectories converge to peripheral eigenvalues and identify the relevant pseudospectrum components, rather than on a large number of predefined points on a rigid grid.

Application 2. *To demonstrate how the procedure works in cases of larger matrices, in this application we examine the matrix* $A = 10^{-7} \cdot \text{Pores2}$*, where Pores2 is a* 1024×1024 *matrix from the Harwell-Boeing sparse matrix collection [22] related to a non–symmetric computational fluid dynamics problem. Here, the factor* 10^{-7} *is used for scaling purposes and is related to the norm–*$\|\cdot\|_1$ *order of the matrix under consideration. Initiating the procedure with 30 equidistributed points on the circle* $\left\{z \in \mathbb{C} : |z| = \frac{1}{2}\|A\|_1\right\}$*, the method required a total of 810 singular value computations for a minimum parameter value of* $\epsilon_0 = 0.005$*; the resulting pseudospectra visualizations for* $\epsilon = 10^{-1}, 10^{-1.5}, 10^{-2}$ *are depicted in Figure 2. For this example, we have opted not to introduce additional points.*

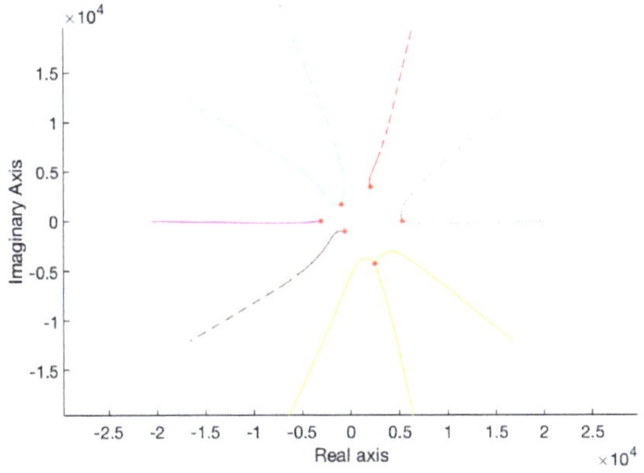

(**a**) Trajectories of 10 sequences converging to $\sigma(A)$.

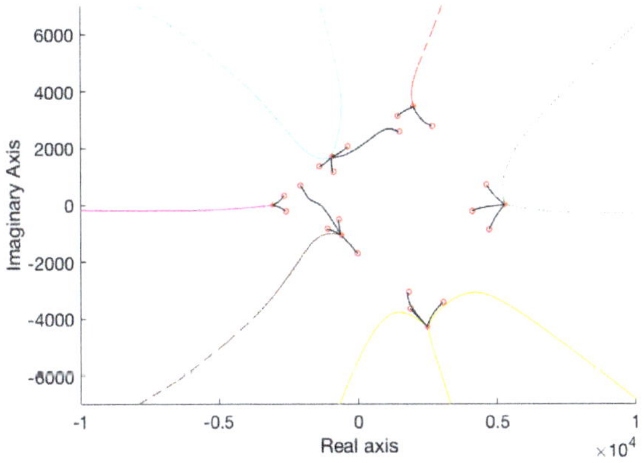

(**b**) Additional interior points (red circles) and relevant trajectories (solid black lines).

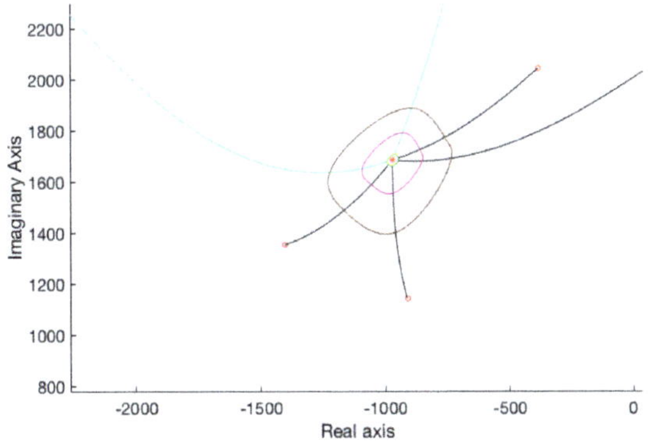

(**c**) Pseudospectrum component in the upper left side for $\epsilon = 1, 5, 10$.

Figure 1. Pseudospectrum computation for random $A \in \mathbb{C}^{6\times 6}$ with spectral gaps, using 10 initial points.

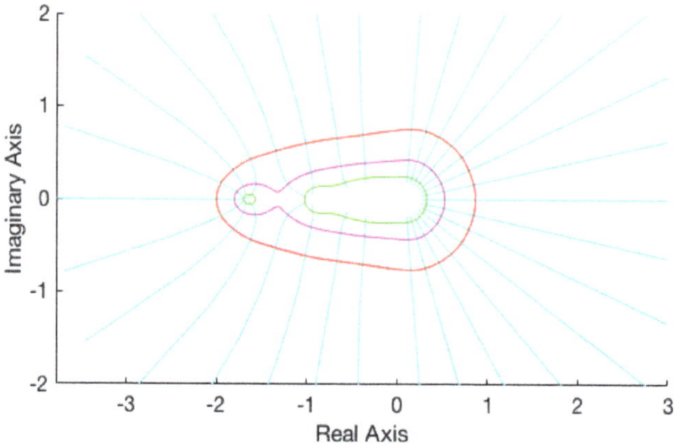

Figure 2. Pseudospectra computations for a non–symmetric sparse matrix of order 1024 from the Harwell-Boeing collection and $\epsilon = 10^{-1}, 10^{-1.5}, 10^{-2}$.

Perron root computation. Applications of non–negative matrices, i.e., matrices with exclusively non–negative real entries, abound in such diverse fields as probability theory, dynamical systems, Internet search engines, tournament matrices etc. In this context, the dominant eigenvalue of non–negative matrices, also referred to as *Perron root*, is of central importance. Localization of the Perron root has been extensively studied in the literature; relevant bounds can be found in [23–27]. Its computation is typically carried out using the power method; the convergence rate of this approach depends on the relative magnitudes of the two dominant eigenvalues. Relevant methods have appeared in [28–30], among others. As a second application of the approximating sequences (2), the following experiment reports an elegant way of approximating Perron roots.

Application 3. *For this experiment, we considered a tuple of 50 non-negative matrices* $\{A_\ell\}_{\ell=1}^{50} \subset \mathbb{R}_+^{500\times 500}$ *with uniformly distributed entries in* $(0, 50)$*. The symmetry of* $\sigma_\epsilon(A_\ell)$ *with respect to the real axis suggests that it suffices to restrict the computations exclusively to the closed upper half–plane. Hence, for each of the matrices* A_ℓ*, we initiated the construction of the sequences (2) from equidistributed initial terms* $\left\{\mu_0^{\ell,j}\right\}_{j=1}^{10} \subset \left\{z \in \mathbb{C} : |z| = 10^4 \cdot \|A_\ell\|_1, \mathrm{Im}(z) \geq 0\right\}$ $(\ell = 1, \ldots 50)$*. As expected, the rightmost of these points formed sequences converging to the Perron root of* A_ℓ*, while each of the remaining ones approximated some other peripheral eigenvalue. In the generic case, the magnitude of the second highest eigenvalue of* A_ℓ *was much smaller than the Perron root. Figure 3 is illustrative of this separation; the blue curve traces the boundary of the numerical range of such a matrix, red points indicate its eigenvalues, while the cyan lines correspond to the trajectories of the constructed sequences. Denoting* $\left\{\mu_k^{\ell,j}\right\}_{k=0}^{n_{\ell,j}}$ $(j = 1, \ldots, s_\ell)$ *those sequences approximating the Perron root* $\lambda_\ell \in \sigma(A_\ell)$ $(\ell = 1, \ldots, 50)$*, then the relative error in each iteration* $\frac{\left|\mu_k^{\ell,j} - \lambda_\ell\right|}{|\lambda_\ell|}$, $k = 0, 1, \ldots, \min(n_{\ell,j})$*, decreases rapidly, even though the initial points* $\mu_0^{\ell,j}$ $(j = 1, \ldots, s_\ell)$ *were chosen to be extremely remote from* $\sigma(A_\ell)$*. Averages*

$$\frac{1}{\ell} \sum_{\ell=1}^{50} \frac{1}{s_\ell} \sum_{j=1}^{s_\ell} \frac{\left|\mu_k^{\ell,j} - \lambda_\ell\right|}{|\lambda_\ell|}$$

of these relative approximation errors over the tuple of matrices for the first $k = 1, 2, \ldots, 5$ *iterations are demonstrated in the first column of Table 1, verifying that a reliable estimate for the Perron root may in the generic case be obtained after the computation of as few as 3 terms in the corresponding trajectories.*

The remaining $(10 - s_\ell)$ *sequences converge to some other peripheral eigenvalues* $\lambda_{\ell,1}, \ldots, \lambda_{\ell,s_\ell} \in \sigma(A_\ell)$*, reasonable approximations of which require a rather larger number of iterations, as can be seen from the second column of Table 1 reporting.*

$$\frac{1}{\ell}\sum_{\ell=1}^{50}\frac{1}{10-s_\ell}\sum_{j=s_\ell+1}^{10}\frac{\left|\mu_k^{\ell,j}-\lambda_{\ell,j}\right|}{\left|\lambda_{\ell,j}\right|}.$$

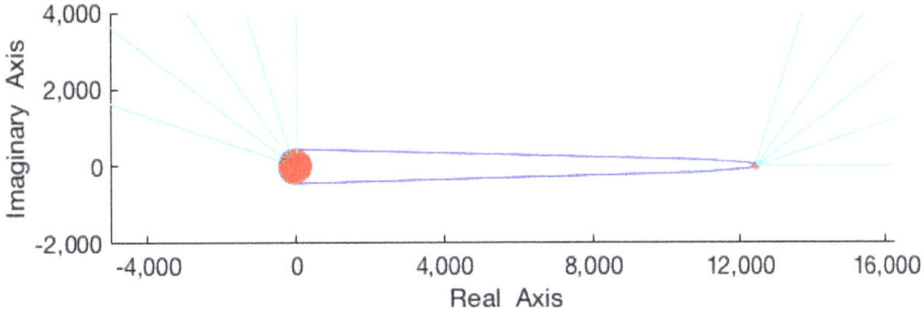

Figure 3. Indicative numerical range of 500 × 500 non–negative matrix and 10 approximating trajectories.

Table 1. Relative approximation errors for Perron root and other peripheral eigenvalues of 500 × 500 non–negative matrices.

# of Iterations	Mean Rel. Error (Perron Root)	Mean Rel. Error (Other Eigenvalues)
1	0.0011	0.4205
2	7.0082×10^{-7}	0.1783
3	4.4907×10^{-10}	0.1030
4	2.8798×10^{-13}	0.0680
5	9.2285×10^{-16}	0.0483

Application 3 suggests that any reasonable upper bound $\mu_0 \in \mathbb{R}$ suffices to yield reliable estimations for the Perron root after computation of only 2–3 terms in the sequence (2).

The previous experiment may seem excessively optimistic. Indeed, there can be instances when the situation is much more demanding.

Application 4. *The Frank matrix is well–known to have ill-conditioned eigenvalues. For this application, we test the behavior of the proposed method on the Frank matrix of order* 32*, the normalized matrix of eigenvectors of which has condition number* 7.81×10^{11}*. Figure 4 depicts the resulting pseudospectra visualizations for* $\epsilon = 0.001, 0.005, 0.01, 0.02, 0.03$*, initiating the procedure from 30 points located on the upper semiellipse centered at* $(40, 0)$ *with semi–major and semi–minor axes lengths equal to 70 and 15, respectively. The depicted trajectories were constructed, so that the final terms in each polygonal chain lie within* $\sigma_{0.001}(A)$*. Then, according to the distances of the final terms of consecutive sequences, at most two additional points are introduced on the line segment connecting these respective final terms. The necessary iterations for the construction of the relevant sequences are reported in Table 2 for different numbers of initial points.*

The approximating quality of the sequences is much compromised when compared to the generic case, requiring many more iterations, especially for the eigenvalues with smallest real parts; these are also the most ill-conditioned ones. In fact, the seven rightmost sequences converging to the Perron root (refer to Figure 4) display the fastest convergence, the second group of thirteen sequences leading to the intermediate eigenvalues being somewhat more compromised, while the leftmost sequences naturally exhibit even more diminished approximation quality. Mean relative approximation errors for these three groups are reported in Table 3.

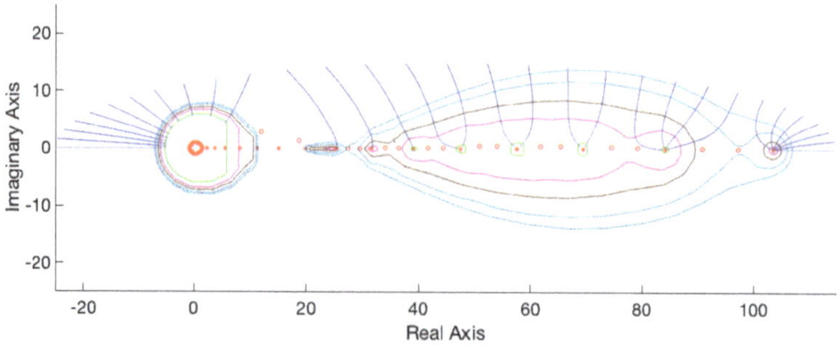

Figure 4. Pseudospectra computation for the Frank matrix of order 32 and $\epsilon = 0.001, 0.005, 0.01, 0.02, 0.03$. Additional points selected between the endpoints of the initial sequences are denoted by red circles, while eigenvalues are denoted by red stars.

Table 2. Number of iterations for different numbers of initial points ($\epsilon_0 = 0.001$).

# of Initial Points	10	15	30
Iterations (initial points)	11,206	18,455	35,159
Iterations (additional points)	16,116	14,872	11,883
Iterations (total)	27,322	33,327	47,042

Table 3. Relative approximation errors for Perron root and other eigenvalues of the Frank matrix of order 32.

# of Iterations	Mean Rel. Error (Perron Root)	Mean Rel. Error (Intermediate Eigenvalues)	Mean Rel. Error (Leftmost Eigenvalues)
1	0.0916	0.2795	11.0866
100	0.0373	0.1507	5.7968
200	0.0192	0.1206	5.3541
300	0.0103	0.1103	5.1174
400	0.0055	0.0956	4.9582
500	0.0029	0.0843	4.8652

For the numerical experiments in this section, we have restricted ourselves to initial points encircling the spectrum. Another option would be to use our method in tandem with randomization techniques for the initial points selection.

3. Matrix Polynomials

The derivation of eigenvalue approximating sequences may be readily extended to account for the general matrix polynomial case

$$P(\lambda) = A_m\lambda^m + A_{m-1}\lambda^{m-1} + \cdots + A_1\lambda + A_0,$$

where $\lambda \in \mathbb{C}$ and $A_j \in \mathbb{C}^{n\times n}$ $(j = 0, 1, \ldots, m)$, with $A_m \neq 0$. Recall that the *spectrum* of $P(\lambda)$ is the set of all its *eigenvalues*; i.e., $\sigma(P) = \{\lambda \in \mathbb{C} : \det P(\lambda) = 0\}$. For a scalar $\lambda_0 \in \sigma(P)$, the nonzero solutions $v_0 \in \mathbb{C}^n$ to the system $P(\lambda_0)v_0 = 0$ are the *eigenvectors* of $P(\lambda)$ corresponding to λ_0.

The ϵ*–pseudospectrum* of $P(\lambda)$ was introduced in [14] for a given parameter $\epsilon > 0$ and a set of nonnegative weights $\mathbf{w} \in \mathbb{R}_+^{m+1}$ as the set

$$\sigma_{\epsilon,\mathbf{w}}(P) = \left\{\lambda \in \mathbb{C} : \det P_\Delta(\lambda) = 0, \left\|\Delta_j\right\| \leq \epsilon w_j, j = 0, 1, \ldots, m\right\} \tag{3}$$

of eigenvalues of all admissible perturbations $P_\Delta(\lambda)$ of $P(\lambda)$ of the form

$$P_\Delta(\lambda) = (A_m + \Delta_m)\lambda^m + (A_{m-1} + \Delta_{m-1})\lambda^{m-1} + \cdots + (A_1 + \Delta_1)\lambda + (A_0 + \Delta_0),$$

where the norms of the matrices $\Delta_j \in \mathbb{C}^{n\times n}$ $(j = 0, 1, \ldots, m)$ satisfy the specified $(\epsilon, \mathbf{w})$-related constraints. In contrast to the constant matrix case, a whole tuple of perturbing matrices Δ_j is involved, which explains the presence of the additional parameter vector $\mathbf{w}$ in the definition of $\sigma_{\epsilon,\mathbf{w}}(P)$. However, considering for some $A \in \mathbb{C}^{n\times n}$ the pencil $P(\lambda) = I_n\lambda - A$, note that (3) reduces to the usual *ϵ–pseudospectrum* of the matrix $A \in \mathbb{C}^{n\times n}$ for the choice of $\mathbf{w} = \{w_0, w_1\} = \{1, 0\}$, since

$$\sigma_{\epsilon,\{1,0\}}(P) = \{\lambda \in \mathbb{C} : \det(I_n\lambda - (A + \Delta_0)) = 0, \|\Delta_0\| \leq \epsilon\} = \sigma_\epsilon(A).$$

In the general case, the nonnegative weights $\{w_j\}_{j=0}^m$ allow freedom in how perturbations are measured; for example, in an absolute sense when $w_0 = w_1 = \cdots = w_m = 1$, or in a relative sense when $w_j = \|A_j\|$ $(j = 0, 1, \ldots, m)$. On the other hand, the choice $\epsilon = 0$ leads to $\sigma_{0,\mathbf{w}}(P) = \sigma(P)$.

From a computational viewpoint, a more convenient characterization [14] (Lemma 2.1) for this set is given by

$$\sigma_{\epsilon,\mathbf{w}}(P) = \{\lambda \in \mathbb{C} : s_{\min}(P(\lambda)) \leq \epsilon q_{\mathbf{w}}(|\lambda|)\},$$

where $s_{\min}(P(\lambda))$ is the minimum singular value of the matrix $P(\lambda)$ and the scalar polynomial

$$q_{\mathbf{w}}(\lambda) = w_m\lambda^m + w_{m-1}\lambda^{m-1} + \cdots + w_1\lambda + w_0,$$

is defined in terms of the weights $\{w_j\}_{j=0}^m$ used in the definition (3) of $\sigma_{\epsilon,\mathbf{w}}(P)$. In fact, since the eigenvalues of $P_\Delta(\lambda)$ are continuous with respect to the entries of its coefficient matrices, the boundary of $\sigma_{\epsilon,\mathbf{w}}(P)$ is expressed as

$$\partial\sigma_{\epsilon,\mathbf{w}}(P) \subseteq \{\lambda \in \mathbb{C} : s_{\min}(P(\lambda)) = \epsilon q_{\mathbf{w}}(|\lambda|)\}; \tag{4}$$

the equality $s_{\min}(P(\lambda)) = \epsilon q_{\mathbf{w}}(|\lambda|)$ is satisfied for some $\epsilon > 0$ only for a finite number of points $\lambda \in \mathrm{int}(\sigma_{\epsilon,\mathbf{w}}(P))$.

Suppose now that we want to approximate an eigenvalue of a matrix polynomial which lies in the neighborhood of some point of interest $\mu_0 \in \mathbb{C}\backslash\sigma(P)$ on the complex plane. Expression (4) suggests that the derivation of a convergent sequence in Section 2 may be readily adapted for our purposes. Indeed, for every scalar $\mu_0 \in \mathbb{C}$, there exists some $\hat{\epsilon}_1 > 0$, such that $\mu_0 \in \partial\sigma_{\hat{\epsilon}_1,\mathbf{w}}$ and then (4) implies $\hat{\epsilon}_1 = \dfrac{s_{\min}(P(\mu_0))}{q_{\mathbf{w}}(|\mu_0|)}$. Moreover, assuming $s_{\min}(P(\mu_0))$ is a simple singular value of the matrix $P(\mu_0)$, we may invoke Theorem 1 to conclude that the function $g_P : \mathbb{C} \to \mathbb{R}_+$ with $g_P(z) = s_{\min}(P(z))$ is real analytic in a neighborhood of $\mu_0 = x_0 + \mathbf{i}y_0$. In fact,

$$\nabla g_P(x_0 + \mathbf{i}y_0) = \left(\mathrm{Re}\left(u_{\min}^* \frac{\partial P(x_0 + \mathbf{i}y_0)}{\partial x} v_{\min}\right), \mathrm{Re}\left(u_{\min}^* \frac{\partial P(x_0 + \mathbf{i}y_0)}{\partial y} v_{\min}\right)\right),$$

where $u_{\min}$ and $v_{\min}$ denote the left and right singular vectors of $P(\mu_0)$ associated to $s_{\min}(P(\mu_0)) = \hat{\epsilon}_1 q_{\mathbf{w}}(|\mu_0|)$, respectively [13] (Corollary 4.2).

As in the constant matrix case, moving from the initial point $\mu_0 \in \partial\sigma_{\hat{\epsilon}_1,\mathbf{w}}$ towards the interior of $\sigma_{\hat{\epsilon}_1,\mathbf{w}}$ in the normal direction to the curve $\partial\sigma_{\hat{\epsilon}_1,\mathbf{w}}$, the scalar

$$\mu_1 = \mu_0 - \hat{\epsilon}_1 \cdot \left.\frac{\nabla[s_{\min}(P(z)) - \hat{\epsilon}_1 q_{\mathbf{w}}(|z|)]}{|\nabla[s_{\min}(P(z)) - \hat{\epsilon}_1 q_{\mathbf{w}}(|z|)]|}\right|_{z=x_0+\mathbf{i}y_0}$$

with $\hat{\epsilon}_1 = \dfrac{s_{\min}(P(\mu_0))}{q_{\mathbf{w}}(|\mu_0|)}$ can be considered to be an estimate of some eigenvalue $\lambda \in \sigma(P)$. In this way, a convergent sequence $\{\mu_k\}_{k\in\mathbb{N}}$ to the eigenvalue $\lambda \in \sigma(P)$ is recursively defined with initial point μ_0 and general term

$$\mu_k = \mu_{k-1} - \frac{s_{\min}(P(\mu_{k-1}))}{q_{\mathbf{w}}(|\mu_{k-1}|)} \cdot \left.\frac{\nabla[s_{\min}(P(z)) - \hat{\epsilon}_{k-1}q_{\mathbf{w}}(|z|)]}{|\nabla[s_{\min}(P(z)) - \hat{\epsilon}_{k-1}q_{\mathbf{w}}(|z|)]|}\right|_{z=\mu_{k-1}=x_{k-1}+\mathbf{i}y_{k-1}}. \quad (5)$$

Numerical Experiments

The steps outlined in Section 2.1.1 are readily modified using the sequences in (5) to yield spectral enclosures for matrix polynomials.

Application 5 ([31], Example 3). *We consider the* 50×50 *matrix polynomial* $P(\lambda) = A_2\lambda^2 + A_1\lambda + A_0$, *where*

$$A_2 = I_{50}, \quad A_1 = \text{tridiag}\{-3, 9, -3\}, \quad A_0 = \text{tridiag}\{-5, 15, -5\},$$

describing a damped mass-spring system [14,32] and set non-negative weights $\mathbf{w} = \{1, 1, 1\}$, *measuring perturbations of the coefficient matrices* $\{A_j\}_{j=0}^2$ *in an absolute sense. We initiate the procedure with 15 equidistributed initial points* $\left\{\mu_0^j\right\}_{j=1}^{15}$ *on the semicircle*

$$\left\{z \in \mathbb{C} : |z| = 15\left(= \text{median}_{j=0,1,2}\left(\|A_j\|_1\right)\right), \text{Im}(z) \geq 0\right\}$$

and proceed to determine eigenvalue approximating sequences $\left\{\mu_k^j\right\}_{k=0}^{n_j}$ $(j = 1, \dots 15)$ *according to (5), so that their final terms all lie in the interior of* $\sigma_{0.01,\mathbf{w}}(P)$. *This computation requires 722 iterations. As in the constant matrix case, interpolation between the values of* ϵ_k^j *such that* $\mu_k^j \in \partial\sigma_{\epsilon_k^j,\mathbf{w}}(P)$ *along the trajectories formed by* $\left\{\mu_k^j\right\}_{k=0}^{n_j}$ $(j = 1, \dots 15)$ *results in approximations of* $\partial\sigma_{\epsilon,\mathbf{w}}(P)$ *for* $\epsilon = 0.1, 0.2, 0.3, 0.4, 0.5$, *as seen in Figure 5a. Note this yields a sufficiently accurate sketch of* $\sigma_{\epsilon,\mathbf{w}}(P)$ *and is very competitive when compared to other methods. For instance, Figure 5b is obtained via the procedure in [31] applied to a* 400×400 *grid on the relevant region* $\Omega = [-20, 5] \times [-15, 15]$. *This latter approach is far more computationally intensive, requiring 71,575 iterations to visualize* $\sigma_{\epsilon,\mathbf{w}}(P)$ *for the same tuple of parameters.*

In case a more detailed spectral localization is desired, our method may be adapted, as in Application 1, to identify individual pseudospectrum components. Our next experiment also serves to illustrate the fact that the number of initial trajectories that are attracted by the individual eigenvalues to form the related clusters is intimately connected to eigenvalue sensitivity.

Application 6 ([13], Example 5.1). *We consider the mass-spring system from ([13], Ex. 5.2) defining the* 3×3 *selfadjoint matrix polynomial*

$$P(\lambda) = A_2\lambda^2 + A_1\lambda + A_0 = \begin{bmatrix} 1 & 0 & 0 \\ 0 & 2 & 0 \\ 0 & 0 & 5 \end{bmatrix}\lambda^2 + \begin{bmatrix} 0 & 0 & 0 \\ 0 & 3 & -1 \\ 0 & -1 & 6 \end{bmatrix}\lambda + \begin{bmatrix} 2 & -1 & 0 \\ -1 & 3 & 0 \\ 0 & 0 & 10 \end{bmatrix}$$

and set $\mathbf{w} = \{1, 1, 1\}$. *As in Application 5, computations are restricted exclusively to the closed upper half-plane. However, the close proximity of the eigenvalues* $-0.08 \pm \mathbf{i}1.45$, $-0.75 \pm \mathbf{i}0.86$, $-0.51 \pm \mathbf{i}1.25$ *(indicated by "*" in Figure 6), as well as the fact that the pair* $\lambda = -0.51 \pm \mathbf{i}1.25$ *is less sensitive than the other two, necessitates the use of many initial points. Indeed, as demonstrated in Figure 6a, initiating the procedure with 40 equidistributed initial points on*

$\left\{z \in \mathbb{C} : |z| = \min\|A_j\|_1, \mathrm{Im(z)} \geq 0\right\}$ *results in* $\sigma(P)$ *being under-represented in the resulting clusters. In order to correctly approximate all three elements of the spectrum on the upper half-plane enforces the use of as many as 80 points on the selected semicircle. The length* n_j *of each sequence* $\left\{\mu_k^j\right\}_{k=0}^{n_j}$ $(j = 1, \ldots 80)$ *is determined, so that all values* $\left\{s_{\min}(P(\mu_{n_j}^j))\right\}_{j=1}^{80}$ *do not exceed the prefixed parameter value of* $\epsilon_0 = 0.01$*; this construction involved 1162 singular value computations. Using the squared Euclidean distance as the metric for computing the cluster evaluation criterion, three distinct groups are correctly identified, each converging to a different eigenvalue in the closed upper half-plane, as in Figure 6b. Note that the least sensitive eigenvalue* $\lambda = -0.51 + \mathbf{i}1.25$ *ends up attracting only one of these sequences; the corresponding group being a singleton. To correctly sketch the boundaries of* $\sigma_{\epsilon,\mathbf{w}}(P)$ *for the triple of* $\epsilon = 0.24, 0.48, 0.73$ $(>\epsilon_0 = 0.01)$*, we introduce six additional points for each cluster. Indeed, denoting* c_1*,* c_2*,* c_3 *the centroids of the clusters, for each cluster* $j = 1, 2, 3$ *we consider the vertices* $\left\{p_i^j\right\}_{i=1}^{6}$ *of a canonical hexagon centered at* c_j *with maximal diameter equal to* $\min\left(|c_j - c_i|\right)_{i \neq j}$*. These vertices are indicated by circles in Figure 6b and are used as starting points to construct the additional trajectories indicated by the black lines in Figure 6c. Note that all three selected parameters* ϵ *= 0.24, 0.48, 0.73 should be possible to interpolate along these additional lines as well, which explains why most of these trajectories have been extended to the opposite directions as well, modifying the definition of the sequences in (5) in each instance accordingly. The construction of the additional sequences requires 202 singular value computations (leading to a total of 1364 iterations), while the resulting approximations of pseudospectra boundaries for* $\epsilon = 0.24, 0.48, 0.73$ *are depicted in Figure 6c.*

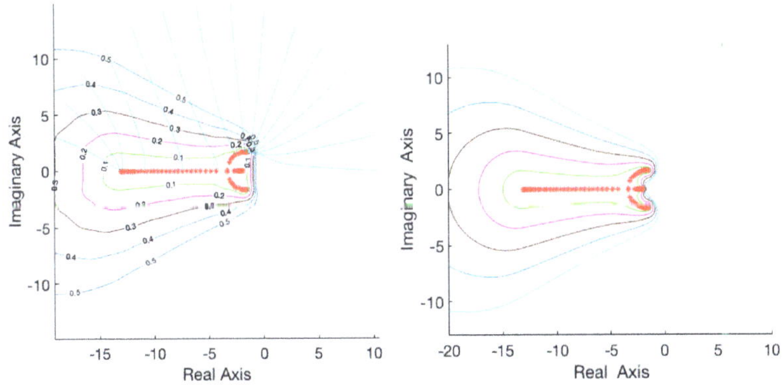

(**a**) (**b**)

Figure 5. Pseudospectrum computation for a damped mass-spring system. (**a**) Approximate pseudospectra visualization, interpolating along 15 trajectories of converging sequences. (**b**) Pseudospectra visualization, using the modified grid algorithm in [31].

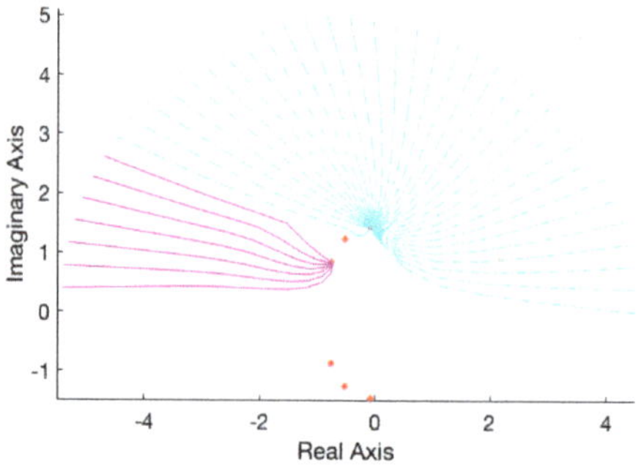

(**a**) Partial spectral identification, due to close eigenvalue proximity.

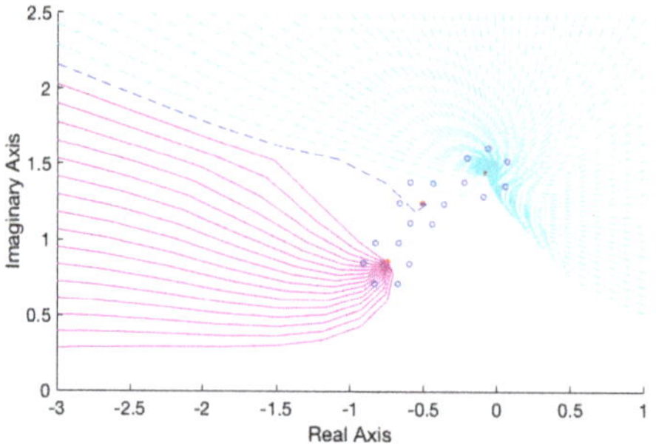

(**b**) Complete spectral identification with increased number of initial points.

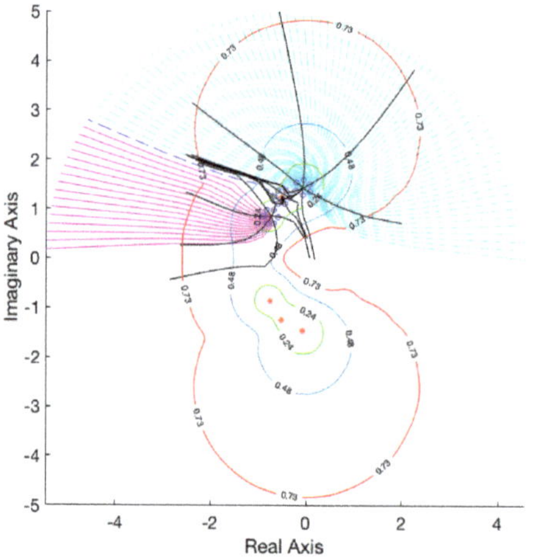

(**c**) Pseudospectra visualizations for $\epsilon = 0.24, 0.48, 0.73$.

Figure 6. Pseudospectra computations for a vibrating system.

Application 7 ([13], Example 5.3)**.** *This experiment tests the behavior of the method on a damped gyroscopic system described by the* 100×100 *matrix polynomial*

$$P(\lambda) = M\lambda^2 + (G + D)\lambda + K,$$

with

$$
\begin{aligned}
M &= I_{10} \otimes \frac{4I_{10} + B + B^T}{6} + 1.30\frac{4I_{10} + B + B^T}{6} \otimes I_{10}, \\
G &= 1.35 I_{10} \otimes (B - B^T) + 1.10(B - B^T) \otimes I_{10}, \\
D &= \text{tridiag}\{-0.1, 0.3, -0.1\}, \\
K &= I_{10} \otimes (B + B^T - 2I_{10}) + 1.20(B + B^T - 2I_{10}) \otimes I_{10}
\end{aligned}
$$

and B the 10×10 nilpotent matrix having ones on its subdiagonal and zeros elsewhere. Note M, K are positive and negative definite respectively, G is skew-symmetric, and the tridiagonal D is a damping matrix.

Starting with 50 points on

$$\{z \in \mathbb{C} : |z| = 15(= \text{median}(\|K\|_1, \|G + D\|_1, \|M\|_1)), \text{Im}(z) \geq 0\}$$

and then 5 additional points on the perpendicular bisector of the line segment defined by the two centroids of the resulting clusters (indicated by the blue circles), the resulting pseudospectrum approximation required 1212 iterations in total with $\epsilon_0 = 0.002$ and can be seen in the left part of Figure 7a. The algorithm in [31] applied to a 300×300 grid on the region $\Omega = [-4, 4] \times [-3, 3]$ required 29,110 iterations for pseudospectra visualization for the same triple $\epsilon = 0.004, 0.02, 0.1$ to obtain comparable results in Figure 7b.

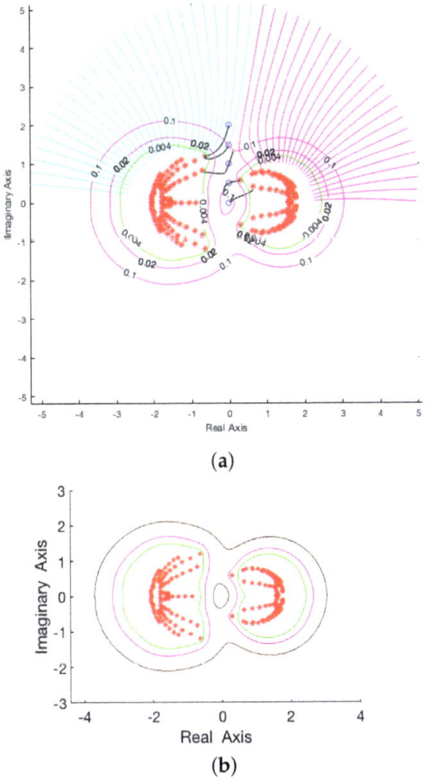

Figure 7. Comparison of pseudospectra computation for a damped gyroscopic system and ϵ = 0.004, 0.02, 0.1. (**a**) Computation using 50 initial points. (**b**) Computation using algorithm in [31].

We conclude this section, examining the behavior of the method on a non-symmetric example.

Application 8 ([31], Example 2). *We consider the* 20×20 *gyroscopic system*

$$P(\lambda) = A_2\lambda^2 + A_1\lambda + A_0 = I_{20}\lambda^2 + \mathbf{i}\begin{bmatrix} I_{10} & 0 \\ 0 & 5I_{10} \end{bmatrix}\lambda + \begin{bmatrix} 1 & -1 & -1 & \cdots & -1 \\ -1 & 1 & -1 & \cdots & -1 \\ \vdots & \vdots & \vdots & \ddots & \vdots \\ -1 & -1 & -1 & \cdots & 1 \end{bmatrix}$$

and $\mathbf{w} = \{1,1,1\}$. *Starting with 21 points on*

$$\{z \in \mathbb{C} : |z| = 25(= \|A_0\|_1 + \|A_1\|_1), \mathrm{Re}(z) \leq 0\}$$

and $\epsilon_0 = 0.001$, *five clusters are detected (Figure 8a) after 1140 iterations. Then, two additional points are introduced on each of the line segments defined by the centroids of the detected clusters (indicated by the blue circles in Figure 8b), causing the iterations to rise to the total number of 2662 in order to determine the 20 corresponding trajectories (indicated by grey lines in Figure 8c). The corresponding visualizations in Figure 8d), obtained via [31] applied to a* 400×400 *grid on the region* $\Omega = [-20, 20] \times [-15, 10]$ *required 88,462 iterations.*

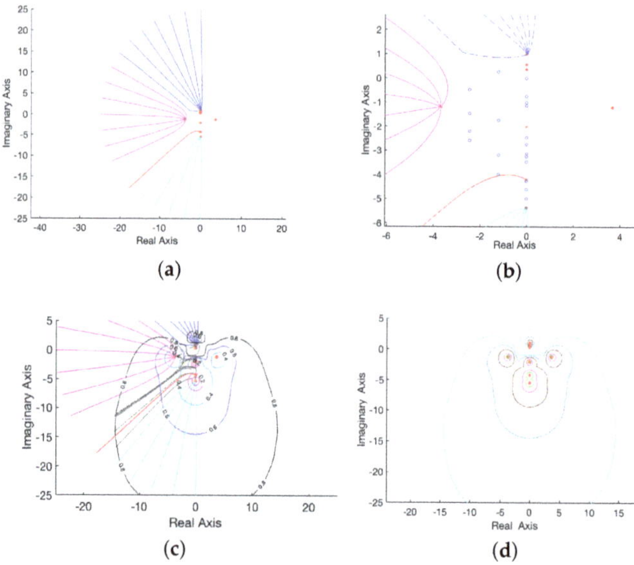

Figure 8. Comparison of pseudospectra computation for a gyroscopic system and $\epsilon = 0.1, 0.2, 0.4, 0.6, 0.8$. (**a**) Cluster detection using 21 initial points. (**b**) Locations of additional points. (**c**) Pseudospectra visualizations interpolating along the trajectories of 21 initial and 20 additional points. (**d**) Pseudospectra visualization, using the modified grid algorithm in [31].

4. Concluding Remarks

In this note, we have shown how to define sequences which, beginning from arbitrary complex scalars, converge to some element of the spectrum of a matrix. This approach can be applied both to constant matrices and to more general matrix polynomials and can be used as a means to obtain estimates for those eigenvalues that lie in the vicinity of the initial term of the sequence. This construction is also useful when no information on the location of the spectrum is a priori known. In such cases, repeating the construction from arbitrary points, it is possible to detect peripheral eigenvalues, localize the spectrum and even obtain spectral enclosures.

As an application, in this paper we used this construction to compute the pseudospectrum of a matrix or a matrix polynomial. Thus, a useful technique for speeding up pseudospectra computations emerges, which is essential for applications. An advantage of the proposed approach is that does not make any assumptions on the location of the spectrum. The fact that all computations are performed on some dynamically chosen locations on the complex plane which converge to the eigenvalues, rather than on a large number of predefined points on a rigid grid, can be seen as improvement over conventional grid algorithms.

Parallel implementation of the method can lead to further computational savings when applied to large matrices. Another option would be to apply this method combined with randomization techniques for the selection of the initial points of the sequences. In the large-scale matrix case, this method may be helpful in obtaining a first impression of the shape and size of pseudospectrum and even computing a rough approximation. Then, if desired, this could be used in conjunction with local versions of the grid algorithm and small local meshes about individual areas of interest.

Author Contributions: All authors have equally contributed to the conceptualization of this paper, to software implementation and to the original draft preparation. Funding acquisition and project administration: P.P. All authors have read and agreed to the submitted version of the manuscript.

Funding: This research is carried out/funded in the context of the project "Approximation algorithms and randomized methods for large-scale problems in computational linear algebra" (MIS 5049095) under the call for proposals *"Researchers' support with an emphasis on young researchers–2nd Cycle'." The project is co-financed by Greece and the European Union (European Social Fund—ESF) by the Operational Programme Human Resources Development, Education and Lifelong Learning 2014–2020.*

Institutional Review Board Statement: Not applicable.

Informed Consent Statement: Not applicable.

Data Availability Statement: Not applicable.

Conflicts of Interest: The authors declare no conflict of interest.

References

1. Landau, H.J. On Szegö's eigenvalue distribution theorem and non–Hermitian kernels. *J. Analyse Math.* **1975**, *28*, 216–222. [CrossRef]
2. Varah, J.M. On the separation of two matrices. *SIAM J. Numer. Anal.* **1979**, *16*, 216–222. [CrossRef]
3. Wilkinson, J.H. Sensitivity of eigenvalues II. *Utilitas Math.* **1986**, *30*, 243–286.
4. Demmel, W. A counterexample for two conjectures bout stability. *IEEE Trans. Aut. Control* **1987**, *32*, 340–342. [CrossRef]
5. Trefethen, L.N. Approximation theory and numerical linear algebra. In *Algorithms for Approximation, II (Shrivenham, 1988)*; Chapman & Hall: London, UK, 1990; pp. 336–360.
6. Nachtigal, N.M.; Reddy, S.C.; Trefethen, L.N. How fast are nonsymmetric matrix iterations? *SIAM J. Matrix. Anal.* **1992**, *13*, 778–795. [CrossRef]
7. Mosier, R.G. Root neighborhoods of a polynomial. *Math. Comput.* **1986**, *47*, 265–273. [CrossRef]
8. Reddy, S.C.; Trefethen, L.N. Lax–stability of fully discrete spectral methods via stability regions and pseudo–eigenvalues. *Comput. Methods Appl. Mech. Eng.* **1990**, *80*, 147–164. [CrossRef]
9. Higham, D.J.; Trefethen, L.N. Stiffness of ODEs. *BIT Numer. Math.* **1993**, *33*, 285–303. [CrossRef]
10. Davies, E.; Simon, B. Eigenvalue estimates for non–normal matrices and the zeros of random orthogonal polynomials on the unit circle. *J. Approx. Theory* **2006**, *141*, 189–213. [CrossRef]
11. Böttcher, A.; Grudsky, S.M. *Spectral Properties of Banded Toeplitz Matrices*; Society for Industrial and Applied Mathematics: Philadelphia, PA, USA, 2005.
12. Van Dorsselaer, J.L.M. Pseudospectra for matrix pencils and stability of equilibria. *BIT Numer. Math.* **1997**, *37*, 833–845. [CrossRef]
13. Lancaster, P.; Psarrakos, P. On the pseudospectra of matrix polynomials. *SIAM J. Matrix Anal. Appl.* **2005**, *27*, 115–129. [CrossRef]
14. Tisseur, F.; Higham, N.J. Structured pseudospectra for polynomial eigenvalue problems with applications. *SIAM J. Matrix Anal. Appl.* **2001**, *23*, 187–208. [CrossRef]
15. Trefethen, L.N.; Embree, M. *Spectra and Pseudospectra: The Behavior of Nonnormal Matrices and Operators*; Princeton University Press: Princeton, NJ, USA, 2005.
16. Brühl, M. A curve tracing algorithm for computing the pseudospectrum. *BIT* **1996**, *36*, 441–454. [CrossRef]
17. Sun, J.-G. A note on simple non–zero singular values. *J. Comput. Math.* **1988**, *62*, 235–267.
18. Kokiopoulou, E.; Bekas, C.; Gallopoulos, E. Computing smallest singular triples with implicitly restarted Lanczos biorthogonalization. *Appl. Num. Math.* **2005**, *49*, 39–61. [CrossRef]

19. Bekas, C.; Gallopoulos, E. Cobra: Parallel path following for computing the matrix pseudospectrum. *Parallel Comput.* **2001**, *27*, 1879–1896. [CrossRef]
20. Bekas, C.; Gallopoulos, E. Parallel computation of pseudospectra by fast descent. *Parallel Comput.* **2002**, *28*, 223–242. [CrossRef]
21. Trefethen, L.N. Computation of pseudospectra. *Acta Numer.* **1999**, *9*, 247–295. [CrossRef]
22. Duff, I.S.; Grimes, R.G.; Lewis, J.G. Sparse matrix test problems. *ACM Trans. Math. Softw.* **1989**, *15*, 1–14. [CrossRef]
23. Kolotilina, L.Y. Lower bounds for the Perron root of a nonnegative matrix. *Linear Algebra Appl.* **1993**, *180*, 133–151. [CrossRef]
24. Liu, S.L. Bounds for the greater characteristic root of a nonnegative matrix. *Linear Algebra Appl.* **1996**, *239*, 151–160. [CrossRef]
25. Duan, X.; Zhou, B. Sharp bounds on the spectral radius of a nonnegative matrix. *Linear Algebra Appl.* **2013**, *439*, 2961–2970. [CrossRef]
26. Xing, R.; Zhou, B. Sharp bounds on the spectral radius of nonnegative matrices. *Linear Algebra Appl.* **2014**, *449*, 194–209. [CrossRef]
27. Liao, P. Bounds for the Perron root of nonnegative matrices and spectral radius of iteration matrices. *Linear Algebra Appl.* **2017**, *530*, 253–265. [CrossRef]
28. Elsner, L.; Koltracht, I.; Neumann, M.; Xiao, D. On accuate computations of the Perron root. *SIAM J. Matrix. Anal.* **1993**, *14*, 456–467. [CrossRef]
29. Lu, L. Perron complement and Perron root. *Linear Algebra Appl.* **2002**, *341*, 239–248. [CrossRef]
30. Dembélé, D. A method for computing the Perron root for primitive matrices. *Numer. Linear Algebra Appl.* **2021**, *28*, e2340. [CrossRef]
31. Fatouros, S.; Psarrakos, P. An improved grid method for the computation of the pseudospectra of matrix polynomials. *Math. Comp. Model.* **2009**, *49*, 55–65. [CrossRef]
32. Tisseur, F.; Meerbergen, K. The quadratic eigenvalue problem. *SIAM Rev.* **1997**, *39*, 383–406. [CrossRef]

mathematics MDPI

Article

Iterative Methods for the Computation of the Perron Vector of Adjacency Matrices †

Anna Concas [1], Lothar Reichel [2,*], Giuseppe Rodriguez [1] and Yunzi Zhang [2]

1 Department of Mathematics and Computer Science, University of Cagliari, Via Ospedale 72, 09124 Cagliari, Italy; anna.concas@unica.it (A.C.); rodriguez@unica.it (G.R.)
2 Department of Mathematical Sciences, Kent State University, Kent, OH 44242, USA; yzhang82@kent.edu
* Correspondence: reichel@math.kent.edu

† Dedicated to Paul Van Dooren on the occasion of his 70th birthday.

Abstract: The power method is commonly applied to compute the Perron vector of large adjacency matrices. Blondel et al. [SIAM Rev. 46, 2004] investigated its performance when the adjacency matrix has multiple eigenvalues of the same magnitude. It is well known that the Lanczos method typically requires fewer iterations than the power method to determine eigenvectors with the desired accuracy. However, the Lanczos method demands more computer storage, which may make it impractical to apply to very large problems. The present paper adapts the analysis by Blondel et al. to the Lanczos and restarted Lanczos methods. The restarted methods are found to yield fast convergence and to require less computer storage than the Lanczos method. Computed examples illustrate the theory presented. Applications of the Arnoldi method are also discussed.

Keywords: networks; perron vector; power method; lanczos method

MSC: 05C50; 65F15

Citation: Concas, A.; Reichel, L.; Rodriguez, G.; Zhang, Y. Iterative Methods for the Computation of the Perron Vector of Adjacency Matrices. *Mathematics* **2021**, 9, 1522. https://doi.org/10.3390/math9131522

Academic Editor: Christine Böckmann

Received: 6 May 2021
Accepted: 23 June 2021
Published: 29 June 2021

1. Introduction

Networks arise in many areas, such as social media, transportation, and chemistry; see [1,2] for many examples. Networks can be represented by graphs $\mathcal{G}$ that are made up of a set of *vertices* or *nodes* $\mathcal{V} = \{v_i\}_{i=1}^n$ and a set of *edges* $\mathcal{E} = \{e_i\}_{i=1}^m$, connecting the nodes. Two distinct nodes, v_i and v_j, are said to be *adjacent* if there is an edge between them. The analysis of graphs by mathematical and computational methods can provide valuable information about the networks they model and is receiving considerable attention.

This paper considers networks that can be represented by simple unweighted graphs, that is, no edge starts and ends at the same node, and there is at most one edge between each pair of distinct nodes. Extension to weighted simple graphs, in which each edge has a positive weight, is straightforward. A graph is said to be undirected if every edge is a "two-way street"; a graph with at least one edge that is a "one-way street" is said to be directed. A directed edge e_k pointing from vertex v_i to vertex v_j can be identified with the ordered pair (v_i, v_j); for an undirected edge, this pair is not ordered. A walk of length k in a graph is a sequence of $k+1$ vertices $v_{i_1}, v_{i_2}, \ldots, v_{i_{k+1}}$ and a sequence of k edges $e_{j_1}, e_{j_2}, \ldots, e_{j_k}$, not necessarily distinct, such that e_{j_p} points from v_{i_p} to $v_{i_{p+1}}$ in a directed graph, or connects v_{i_p} to $v_{i_{p+1}}$ in an undirected graph, for $p = 1, 2, \ldots, k$. A path is a walk in which all the nodes are distinct.

An unweighted simple graph $\mathcal{G}$ with n nodes can be represented by its adjacency matrix $A = [a_{ij}]_{i,j=1}^n \in \mathbb{R}^{n \times n}$, where $a_{ij} = 1$ when there is an edge from vertex v_i to vertex v_j; otherwise, $a_{ij} = 0$. In particular, $a_{ii} = 0$ for all i. Undirected graphs are associated with symmetric adjacency matrices, while the adjacency matrix for a directed graph is non-symmetric. Typically, the number of edges, m, is much smaller than n^2. This makes the adjacency matrix A sparse. An undirected graph is said to be *connected* if there is a path connecting each pair of nodes. A directed graph is referred to as *strongly connected* if there is a directed path from v_i to v_j and vice versa for every pair of distinct nodes. The adjacency matrix A associated with an undirected graph $\mathcal{G}$ is irreducible if and only if $\mathcal{G}$ is connected. Similarly, the adjacency matrix A associated with a directed graph $\mathcal{G}$ is irreducible if and only if $\mathcal{G}$ is strongly connected.

A problem of considerable interest in network analysis is the determination of the most important vertices of a network. The notion of centrality can be used to identify these vertices. There are many centrality measures available, including degree centrality [1,2], betweenness centrality [3], hub-and-authority centrality [4], and eigenvector centrality [5].

We are interested in investigating the performance of iterative methods for determining the eigenvector centrality of vertices belonging to certain structured graphs $\mathcal{G}$ with many nodes n. The eigenvector centrality was introduced by Bonacich for quantifying the influence a node has in a network [5], beyond its nearest neighbors, in terms of spectral properties of the associated adjacency matrix. According to the Perron–Frobenius theorem, the largest eigenvalue, ρ, which is known as the *Perron root*, of a nonnegative irreducible matrix A, is unique and has a unique eigenvector $\mathbf{w} = [w_1, w_2, \ldots, w_n]^T \in \mathbb{R}^n$ (up to scaling) with positive components w_i. This vector is commonly referred to as the *Perron vector* of A; see, for example, Meyer ([6] Section 8.3). For notational simplicity, we may assume that $\mathbf{w}$ is scaled so that $\|\mathbf{w}\| = 1$. Here and throughout this paper, $\|\cdot\|$ denotes the Euclidean vector norm. The eigenvector centrality of the vertex v_i is given by the entry w_i of the Perron vector $\mathbf{w}$ of the adjacency matrix A. A vertex v_i is considered a central, that is, important, vertex of the graph $\mathcal{G}$ if w_i is the largest entry of $\mathbf{w}$. This centrality measure also takes into account the centralities of those nodes to which v_i is connected [7].

Blondel et al. [8] investigated the performance of the power method when applied to determining the Perron vector of a matrix of the form

$$M = \begin{bmatrix} 0 & A \\ A^T & 0 \end{bmatrix} \in \mathbb{R}^{2n \times 2n}, \tag{1}$$

where $A \in \mathbb{R}^{n \times n}$ is the adjacency matrix for a graph $\mathcal{G}$ with n nodes, and the superscript T denotes transposition. M can be interpreted as the adjacency matrix of a bipartite graph containing $2n$ vertices partitioned into two disjoint vertex subsets, whose connections are described by A and occur only across, but not within, the two groups.

There are numerous methods for partitioning the vertex set of a bipartite graph $\mathcal{G}$ so that its adjacency matrix is of the form (1); see [2,9,10] and references therein. The Perron vector of the matrix (1) is used to determine the hub-and-authority centralities for the vertices of $\mathcal{G}$ [2,4] and its components give similarity scores between graph nodes. These scores were introduced by Blondel et al. [8]. There are several applications of similarity scores. These applications lead to the construction of a self-similarity matrix associated with a graph, which measures how vertices are similar to each other [8]; see [11] for an application in archaeology of the similarity matrix associated with a bipartite graph and for an algorithm for solving the seriation problem. The latter is a fundamental ordering problem that aims at finding the best enumeration order of a set of units so that in the resulting sequence, elements having higher similarity are placed close to each other.

Given an initial vector $\mathbf{z}_0 \in \mathbb{R}^{2n}$ with positive entries, the power method applied to the matrix M generates the sequence of vectors

$$\mathbf{z}_k = \frac{M\mathbf{z}_{k-1}}{\|M\mathbf{z}_{k-1}\|_2}, \quad k = 1, 2, \ldots. \tag{2}$$

When applied to a real square matrix with a single largest eigenvalue of maximal magnitude, the power method is known to determine a sequence of vectors that converge to the span of the eigenvector associated with this eigenvalue for almost all initial vectors; see, for example, Saad ([12] Section 4.1). The following result, which highlights the property of the adjacency matrix of a bipartite graph of having a spectrum symmetric with respect to the origin ([13] Theorem 3.14), shows why the application of the power method to the matrix (1) is not straightforward.

Proposition 1. *The matrix* (1) *has distinct eigenvalues of the largest magnitude.*

Proof. Partition the Perron vector $\mathbf{x} = [\mathbf{x}_1^T, \mathbf{x}_2^T]^T \in \mathbb{R}^{2n}$ of the matrix M defined by (1), where $\mathbf{x}_i \in \mathbb{R}^n$, $i = 1, 2$. Let λ denote the Perron root of M. Then, $M\mathbf{x} = \lambda\mathbf{x}$ implies that

$$M\begin{bmatrix} \mathbf{x}_1 \\ -\mathbf{x}_2 \end{bmatrix} = -\lambda\begin{bmatrix} \mathbf{x}_1 \\ -\mathbf{x}_2 \end{bmatrix}.$$

Thus, the negative Perron root is also an eigenvalue of M. □

The presence of more than one eigenvalue of the largest magnitude of M suggests that the sequence of vectors, $\mathbf{z}_1, \mathbf{z}_2, \mathbf{z}_3, \ldots$, might not converge to the Perron vector. Indeed, Blondel et al. [8] show that both the limits

$$\lim_{k\to\infty} \mathbf{z}_{2k} \quad \text{and} \quad \lim_{k\to\infty} \mathbf{z}_{2k-1} \tag{3}$$

exist, but they might not be the same. The limits depend on the initial vector $\mathbf{z}_0$ for the power iteration and none of the limits might be the Perron vector for M. Throughout this paper, $\mathbf{e} = [1, 1, \ldots, 1]^T$ denotes the vector with all entries 1 of a suitable dimension. Blondel at al. ([8] Theorem 2) show that when $\mathbf{z}_0 = \mathbf{e}/\|\mathbf{e}\|$, the limit on the left-hand side of (3) is the Perron vector for M.

An advantage of the power method, when compared to other methods for computing the Perron vector of a matrix with only nonnegative entries, is that only two vectors, $\mathbf{z}_k$ and $M\mathbf{z}_k$, have to be stored simultaneously during the computations. The low storage requirement may be important for very large matrices; however, convergence of the power method can also be very slow when there is only one eigenvalue of the largest magnitude. The rate of convergence decreases with the distance between the Perron root and the magnitude of the second largest eigenvalue in modulus; see, for example, ([12] Section 4.1). It is therefore interesting to investigate the convergence properties of methods that converge faster, such as the Lanczos or restarted Lanczos methods, when applied to matrices of the form (1) and generalizations thereof. It is the purpose of the present paper to study the convergence of the Lanczos and restarted Lanczos methods when applied to the computation of the Perron vector of matrices of the form (1) and some generalizations. Our analysis is based on results by Blondel et al. [8]. We also discuss the computation of the Perron vector of structured matrices, somewhat related to the matrix M, and by application of the Arnoldi method to the submatrix A in (1). These particular matrices represent graphs with a chained structure that refine the notion of bipartivity [14].

This paper is organized as follows: Section 2 introduces undirected chained graphs. The adjacency matrix for this kind of graph has a staircase structure, which generalizes the structure (1). Chained graphs have been shown to be bipartite in [14], which implies that the eigenvalues of their associated adjacency matrices appear in ± pairs. Section 3 studies the performance of the Lanczos and restarted Lanczos methods when applied to computing the Perron vector for these and other symmetric adjacency matrices. The Arnoldi method and its application to estimating the Perron vector for a symmetric matrix considered by Blondel et al. [8] are described in Section 4. A few computed examples are presented in Section 5, and Section 6 contains concluding remarks.

2. Undirected Chained Graphs

This section describes ℓ-chained undirected graphs and the structure of their adjacency matrices. These graphs, which are particular bipartite graphs, were introduced in [14] and are defined as follows.

Definition 1. *An undirected graph $\mathcal{G} = \{\mathcal{V}, \mathcal{E}\}$ is said to be ℓ_i-chained with initial vertex v_i if the set of vertices can be subdivided into ℓ_i disjoint non-empty subsets*

$$\mathcal{V} = \mathcal{V}_1 \cup \mathcal{V}_2 \cup \cdots \cup \mathcal{V}_{\ell_i},$$

such that $v_i \in \mathcal{V}_1$, and all vertices in the set $\mathcal{V}_j$, are adjacent only to vertices in the sets $\mathcal{V}_{j-1}$ or $\mathcal{V}_{j+1}$ for $j = 2, 3, \ldots, \ell_i - 1$, where the chain length ℓ_i is the largest number of vertex subsets $\mathcal{V}_j$ with this property. Moreover, the vertices in $\mathcal{V}_1$ and $\mathcal{V}_{\ell_i}$ are adjacent only to vertices in $\mathcal{V}_2$ and $\mathcal{V}_{\ell_i-1}$, respectively. Vertex sets $\mathcal{V}_j$ with consecutive indices are said to be adjacent.

Chained graphs arise in various applications; see [8,14,15] and Section 5.

Consider an undirected ℓ-chained graph $\mathcal{G} = (\mathcal{V}, \mathcal{E})$ with vertex set partitioning $\mathcal{V} = \mathcal{V}_1 \cup \mathcal{V}_2 \cup \cdots \cup \mathcal{V}_\ell$. Let n_i be the cardinality of the vertex subset $\mathcal{V}_i$ for $i = 1, 2, \ldots, \ell$. Thus, the graph $\mathcal{G}$ has $n = \sum_{i=1}^{\ell} n_i$ nodes. Order the vertices v_j of $\mathcal{G}$ so that the vertices in $\mathcal{V}_i$ precede those in $\mathcal{V}_{i+1}$ for $i = 1, 2, \ldots, \ell - 1$, and define the matrix $A_i \in \mathbb{R}^{n_i \times n_{i+1}}$ that describes the connections between the vertices in $\mathcal{V}_i$ and the vertices in $\mathcal{V}_{i+1}$ for $i = 1, 2, \ldots, \ell - 1$. Then, the adjacency matrix $M \in \mathbb{R}^{n \times n}$, associated with $\mathcal{G}$, has the staircase structure

$$M = \begin{bmatrix} O & A_1 & & & \\ A_1^T & O & A_2 & & \\ & A_2^T & \ddots & \ddots & \\ & & \ddots & O & A_{\ell-1} \\ & & & A_{\ell-1}^T & O \end{bmatrix}. \tag{4}$$

Theorem 1 ([14])**.** *An ℓ-chained graph is bipartite. Conversely, if a graph is bipartite, then the graph is ℓ-chained for some $\ell \geq 2$.*

From Theorem 1 it follows that, for a suitable permutation matrix $P \in \mathbb{R}^{n \times n}$, the adjacency matrix (4) can be permuted to the form

$$PMP^T = \left[\begin{array}{c|c} O & C \\ \hline C^T & O \end{array}\right], \tag{5}$$

with $C \in \mathbb{R}^{n_o \times n_e}$, where

$$n_o = \sum_{i=1}^{\lfloor(\ell+1)/2\rfloor} n_{2i-1}, \qquad n_e = \sum_{i=1}^{\lfloor \ell/2 \rfloor} n_{2i}.$$

Here, $\lfloor \alpha \rfloor$ denotes the integer part of $\alpha \geq 0$. The structure (5) is the same as (1). It follows from Proposition 1 that the adjacency matrix for an ℓ-chained undirected graph has pairs of eigenvalues of the opposite sign, which include the Perron root.

Example 1. *Consider the* 3*-chained graph with adjacency matrix*

$$M = \begin{bmatrix} O & A & O \\ A^T & O & A \\ O & A^T & O \end{bmatrix} \in \mathbb{R}^{3n \times 3n}, \tag{6}$$

where $A \in \mathbb{R}^{n \times n}$. Then

$$M^2 = \begin{bmatrix} AA^T & O & AA \\ O & A^TA + AA^T & O \\ A^TA^T & O & A^TA \end{bmatrix}. \tag{7}$$

Introduce the permutation matrix

$$P = \begin{bmatrix} I_n & O & O \\ O & O & I_n \\ O & I_n & O \end{bmatrix},$$

where $I_n \in \mathbb{R}^{n\times n}$ *is the identity matrix. Then, the matrix* $C \in \mathbb{R}^{2n\times n}$ *is defined by*

$$PMP^T = \left[\begin{array}{cc|c} O & O & A \\ O & O & A^T \\ \hline A^T & A & O \end{array}\right] = \left[\begin{array}{c|c} O & C \\ \hline C^T & O \end{array}\right].$$

It follows that the $\pm$ *singular values of* C *are eigenvalues of* M*. This yields* $2n$ *of the eigenvalues of* M*. The remaining* n *eigenvalues vanish. We will discuss the computation of the Perron vector of matrices of the form (6), as well as of matrices of the form (4), in the following section.*

3. The Lanczos and Restarted Lanczos Methods

This section discusses the application of the Lanczos and restarted Lanczos methods to the computation of the Perron vector of an undirected connected graph. We first consider the Lanczos method and subsequently turn to restarted variants.

The Lanczos method reduces a large symmetric matrix to a usually much smaller symmetric tridiagonal matrix by computing an orthogonal projection onto a Krylov subspace of fairly low dimension. It is a commonly used method for determining approximations of a few large eigenvalues and associated eigenvectors of a large symmetric matrix; see, for example, [12] for a discussion of this method.

Consider an undirected connected graph $\mathcal{G}$ with associated adjacency matrix $A \in \mathbb{R}^{n\times n}$. Application of $1 \le k \ll n$ steps of the Lanczos method to A with initial vector $\mathbf{v} \in \mathbb{R}^n \backslash \{\mathbf{0}\}$ yields, generically, the Lanczos decomposition

$$AQ_k = Q_k T_k + \beta_k \mathbf{q}_{k+1}\mathbf{e}_k^T, \tag{8}$$

where the columns of the matrix $Q_k = [\mathbf{q}_1, \mathbf{q}_2, \dots, \mathbf{q}_k] \in \mathbb{R}^{n\times k}$ form an orthonormal basis for the Krylov subspace,

$$\mathcal{K}_k(A, \mathbf{v}) = \text{span}\{\mathbf{v}, A\mathbf{v}, A^2\mathbf{v}, \dots, A^{k-1}\mathbf{v}\}, \quad k = 1, 2, \dots,$$

with $\mathbf{q}_1 = \mathbf{v}/\|\mathbf{v}\|$. Throughout this paper, $\mathbf{e}_k = [0, \dots, 0, 1, 0, \dots, 0]^T$ denotes the kth axis vector of the suitable dimension. Moreover,

$$T_k = \begin{bmatrix} \alpha_1 & \beta_1 & & & \\ \beta_1 & \alpha_2 & \beta_2 & & \\ & \ddots & \ddots & \ddots & \\ & & \beta_{k-2} & \alpha_{k-1} & \beta_{k-1} \\ & & & \beta_{k-1} & \alpha_k \end{bmatrix} \in \mathbb{R}^{k\times k}$$

is a symmetric tridiagonal matrix, the coefficient β_k in (8) is positive, and the vector $\mathbf{q}_{k+1} \in \mathbb{R}^n$ satisfies $Q_k^T \mathbf{q}_{k+1} = \mathbf{0}$ and $\|\mathbf{q}_{k+1}\| = 1$. We tacitly assume that the number of steps k of the Lanczos method is small enough so that the decomposition (8) with the stated properties exists. This is the generic situation.

Let ρ_k denote the largest eigenvalue of T_k, and let $\mathbf{y}_k \in \mathbb{R}^k$ be an associated unit eigenvector. Then, ρ_k and $Q_k\mathbf{y}_k$ are commonly referred to as a Ritz value and a Ritz vector, respectively, of A.

Theorem 2. *Consider an undirected connected graph* $\mathcal{G}$ *with adjacency matrix* $M \in \mathbb{R}^{n\times n}$*. Then,* M *is symmetric and nonnegative. Let* ρ *denote the Perron root of* M *and let* $\mathbf{w}$ *be the associated*

Perron vector. Apply k steps of the Lanczos method to M with initial vector $\mathbf{e} = [1, 1, \ldots, 1]^T \in \mathbb{R}^n$. *This produces the decompositions*

$$MQ_k = Q_k T_k + \beta_k \mathbf{q}_{k+1} \mathbf{e}_k^T, \quad k = 0, 1, \ldots . \tag{9}$$

Let ρ_k *denote the largest eigenvalue of* T_k *with the associated Perron vector* $\mathbf{y}_k$. *Then, the Ritz values* ρ_k *converge to the Perron root* ρ *of M and the Ritz vectors* $\mathbf{w}_k = Q_k \mathbf{y}_k$ *converge to* $\mathbf{w}$ *as k increases. If the Lanczos method breaks down at iteration* ℓ, *then* $\mathbf{w}_\ell$ *is the Perron vector.*

Proof. The eigenvectors of M are stationary points of the Rayleigh quotient

$$r(\mathbf{x}) = \frac{\mathbf{x}^T M \mathbf{x}}{\mathbf{x}^T \mathbf{x}}, \qquad \mathbf{x} \in \mathbb{R}^n \backslash \{\mathbf{0}\},$$

and the eigenvalues of M are the values of $r(\mathbf{x})$ at these stationary points. The Perron root ρ is the maximum value of $r(\mathbf{x})$. The largest eigenvalue of T_k is the maximum value ρ_k of $r(\mathbf{x})$ over the k-dimensional Krylov subspace $\mathcal{K}_k(M, \mathbf{e})$. It follows that $\rho_k \leq \rho$.

Blondel et al. ([8] Theorem 2) show that, using the initial vector $\mathbf{e}/\|\mathbf{e}\|$, the sequence $\mathbf{z}_{2k}$ in (2) generated by the power method converges to the Perron vector $\mathbf{w}$ of M. The unit vector $\mathbf{z}_{2k}$ lives in $\mathcal{K}_{2k}(M, \mathbf{e})$. Clearly,

$$\mathbf{z}_{2k}^T M \mathbf{z}_{2k} \leq \rho_{2k} \leq \rho. \tag{10}$$

Since the Krylov subspaces $\mathcal{K}_j(M, \mathbf{e})$, $j = 1, 2, \ldots$ are nested, it follows that

$$\rho_{2k-2} \leq \rho_{2k-1} \leq \rho_{2k}. \tag{11}$$

It is a consequence of the mentioned result by Blondel et al. [8] that the Lanczos method does not break down until the Perron vector has been determined. Assume, to the contrary, that the Lanczos method breaks down at step k. Then, the relation (9) is replaced by

$$MQ_k = Q_k T_k,$$

which shows that the range of Q_k forms an invariant subspace of M. This implies that the vector $M\mathbf{z}_k$, determined by the power method in the next step, lives in the range of Q_k. This would imply that the Perron root of M is the Perron root of T_k, and therefore the Lanczos method determines the Perron root and Perron vector.

It follows from (10) that ρ_{2k} converges to ρ and, due to (11), the sequence ρ_j converges monotonically to ρ (from below) as j increases. Let $\mathbf{y}_j \in \mathbb{R}^j$ be the Perron vector of T_j. Since T_j is an irreducible symmetric tridiagonal matrix, the unit vector $\mathbf{y}_j$ is uniquely determined. Then, the associated Ritz vectors $\mathbf{w}_j = Q_j \mathbf{y}_j$ converge to the Perron vector of M as j increases. We remark that the Ritz vectors $\mathbf{w}_j$ so obtained, $j \geq 1$, may have small negative entries. This is of no importance, since we are interested in determining the largest component(s) of these vectors. □

The iterations of the Lanczos method applied to M are terminated as soon as two consecutive approximations $\mathbf{w}_{k-1}$ and $\mathbf{w}_k$ of the Perron vector are close enough, that is, as soon as

$$\|\mathbf{w}_k - \mathbf{w}_{k-1}\| \leq \epsilon, \tag{12}$$

for some user-specified (small) value of $\epsilon > 0$. Note that

$$\|\mathbf{w}_k - \mathbf{w}_{k-1}\| = \|Q_k \mathbf{y}_k - Q_{k-1} \mathbf{y}_{k-1}\| = \left\| \mathbf{y}_k - \begin{bmatrix} \mathbf{y}_{k-1} \\ 0 \end{bmatrix} \right\|.$$

Thus, it suffices to choose a k large enough so that

$$\left\| \mathbf{y}_k - \begin{bmatrix} \mathbf{y}_{k-1} \\ 0 \end{bmatrix} \right\| \leq \epsilon.$$

The Lanczos iteration is described by Algorithm 1. The algorithm applies the Lanczos method to a general real symmetric matrix $M \in \mathbb{R}^{n \times n}$. In Line 14 of the algorithm, the symmetric tridiagonal matrix $T_{k-1} \in \mathbb{R}^{(k-1)\times(k-1)}$ is augmented by appending a row and a column to obtain the new symmetric tridiagonal matrix $T_k \in \mathbb{R}^{k \times k}$.

Algorithm 1 Determine the Perron vector of the matrix M by the Lanczos method.

Require: Adjacency matrix $M \in \mathbb{R}^{n \times n}$ and initial vector $\mathbf{e} = \mathbf{1}$.
Ensure: Approximation $\mathbf{w}$ of the Perron vector of M.

1: $\beta_0 = 0, \mathbf{q}_0 = \mathbf{0}, \mathbf{q}_1 = \frac{\mathbf{e}}{\|\mathbf{e}\|}, \mathbf{w}_0 = \mathbf{0}, k = 1$
2: $\alpha_1 = \mathbf{q}_1^T M \mathbf{q}_1$
3: $\mathbf{r} = M\mathbf{q}_1 - \alpha_1 \mathbf{q}_1$
4: $\beta_1 = \|\mathbf{r}\|$
5: $\mathbf{q}_2 = \mathbf{r}/\beta_1$
6: $T_1 = \alpha_1$
7: $Q_1 = \mathbf{q}_1, \mathbf{w}_1 = \mathbf{q}_1$
8: **while** $\|\mathbf{w}_k - \mathbf{w}_{k-1}\| > \epsilon$ **do**
9: $\quad k = k + 1$
10: $\quad \alpha_k = \mathbf{q}_k^T M \mathbf{q}_k$
11: $\quad \mathbf{r} = M\mathbf{q}_k - \alpha_k \mathbf{q}_k - \beta_{k-1}\mathbf{q}_{k-1}$
12: $\quad \beta_k = \|\mathbf{r}\|$
13: $\quad \mathbf{q}_{k+1} = \mathbf{r}/\beta_k$
14: $\quad T_k = \begin{bmatrix} T_{k-1} & \beta_{k-1}\mathbf{e}_{k-1} \\ \beta_{k-1}\mathbf{e}_{k-1}^T & \alpha_k \end{bmatrix}$
15: $\quad Q_k = [Q_{k-1} \ \ \mathbf{q}_k]$
16: $\quad$ Compute the Perron vector $\mathbf{y}_k$ of T_k
17: $\quad \mathbf{w}_k = Q_k \mathbf{y}_k$
18: **end while**
19: $\mathbf{w} = \mathbf{w}_k$

The following example compares the results of finding the most important vertices of each vertex subset of an undirected 4-chained graph by the power method and the Lanczos method with initial vector $\mathbf{e}$. In this comparison, we terminate the iterations with the power method as soon as two consecutive approximations $\mathbf{z}_{2k}$ and $\mathbf{z}_{2(k-1)}$ of the Perron vector are sufficiently close, that is, as soon as

$$\|\mathbf{z}_{2k} - \mathbf{z}_{2(k-1)}\| \leq \epsilon. \tag{13}$$

Example 2. *This example uses the Citeseer Index data set downloaded on June 2007 from the Citeseer*^{X} *website [16]. The data set consists of a list of papers with some information such as authors, journals, and institutions. We extracted an undirected 4-chained network from this data set. It shows relations between the vertex subsets institutions, authors, papers and journals. The number of vertices that represent institutions, authors, papers and journals are 20, 58, 26 and 21, respectively. The power method and the Lanczos method are applied with the stopping criteria (13) and (12), respectively, with* $\epsilon = 10^{-4}$.

Both the power and Lanczos methods identify vertex v_1 *as the most important university, vertices* v_{21} *and* v_{22} *as the most important authors, vertex* v_{81} *as the most important paper, and vertex* v_{108} *as the most important journal. The power method terminates the iterations after step 364, while the Lanczos method stops at step 26. Thus, the Lanczos method requires the evaluation of significantly fewer matrix–vector products with the matrix M than the power method to determine the most important vertices of each vertex subset.*

Typically, the Lanczos method yields much faster convergence to the Perron vector of a symmetric nonnegative matrix M than the power method. However, it has the drawback of requiring storage space for the matrix Q_k in (9). The need to store the matrix Q_k may make it difficult to apply the Lanczos method to compute the Perron vector of very large adjacency matrices. We describe two standard approaches for circumventing this difficulty. They restart the Lanczos iterations in different ways.

(i) Carry out the Lanczos iterations twice: First generate the tridiagonal matrix T_k for a suitably chosen k (see below) and discard the columns of the matrix Q_k that are not required by the Lanczos method for determining the next column. Indeed, to compute column $\mathbf{q}_{j+1}$ for $j \geq 2$ only the columns $\mathbf{q}_j$ and $\mathbf{q}_{j-1}$ are needed. Thus, the storage demand is modest and bounded independently of the number of Lanczos steps k. Having computed the Perron vector $\mathbf{y}_k$ for T_k, we have to evaluate the corresponding Ritz vector $\mathbf{w}_k = Q_k\mathbf{y}_k$. This can be done by regenerating the columns of Q_k. Thus, we determine these columns by applying the recursion formula of the Lanczos method again and discard the columns $\mathbf{q}_j$ as soon as their contribution to the Ritz vector $\mathbf{w}_k$ have been evaluated. The inner products that determine the nontrivial entries of T_k do not have to be recomputed. This approach of reducing the storage amount is straightforward, but it doubles the number of matrix–vector product evaluations with M. This method is described by Algorithm 2. The iterations are terminated similarly as in Algorithm 1.

(ii) Restart the Lanczos method, that is, compute an approximation of the Perron vector every k iteration, and use this approximation as a new initial vector when restarting the Lanczos iterations. The vector $\mathbf{e}$ is used to initialize the very first k Lanczos steps. The method is restarted until the stopping criterion is satisfied. The storage requirement of this restarted Lanczos method is limited to essentially the matrix Q_k, independently of the number of iterations that are carried out. However, the rate of convergence of computed approximations of the Perron vector may be slower than for the un-restarted Lanczos method. This method is discussed in Theorem 3 below.

Example 3. *We applied Algorithm 2 to the adjacency matrix of the 4-chained network described in Example 2, with $\epsilon = 10^{-4}$. The stopping criterion was satisfied at step 20. The algorithm determined the same vertices as the standard Lanczos method in Example 2. The main differences between Algorithm 1 and Algorithm 2 are that the latter requires less computer storage, but more matrix–vector product evaluations with M (40 vs. 26). The difference in the number of steps required by Algorithms 1 and 2 depends in part on the different stopping criteria used. In Algorithm 1, the iterations are terminated when two consecutive Ritz vectors are close enough, while Algorithm 2 is terminated when two consecutive Ritz values are sufficiently close.*

We turn to computing the Perron vector of M by the restarted Lanczos method described in (ii). This method applies k steps of the Lanczos method to the matrix M with initial vector $\mathbf{e}$ to determine the decomposition (9), and computes the Perron vector $\mathbf{y}^{(1)} \in \mathbb{R}^k$ of the symmetric tridiagonal matrix T_k in this decomposition. We denote the Perron root of T_k by $\rho^{(1)}$. Then, $Q_k\mathbf{y}^{(1)}$ is the Ritz vector of M that best approximates the Perron vector, and $\rho^{(1)}$ is the corresponding Ritz value. The computed Ritz vector may have negative entries, while the Perron vector of M is known to only have strictly positive entries. We therefore set all entries of $Q_k\mathbf{y}^{(1)}$ that are smaller than a small $\delta > 0$, say $\delta = 10^{-8}$, to δ, and refer to the vector so obtained as $\widehat{\mathbf{z}}^{(1)}$.

Algorithm 2 Determine the Perron vector of the matrix M by applying twice the Lanczos recursions.

Require: Adjacency matrix $M \in \mathbb{R}^{n \times n}$ and initial vector $\mathbf{e} = \mathbf{1}$.
Ensure: Approximation $\mathbf{w}$ of the Perron vector of M.

$\beta_0 = 0, \mathbf{q}_1 = \mathbf{e}/\|\mathbf{e}\|, \rho_0 = 0, k = 1$
$\alpha_1 = \mathbf{q}_1^T M \mathbf{q}_1$
$\mathbf{r} = M\mathbf{q}_1 - \alpha_1 \mathbf{q}_1$
$\beta_1 = \|\mathbf{r}\|$
$\mathbf{q}_0 = \mathbf{q}_1$
$\mathbf{q}_1 = \mathbf{r}/\beta_1$
$T_1 = \alpha_1, \rho_1 = \alpha_1$
while $|\rho_k - \rho_{k-1}| > \epsilon$ **do**
  $k = k + 1$
  $\alpha_k = \mathbf{q}_1^T M \mathbf{q}_1$
  $\mathbf{r} = M\mathbf{q}_1 - \alpha_k \mathbf{q}_1 - \beta_{k-1}\mathbf{q}_0$
  $\beta_k = \|\mathbf{r}\|$
  $\mathbf{q}_0 = \mathbf{q}_1$
  $\mathbf{q}_1 = \mathbf{r}/\beta_k$
  $T_k = \begin{bmatrix} T_{k-1} & \beta_{k-1}\mathbf{e}_{k-1} \\ \beta_{k-1}\mathbf{e}_{k-1}^T & \alpha_k \end{bmatrix}$
  Compute the largest eigenvalue ρ_k of T_k
end while
Compute the Perron vector $\mathbf{y}_k = [\mathbf{y}_k^{(1)}, \mathbf{y}_k^{(2)}, \cdots, \mathbf{y}_k^{(k)}]$ of matrix T_k
$\mathbf{q}_0 = \mathbf{0}, \mathbf{q}_1 = \mathbf{e}/\|\mathbf{e}\|$
$\mathbf{w} = \mathbf{y}_k^{(1)}\mathbf{q}_1$
for $i = 1, \ldots, k-1$ **do**
  $\mathbf{r} = M\mathbf{q}_1 - \alpha_i \mathbf{q}_1 - \beta_{i-1}\mathbf{q}_0$
  $\mathbf{q}_0 = \mathbf{q}_1$
  $\mathbf{q}_1 = \mathbf{r}/\beta_i$
  $\mathbf{w} = \mathbf{w} + \mathbf{y}_k^{(i+1)}\mathbf{q}_1$
end for

The vector $\widehat{\mathbf{z}}^{(1)}$ is used to determine an improved approximation of the Perron vector of M. Thus, we apply k steps of the Lanczos method to M with initial vector $\widehat{\mathbf{z}}^{(1)}$. This gives a decomposition analogous to (9). We compute the Perron vector $\mathbf{y}^{(2)} \in \mathbb{R}^k$ and the Perron root $\rho^{(2)}$ of the symmetric tridiagonal matrix in this decomposition. Proceeding similarly as described above, we obtain a new approximation of the Perron vector of M. We denote this approximation by $\widehat{\mathbf{z}}^{(2)}$. The latter vector is used as an initial vector for k steps of the Lanczos method applied to M, which yields a new approximation, $\widehat{\mathbf{z}}^{(3)}$, of the Perron vector and a new approximation $\rho^{(3)}$ of the Perron root of M. This approximate Perron vector is computed, similarly, as $\widehat{\mathbf{z}}^{(2)}$. We determine approximate Perron vectors $\widehat{\mathbf{z}}^{(i)}$ and Perron roots $\rho^{(i)}$ for $i = 2, 3, \ldots$, until two consecutive Perron vector approximations are sufficiently close, that is, until

$$\|\widehat{\mathbf{z}}^{(i)} - \widehat{\mathbf{z}}^{(i-1)}\| \leq \epsilon, \tag{14}$$

for a user-supplied tolerance $\epsilon > 0$.

The following result shows that the vectors $\widehat{\mathbf{z}}^{(i)}$ converge to the Perron vector of M when the number of Lanczos steps, k, used to determine $\widehat{\mathbf{z}}^{(i)}$ from $\widehat{\mathbf{z}}^{(i-1)}$ for $i = 2, 3, \ldots$, is large enough and the stopping criterion (14) is not applied.

Theorem 3. *Let $M \in \mathbb{R}^{n \times n}$ be the adjacency matrix of an undirected connected graph $\mathcal{G}$, and let ρ and $\mathbf{w}$ denote the Perron root and Perron vector of M, respectively. Apply the restarted Lanczos method described above with initial vector $\mathbf{e}$ and without the stopping criterion (14). If the number of Lanczos steps between restarts, k, is large enough, then the computed sequence $\widehat{\mathbf{z}}^{(i)}$, $i = 1, 2, \ldots$,* *of approximations of the Perron vector converges to* $\mathbf{w}$ *as i increases. Similarly, the computed sequence* $\rho^{(i)}$ *for* $i = 1, 2, \ldots,$ *of approximations of the Perron root* ρ*, converges to* ρ *as i increases.*

Proof. Blondel et al. ([8] Theorem 2) show that, given a strictly positive initial vector, the sequence $\mathbf{z}_{2k}$, $k = 1, 2, \ldots,$ in Equation (2) generated by the power method, converges to the Perron vector of M. It follows that Theorem 2 also holds when the initial vector $\mathbf{e}$ is replaced by any vector with all entries being strictly positive. In particular, Theorem 2 holds for all the initial vectors $\widehat{\mathbf{z}}^{(i)}$, $i = 0, 1, 2, \ldots,$ used in the restarted Lanczos method. Let us set $\widehat{\mathbf{z}}^{(0)} = \mathbf{e}$.

The Ritz value $\rho^{(i)}$, determined by the restarted Lanczos method, satisfies

$$\rho^{(i)} = \max_{\mathbf{x} \in \mathcal{K}_k(M, \widehat{\mathbf{z}}^{(i-1)})} \frac{\mathbf{x}^T M \mathbf{x}}{\mathbf{x}^T \mathbf{x}}.$$

It follows that, unless $\widehat{\mathbf{z}}^{(i-1)}$ is a stationary point of the Rayleigh quotient, $\rho^{(i)} > \rho^{(i-1)}$. According to Theorem 2, the vector $\widehat{\mathbf{z}}^{(i-1)}$ can be a stationary point only if it is the Perron vector. Thus, we may assume that $\rho^{(i)} > \rho^{(i-1)}$.

The vector $\widehat{\mathbf{z}}^{(i)}$ used in the next restart is not the Ritz vector of M that corresponds to the Rayleigh quotient $\rho^{(i)}$, because all entries smaller than some tiny $\delta > 0$ in this Ritz vector are set to δ. This means that the Rayleigh quotient

$$\rho^{(i)}_{\text{mod}} = \frac{(\widehat{\mathbf{z}}^{(i-1)})^T M \widehat{\mathbf{z}}^{(i-1)}}{(\widehat{\mathbf{z}}^{(i-1)})^T \widehat{\mathbf{z}}^{(i-1)}}$$

may be smaller than $\rho^{(i)}$. We have to choose the number of Lanczos steps between restarts, k, large enough so that $\rho^{(i)}_{\text{mod}}$ is significantly larger than $\rho^{(i-1)}$ for every i. This secures the convergence of the vectors $\widehat{\mathbf{z}}^{(i)}$ to the Perron vector $\mathbf{w}$ of M as i increases. □

Example 4. *We apply the restarted Lanczos method to the same adjacency matrix M as in Example 2 to compute its Perron vector and to identify the most important vertices of the associated graph. We let* $\epsilon = 10^{-4}$ *in (14) and carry out* $k = 10$ *steps of the Lanczos method between restarts. All entries smaller than* $\delta = 10^{-8}$ *in the Ritz vectors of M associated with the Perron roots of consecutively generated symmetric tridiagonal matrices are set to* δ*. For the present example, the restarted Lanczos method requires seven restarts, thus, 70 matrix–vector product evaluations are carried out. The computational load is larger than for Algorithm 1, but the storage requirement of the restarted method is smaller and is independent of the number of restarts necessary.*

4. The Arnoldi Method

The Arnoldi method can be applied to compute approximations of a few eigenvalues and associated eigenvectors of a large non-symmetric matrix $A \in \mathbb{R}^{n \times n}$. We will describe a novel application to the computation of the Perron vector of a large symmetric matrix. A thorough discussion of the Arnoldi method and its properties is provided by Saad ([12] Chapter 6). Here, we only provide a brief outline.

The application of $1 \leq k \ll n$ steps of the Arnoldi method applied to a large matrix $A \in \mathbb{R}^{n \times n}$ with initial vector $\mathbf{v} \in \mathbb{R}^n \backslash \{\mathbf{0}\}$ gives, generically, the Arnoldi decomposition

$$AQ_k = Q_k H_k + h_{k+1,k} \mathbf{q}_{k+1} \mathbf{e}_k^T, \tag{15}$$

where

$$H_k = \begin{bmatrix} h_{11} & h_{12} & h_{13} & \cdots & h_{1k} \\ h_{21} & h_{22} & h_{23} & \cdots & h_{2k} \\ & h_{321} & h_{33} & \cdots & h_{3k} \\ & & \ddots & \ddots & \vdots \\ & & & h_{k,k-1} & h_{kk} \end{bmatrix} \in \mathbb{R}^{k \times k}$$

is an upper Hessenberg matrix with positive subdiagonal entries, the matrix $Q_k \in \mathbb{R}^{n\times k}$ has orthonormal columns, $\mathbf{q}_{k+1} \in \mathbb{R}^n$ is a unit vector such that $Q_k^T\mathbf{q}_{k+1} = \mathbf{0}$, and $h_{k+1,k}$ is a nonnegative scalar. Each step of the Arnoldi method requires the evaluation of one matrix vector product with A. The decomposition (15) exists, provided that the Arnoldi method, outlined in Algorithm 3, does not break down because of a division by zero. This situation is very rare; we therefore will not dwell on it further.

Let ρ_k denote the largest eigenvalue of H_k, and let $\mathbf{y}_k \in \mathbb{R}^k$ be an associated unit eigenvector. Then, ρ_k and $\mathbf{w}_k = Q_k\mathbf{y}_k$ are the corresponding Ritz value and Ritz vector of A, respectively. The iterations with the Arnoldi method are terminated when two consecutive approximations of the Perron vector are sufficiently close, that is, when

$$\|\mathbf{w}_k - \mathbf{w}_{k-1}\| \leq \epsilon$$

for some user-specified tolerance $\epsilon > 0$. Algorithm 3 describes the Arnoldi method with initial vector $\mathbf{e}$.

Algorithm 3 Estimate the Perron vector of matrix A with the Arnoldi method with initial vector $\mathbf{e}$.

Require: Adjacency matrix $A \in \mathbb{R}^{n\times n}$ and initial vector $\mathbf{e} = \mathbf{1}$.
Ensure: Ritz vector $\mathbf{w}_k$ of the adjacency matrix A.

$\mathbf{q}_1 = \mathbf{e}/\|\mathbf{e}\|$, $\mathbf{w}_0 = \mathbf{0}$, $k = 1$
$h_{11} = \mathbf{q}_1^T A\mathbf{q}_1$
$\mathbf{r} = A\mathbf{q}_1 - h_{11}\mathbf{q}_1$
$h_{21} = \|\mathbf{r}\|$
$\mathbf{q}_2 = \mathbf{r}/h_{21}$
$H_1 = h_{11}$
$Q_1 = \mathbf{q}_1$, $\mathbf{w}_1 = \mathbf{q}_1$
while $\|\mathbf{w}_k - \mathbf{w}_{k-1}\| > \epsilon$ **do**
  $k = k+1$
  $r = A\mathbf{q}_k$
  for $i = 1, 2, \ldots, k$ **do**
    $h_{ik} = \mathbf{q}_i^T r$
    $\mathbf{r} = \mathbf{r} - h_{ik}\mathbf{q}_i$
  end for
  $h_{k+1,k} = \|\mathbf{r}\|$
  $\mathbf{q}_{k+1} = \mathbf{r}/h_{k+1,k}$
  $H_k = \begin{bmatrix} H_{k-1} & \{h_{ik}\}_{i=1}^{k-1} \\ h_{k,k-1}\mathbf{e}_{k-1}^T & h_{k,k} \end{bmatrix}$
  $Q_k = [Q_{k-1} \quad \mathbf{q}_k]$
  Compute the Perron vector $\mathbf{y}_k$ of H_k
  $\mathbf{w}_k = Q_k\mathbf{y}_k$
end while
$\mathbf{w} = \mathbf{w}_k$

Blondel et al. consider the computation of the Perron vector of the central block

$$C = A^T A + AA^T \tag{16}$$

of the matrix (7), where the matrix $A \in \mathbb{R}^{n\times n}$ may be non-symmetric; see [8] Theorem 6. One approach is to apply the Lanczos method to C. Then, each iteration requires the evaluation of two matrix–vector products with A and two with A^T. We will compare this approach to the application of k steps of the Arnoldi method to A.

The Arnoldi decomposition suggests the approximation $A \approx Q_k H_k Q_k^T$, from which we obtain

$$A^T A + AA^T \approx Q_k(H_k^T H_k + H_k H_k^T)Q_k^T. \tag{17}$$

Let ρ_k be the largest eigenvalue of $H_k^T H_k + H_k H_k^T$ and let $\mathbf{y}_k$ be the associated Perron vector. Then, the vector $\mathbf{w}_k = Q_k \mathbf{y}_k$ provides an approximation of the Perron vector of the matrix $A^T A + AA^T$. The main advantage of using this approximation, when compared to the application of the Lanczos method to the matrix (16), is that the computation of the approximation (17) only requires the evaluation of k matrix–vector products with A, while the computation of k steps of the Lanczos method to the matrix (16) demands the evaluation of $4k$ matrix–vector products with A or A^T. For many matrices A, the right-hand side of (17) gives an accurate approximation of the Perron vector for a few Arnoldi steps. We provide an illustration below. However, the use of (17) is not always beneficial as the next example shows.

Example 5. *Let $A \in \mathbb{R}^{n \times n}$ be a Jordan block with the eigenvalue zero. Then, A is an adjacency matrix associated with a simple directed graph. The graph and the matrix are displayed in Figure 1.*

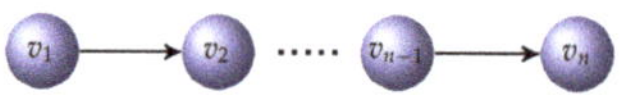

$$A = \begin{bmatrix} 0 & 1 & & & & \\ & 0 & 1 & & & \\ & & 0 & 1 & & \\ & & & \ddots & \ddots & \\ & & & & 0 & 1 \\ & & & & & 0 \end{bmatrix}.$$

Figure 1. A directed graph $\mathcal{G}$ and its adjacency matrix A.

The Perron root of A is 0, with Perron vector $\mathbf{e}_1 = [1, 0, \ldots, 0]^T$. When applying the Arnoldi method to A with initial vector $\mathbf{e}$, the k-dimensional Krylov subspace $\mathcal{K}_k(A, \mathbf{e})$ is spanned by the first k vectors of

$$\mathcal{K}_n(A, \mathbf{e}) = \operatorname{span}\{\mathbf{e}, A\mathbf{e}, A^2\mathbf{e}, \ldots, A^{n-1}\mathbf{e}\} = \operatorname{span}\left\{ \begin{bmatrix} 1 \\ 1 \\ \vdots \\ 1 \\ 1 \end{bmatrix}, \begin{bmatrix} 1 \\ 1 \\ \vdots \\ 1 \\ 0 \end{bmatrix}, \ldots, \begin{bmatrix} 1 \\ 0 \\ \vdots \\ 0 \\ 0 \end{bmatrix} \right\}.$$

In particular, the Perron vector is not contained in the subspaces $\mathcal{K}_k(A, \mathbf{e})$ for $k = 1, 2, \ldots, n-1$. This implies that one has to carry out n steps with the Arnoldi algorithm to determine an accurate approximation of the Perron vector of A. For the present matrix A, Formula (17) requires n steps of the Arnoldi algorithm applied to A to give an accurate approximation of a Perron vector of (16).

We turn to the spectral factorization of the matrix (16). This matrix is diagonal with eigenvalue 2 of multiplicity $n-2$. The corresponding eigenvectors form the eigenspace

$$\operatorname{span}\{\mathbf{e}_2, \mathbf{e}_3, \ldots, \mathbf{e}_{n-1}\}.$$

Example 6. *Let $A \in \mathbb{R}^{n \times n}$ represent the adjacency matrix of a directed circular graph. The adjacency matrix and the associated graph are displayed in Figure 2.*

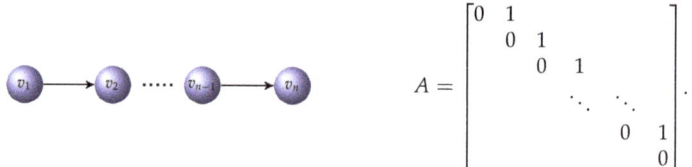

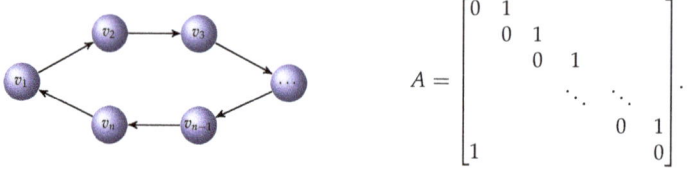

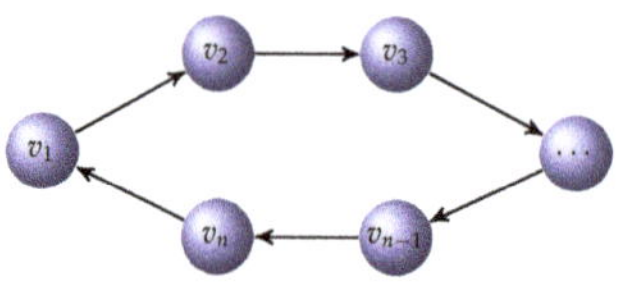

$$A = \begin{bmatrix} 0 & 1 & & & & \\ & 0 & 1 & & & \\ & & 0 & 1 & & \\ & & & \ddots & \ddots & \\ & & & & 0 & 1 \\ 1 & & & & & 0 \end{bmatrix}.$$

Figure 2. A directed circular graph $\mathcal{G}$ and its adjacency matrix A.

In this example, the matrix (16) is diagonal, with Perron root 2 of multiplicity n. In particular, the vector **e** *is a Perron vector. Application of one step of the Arnoldi algorithm to the the circulant matrix A with initial vector* **e** *yields the eigenvector* **e***. Thus, the Arnoldi algorithm performs well.*

Example 7. *Consider the up-shift matrix on the right-hand side of Figure 1 of order* 1000. *By adding the perturbation* $\gamma = 10^{-3}$ *to the entry* $(1000, 1)$, *we obtain an adjacency matrix A that represents a weighted directed circular graph. Thus, the graph is strongly connected. The associated matrix (16) is diagonal with Perron root 2 with eigenspace* $\text{span}\{\mathbf{e}_2, \mathbf{e}_3, \ldots, \mathbf{e}_{n-1}\}$. *When applying the Arnoldi algorithm to A with initial vector* **e**, 1000 *steps are required to approximate the Perron vector. In this case, the Arnoldi algorithm performs poorly.*

We conclude that the Arnoldi method may not provide useful approximations of the Perron vector of certain non-symmetric adjacency matrices A in a reasonable number of steps. The application of the Arnoldi method to A to compute the Perron vector of the matrix (16) can be competitive with the application of the Lanczos method to the latter matrix, but this is not guaranteed. The closer the adjacency matrix A is to the set of symmetric matrices, the better the Arnoldi method, applied to A, can be expected to perform.

5. Application to Real World Networks

In this section, we apply the iterative methods discussed in this paper to the computation of the Perron vector of large real-world networks, and compare the results obtained.

We start by analyzing a particular 3-chained network and seek to determine the most important vertices of each index subset according to the eigenvector centrality. Some social bookmarking services, such as Delicious, allow their users to put tags on web pages. The relationship between users, web pages and tags, can be represented by a 3-chained network [15]. A data set of Delicious bookmarks, which contains 105,000 bookmarks and 1867 users, is available at the Grouplens web site [17]. We selected data from January 2010 to February 2010 and constructed a 3-chained graph $\mathcal{G}$ with the three vertex subsets: 456 users, 4253 web pages, and 5962 tags. The total numbers of vertices and edges are 10,671 and 23,550 respectively. The 3-chained network is undirected and represented by the adjacency matrix $M \in \mathbb{R}^{10671 \times 10671}$.

We used the power method, Lanczos iteration, and restarted the Lanczos iteration to estimate the Perron vector of M and to find the most important vertices of each vertex subset. Denote the computed approximations of the Perron vectors of M, obtained by applying the methods mentioned, by $\mathbf{s}_P$, $\mathbf{s}_L$, and $\mathbf{s}_{RL}$, respectively. Let the initial vector be **e** and the tolerance be 10^{-10} for all the methods. To estimate the accuracy of the methods, we consider as exact the principal eigenvector $\mathbf{s}_{\text{exact}}$ of M computed by the built-in function `eigs` from MATLAB.

Before determining the most important vertices, we first check the accuracy of the approximations of the Perron vector of M computed by the above mentioned methods. We calculate the error, that is, the 2-norm of the difference between each computed approximation of the Perron vector and $\mathbf{s}_{\text{exact}}$. The errors of the estimated Perron vectors are 0.3461 for the power method 3.22×10^{-5} for Lanczos iteration, and 6.69×10^{-8} for restarted Lanczos iteration. From the errors, we observe that the Ritz vector obtained from the restarted Lanczos method is the most accurate estimator. The Ritz vector from the Lanczos algorithm is moderately accurate, while the vector found by the power method is fairly different from the exact Perron vector $\mathbf{s}_{\text{exact}}$.

Let us now look at the performances of each method for finding the most important vertices in the three subsets "users", "web pages" and "tags". The results determined by the above methods and the number of iterations required are displayed in Table 1. The most important vertices determined by $\mathbf{s}_{\text{exact}}$ are displayed in the "Built-in" column. All of the methods identify the vertices v_{142}, v_{1368} and v_{4796} as the most important user, web page and tag, respectively. The last row, "iterations", shows that the standard Lanczos method requires 17 matrix–vector product evaluations with A. For the restarted Lanczos, labeled ResLanc, 10 Lanczos steps are performed between each restart. Thus, it requires in this case 30 matrix–vector products. The power method requires the largest number of matrix–vector products. The rate of convergence of the approximation of the Perron vector of M computed by the Lanczos method is faster than those of the other two methods. The Ritz vector of the restarted Lanczos iteration converges more slowly but the computations require less storage space.

Table 1. The most important vertices found by the methods discussed for each vertex set, and the number of iterations required by each method.

	Built-In	Power	Lanczos	ResLanc_{10}
"users"	142	142	142	142
"web pages"	1368	1368	1368	1368
"tags"	4796	4796	4796	4796
iterations		34	17	3

To better understand the numerical performance of the methods, we applied them to six undirected networks of different sizes. They are listed, together with their number of nodes, in the first column of Table 2:

`autobahn` describes the German highway system network; it is available at [18].

`ndyeast` models the protein interaction network for yeast. The data set was originally included in the Notre Dame Networks Database and is available at [19].

`power` is a representation of the U.S.A. western states power grid; see [20]. It can be found at [21].

`geom` is a weighted graph, extracted from the Computational Geometry Database *geombib* by B. Jones (version 2002) and is available at [19]. The entry (i, j) of the adjacency matrix is the number of papers coauthored by authors i and j.

`internet` is a snapshot of the structure of the Internet at the level of autonomous systems, created by Mark Newman from data for 22 July 2006 [21].

`facebook` describes the *friendship* links of the New Orleans Facebook network resulting from a particular snapshot. The dataset was studied in [22] and is available at [23].

Table 2 displays the number of matrix–vector product evaluations carried out by the methods considered to reach convergence. We also report the results obtained for the `delicious` network for comparison. The label Lanczos2 denotes the results obtained by Algorithm 2, that is, by applying the Lanczos recursion twice to save storage space. In this case, the number of matrix–vector product evaluations is roughly twice the number of iterations required by the standard algorithm (Algorithm 1) if the stopping criterion is adjusted to produce the same accuracy in the approximation of the Perron vector. The restarted Lanczos method (ResLanc) was executed with both ten and five iterations between each restart, so the number of matrix–vector product evaluations is obtained by multiplying the number of iterations by ten and five, respectively. For the other methods, the number of matrix–vector product evaluations coincides with the number of iterations. Table 3 reports the 2-norm errors for each method. The Perron vector returned by the function `eigs` of MATLAB is considered the exact vector.

Table 2. Number of matrix–vector product evaluations required by the methods to reach convergence.

Network	Size	Power	Lanczos	Lanczos2	ResLanc_{10}	ResLanc_{5}
`autobahn`	1168	163	29	53	60	85
`ndyeast`	2114	1029	27	53	60	80
`power`	4941	49	18	35	30	35
`geom`	7343	19	11	23	20	20
`delicious`	10,671	35	17	33	30	30
`internet`	22,963	35	12	25	30	25
`facebook`	63,731	41	13	27	30	25

Table 3. Errors produced by the methods with respect to the Perron vector computed by the `eigs` function of MATLAB.

Network	Size	Power	Lanczos	Lanczos2	ResLanc$_{10}$	ResLanc$_5$
autobahn	1168	1.09×10^{-3}	7.62×10^{-5}	2.42×10^{-4}	9.60×10^{-6}	7.46×10^{-5}
ndyeast	2114	1.47×10^{-2}	7.96×10^{-5}	7.96×10^{-5}	2.37×10^{-6}	7.59×10^{-5}
power	4941	2.76×10^{-4}	3.66×10^{-5}	3.66×10^{-5}	9.77×10^{-8}	8.18×10^{-6}
geom	7343	1.66×10^{-5}	6.53×10^{-6}	1.28×10^{-6}	2.60×10^{-10}	5.10×10^{-8}
delicious	10,671	3.46×10^{-1}	3.22×10^{-5}	3.22×10^{-5}	6.73×10^{-8}	5.42×10^{-6}
internet	22,963	6.77×10^{-5}	3.15×10^{-5}	8.97×10^{-6}	1.51×10^{-11}	2.36×10^{-7}
facebook	63,731	9.74×10^{-5}	2.37×10^{-5}	6.86×10^{-6}	2.38×10^{-10}	1.05×10^{-6}

We see that the power method requires more iterations than the Lanczos algorithm (Algorithm 1) and delivers approximations of the Perron vector of worse accuracy. Applying the Lanczos method twice by Algorithm 2 saves storage but results in a heavier computational load in order to produce the same accuracy of the computed approximation of the Perron vector. The restarted Lanczos approach has the remarkable feature of requiring the same number of matrix products when it is executed, performing ten and five iterations between consecutive restarts. This means that just a few iterations are sufficient to guarantee convergence. The computer storage requirement is much smaller than for the Lanczos method. The errors in the computed approximations of the Perron vector achieved by the restarted Lanczos method are smaller than the errors obtained with the Lanczos methods (Algorithms 1 and 2). Table 2 indicates that the restarted Lanczos method can be competitive.

6. Conclusions

This paper compares the computational effort and storage requirements of the power method, Lanczos method, and the restarted Lanczos method to determine the Perron vector for a large symmetric adjacency matrix. The application of the Arnoldi iteration is also considered. The power method yields quite a slow convergence, much slower than that of the Lanczos method. However, due to its large storage requirement for large adjacency matrices, the latter method is not practical to use for large-scale networks. Different ways of restarting the Lanczos iterations are considered and found to combine faster convergence than the power method with less storage requirement than the Lanczos method.

Author Contributions: Methodology, A.C., L.R., G.R. and Y.Z. All authors have read and agreed to the published version of the manuscript.

Funding: A.C. and G.R. were supported by the INdAM-GNCS research project "Tecniche numeriche per l'analisi delle reti complesse e lo studio dei problemi inversi" and and the Regione Autonoma della Sardegna research project "Algorithms and Models for Imaging Science (AMIS)" [RASSR57257]. L.R. was supported by NSF grant DMS-1720259.

Institutional Review Board Statement: Not applicable.

Informed Consent Statement: Not applicable.

Data Availability Statement: Not applicable.

Conflicts of Interest: The authors declare no conflict of interest.

References

1. Estrada, E. *The Structure of Complex Networks: Theory and Applications*; Oxford University Press: Oxford, UK, 2012.
2. Newman, M.E.J. *Networks: An Introduction*; Oxford University Press: Oxford, UK, 2010.
3. Brandes, U. A faster algorithm for betweenness centrality. *J. Math. Sociol.* **2001**, *25*, 163–177. [CrossRef]
4. Kleinberg, J.M. Authoritative sources in a hyperlinked environment. *J. ACM* **1999**, *46*, 604–632. [CrossRef]
5. Bonacich, P. Power and centrality: A family of measures. *Am. J. Sociol.* **1987**, *92*, 1170–1182. [CrossRef]
6. Meyer, C.D. *Matrix Analysis and Applied Linear Algebra*; SIAM: Philadelphia, PA, USA, 2000.
7. Estrada, E.; Knight, P.A. *A First Course in Network Theory*; Oxford University Press: Oxford, UK, 2015.

8. Blondel, V.D.; Gajardo, A.; Heymans, M.; Senellart, P.; Van Dooren, P. A measure of similarity between graph vertices: Applications to synonym extraction and web searching. *SIAM Rev.* **2004**, *46*, 647–666. [CrossRef]
9. Bondy, J.A.; Murty, U.S.R. *Graph Theory with Applications*; Macmillan: London, UK, 1976.
10. Concas, A.; Noschese, S.; Reichel, L.; Rodriguez, G. A spectral method for bipartizing a network and detecting a large anti-community. *J. Comput. Appl. Math.* **2020**, *373*, 112306. [CrossRef]
11. Concas, A.; Fenu, C.; Rodriguez, G. `PQser`: A Matlab package for spectral seriation. *Numer. Algorithms* **2019**, *80*, 879–902. [CrossRef]
12. Saad, Y. *Numerical Methods for Large Eigenvalue Problems*, 2nd ed.; SIAM: Philadelphia, PA, USA, 2011.
13. Bapat, R.B. *Graphs and Matrices*; Springer: London, UK, 2010.
14. Concas, A.; Reichel, L.; Rodriguez, G.; Zhang, Y. Chained graphs and some applications. *Appl. Netw. Sci.* **2021**, *6*, 39. [CrossRef]
15. Ikematsu, K.; Murata, T. A fast method for detecting communities from tripartite networks. In Proceedings of the International Conference on Social Informatics, Kyoto, Japan, 25–27 November 2013; Springer: Cham, Switzerland, 2013; pp. 192–205.
16. CITESEERX, Computer and Information Science Papers. CiteSeer Publications ResearchIndex. Available online: https://citeseerx.ist.psu.edu/index (accessed on 5 May 2021).
17. Grouplens. Available online: https://grouplens.org/datasets/hetrec-2011 (accessed on 5 May 2021).
18. Biological Networks Data Sets of Newcastle University. Available online: http://www.biological-networks.org/ (accessed on 5 May 2021).
19. Batagelj, V.; Mrvar, A. Pajek Data Sets. Available online: http://vlado.fmf.uni-lj.si/pub/networks/data/ (accessed on 5 May 2021).
20. Watts, D.J.; Strogatz, S.H. Collective dynamics of 'small-world'networks. *Nature* **1998**, *393*, 440–442. [CrossRef] [PubMed]
21. Mark Newman's Web Page. Available online: http://www-personal.umich.edu/~mejn/netdata/ (accessed on 5 May 2021).
22. Viswanath, B.; Mislove, A.; Cha, M.; Gummadi, K.P. On the evolution of user interaction in Facebook. In Proceedings of the 2nd ACM Workshop on Online Social Networks (WOSN'09), Barcelona, Spain, 17 August 2009; pp. 37–42.
23. The Max Plank Institute for Software Systems. Available online: http://socialnetworks.mpi-sws.org/data-wosn2009.html (accessed on 5 May 2021).

mathematics

MDPI

Article

Estimating the Quadratic Form $x^T A^{-m} x$ for Symmetric Matrices: Further Progress and Numerical Computations

Marilena Mitrouli [1,†], Athanasios Polychronou [1,†], Paraskevi Roupa [1,†] and Ondřej Turek [2,*,†]

1 Department of Mathematics, National and Kapodistrian University of Athens, Panepistimiopolis, 15784 Athens, Greece; mmitroul@math.uoa.gr (M.M.); apolychronou@math.uoa.gr (A.P.); parask_roupa@math.uoa.gr (P.R.)

2 Department of Mathematics, University of Ostrava, 701 03 Ostrava, Czech Republic

* Correspondence: ondrej.turek@osu.cz

† These authors contributed equally to this work.

Abstract: In this paper, we study estimates for quadratic forms of the type $x^T A^{-m} x$, $m \in \mathbb{N}$, for symmetric matrices. We derive a general approach for estimating this type of quadratic form and we present some upper bounds for the corresponding absolute error. Specifically, we consider three different approaches for estimating the quadratic form $x^T A^{-m} x$. The first approach is based on a projection method, the second is a minimization procedure, and the last approach is heuristic. Numerical examples showing the effectiveness of the estimates are presented. Furthermore, we compare the behavior of the proposed estimates with other methods that are derived in the literature.

Keywords: quadratic form; estimates; upper bounds

Citation: Mitrouli, M.; Polychronou, A.; Roupa, P.; Turek, O. Estimating the Quadratic Form $x^T A^{-m} x$ for Symmetric Matrices: Further Progress and Numerical Computations. *Mathematics* **2021**, *9*, 1432. https://doi.org/10.3390/math9121432

Academic Editor: Mariano Torrisi

Received: 31 May 2021
Accepted: 16 June 2021
Published: 19 June 2021

Publisher's Note: MDPI stays neutral with regard to jurisdictional claims in published maps and institutional affiliations.

1. Introduction

Let $A \in \mathbb{R}^{n \times n}$ be a given symmetric positive definite matrix and $x \in \mathbb{R}^n$. We are interested in estimating the quadratic forms of the type $x^T A^{-m} x$, $m \in \mathbb{N}$. Our main goal was to find an efficient and cheap approximate evaluation of the desired quadratic form without the direct computation of the matrix A^{-m}. As such, we revisited the approach for estimating the quadratic form $x^T A^{-1} x$, developed in [1], and extended it to the case of an arbitrary negative power of A.

The computation of quadratic forms is a mathematical problem with many applications. Indicatively, we refer to some usual applications.

- Statistics: The inverse of the covariance matrix, which is referred to as a precision matrix, usually appears in statistics. The covariance matrix reveals marginal correlations between the variables, whereas the precision matrix represents the conditional correlations between two data variables of the other variables [2]. The diagonal of the inverse of covariance matrices provides information about the quality of data in uncertainty quantification [3].
- Network analysis: The determination of the importance of the nodes of a graph is a major issue in network analysis. Information for these details can be extracted by the evaluation of the diagonal elements of the matrix $(I_n - aA)^{-1}$, where A is the adjacency matrix of the network, $0 < a < \frac{1}{\rho(A)}$, and $\rho(A)$ is the spectral radius of A. This matrix is referred to as a resolvent matrix, see, for example, [4] and the references therein.
- Numerical analysis: Quadratic forms arise naturally in the context of the computation of the regularization parameter in Tikhonov regularization for solving ill-posed problems. In this case, the matrix has the form $AA^T + \lambda I_n$, $\lambda > 0$. In the literature, many methods have been proposed for the selection of the regularization parameter λ, such

as the discrepancy principle, cross-validation, generalized cross-validation (GCV), L-curve, and so forth; see, for an example, [5] (Chapter 15) and references therein. These methods involve quadratic forms of type $x^T(AA^T + \lambda I_n)^{-m}x$, with $m = 1, 2, 3$.

In practice, exact computation of a quadratic form is often replaced using an estimate that is faster to evaluate. Regarding its numerous applications, the estimation of quadratic forms is an important practical problem that has been frequently studied in the literature. Let us indicatively refer to some well-known methods. A widely used method is based on Gaussian quadrature [5] (Chapter 7) and [6]. Moreover, extrapolation procedures have been proposed. Specifically, in [7], families of estimates for the bilinear form $x^T A^{-1} y$ for any invertible matrix, and in [8], families of estimates for the bilinear form $y^* f(A)x$ for a Hermitian matrix were developed.

In the present work, we consider alternative approaches to this problem. To begin, notice that the value of the quadratic form $(x, A^{-m}x)$ is proportional to the second power of the norm of x. Therefore, the task of estimating $(x, A^{-m}x)$ consists of two steps:

1. Finding an α such that
$$(x, A^{-m}x) \approx \alpha\|x\|^2. \tag{1}$$
2. Assessing the absolute error of the above estimate, i.e., determining a bound for the quantity
$$\left|\alpha\|x\|^2 - (x, A^{-m}x)\right|. \tag{2}$$

In Section 2, we present the upper bounds for the absolute error (2) for any given α. Section 3 is devoted to estimates of the value α in (1) using a projection method. In Section 4, we use bounds from Section 2 as a stepping stone for estimating $x^T A^{-m} x$ using the minimization method. A heuristic approach is outlined in Section 5. In Section 6, we briefly describe two methods that were used in previous studies, namely, an extrapolation approach and another one based on Gaussian quadrature. Section 7 is focused on adapting the proposed estimates to the case of the matrix of form $AA^T + \lambda I_n$. Numerical examples that illustrate the performance of the derived estimates are found in Section 8. We end this work with several concluding remarks in Section 9.

2. Bounds on the Error

In Proposition 1 below, we derive an upper bound on the error (2) for a given estimate $\alpha\|x\|^2$ of the quadratic form $x^T A^{-m} x$. The first three expressions for the bounds (UB1–UB3) are a direct generalization of a result from [1].

Proposition 1. *Let $A \in \mathbb{R}^{n\times n}$ be a symmetric positive definite matrix and $x \in \mathbb{R}^n$ and $est = \alpha\|x\|^2$ be an estimate of the quadratic form $x^T A^{-m} x$. If we denote $b = \alpha A^m x - x$, the absolute error of the estimate $|\alpha\|x\|^2 - (x, A^{-m}x)|$ is bounded from above by the following expressions:*

UB1. $\dfrac{\|x\|^2\|b\|}{2\|A^m x\|}\left(\kappa^m + \dfrac{1}{\kappa^m}\right)$

UB2. $\dfrac{\|x\| \cdot \|b\|^2}{2\|A^m b\|}\left(\kappa^m + \dfrac{1}{\kappa^m}\right)$

UB3. $\dfrac{\|x\|^2\|b\|^2}{4\sqrt{x^T A^m x} \cdot \sqrt{b^T A^m b}}\left(\kappa^{m/2} + \dfrac{1}{\kappa^{m/2}}\right)^2$

UB4. $\dfrac{\|x\| \cdot \|b\|}{\lambda_{\min}^m}$

UB5. For estimates satisfying $\alpha\|x\|^2 \le (x, A^{-m}x)$, we have also the family of error bounds
$$\frac{\|x\|^2}{2\|A^m x\| \cdot \|A^p x\|}\left(\kappa^m + \frac{1}{\kappa^m}\right)\sqrt{\|A^p x\|^2\|b\|^2 - (A^p x, b)^2},$$
where $p \ge 0$ can be chosen as any integer such that $\frac{(x, A^p x)}{(A^m x, A^p x)} < \alpha$.

Proof.

UB1.

The matrix A^{-m} is symmetric because A is symmetric, and it holds that

$$|x^T A^{-m} b| = |(x, A^{-m} b)| = |(A^{-m} x, b)| \leq \|A^{-m} x\| \cdot \|b\|,$$

by the Cauchy–Schwarz inequality.

Moreover, we have

$$\|A^{-m} x\| = \sqrt{(A^{-m} x, A^{-m} x)} = \sqrt{(x, A^{-2m} x)}. \tag{3}$$

Using the Kantorovich inequality for the matrix A^m and considering that $\lambda_{\min}(A^{2m}) = \lambda_{\min}^{2m}$, $\lambda_{\max}(A^{2m}) = \lambda_{\max}^{2m}$, we have

$$\begin{aligned}
& \frac{(x^T x)^2}{(x^T A^{2m} x)(x^T (A^{2m})^{-1} x)} \geq \frac{4\lambda_{\min}(A^{2m})\lambda_{\max}(A^{2m})}{(\lambda_{\min}(A^{2m}) + \lambda_{\max}(A^{2m}))^2} \\
\Rightarrow \quad & \frac{\|x\|^4}{(x^T A^{2m} x)(x^T A^{-2m} x)} \geq \frac{4\lambda_{\min}^{2m}\lambda_{\max}^{2m}}{(\lambda_{\min}^{2m} + \lambda_{\max}^{2m})^2} \\
\Rightarrow \quad & x^T A^{-2m} x \leq \frac{\|x\|^4}{(x, A^{2m} x)} \frac{(\lambda_{\min}^{2m} + \lambda_{\max}^{2m})^2}{4\lambda_{\min}^{2m}\lambda_{\max}^{2m}} \\
\Rightarrow \quad & x^T A^{-2m} x \leq \frac{\|x\|^4}{4\|A^m x\|^2} \left(\frac{\lambda_{\min}^m}{\lambda_{\max}^m} + \frac{\lambda_{\max}^m}{\lambda_{min}^m} \right)^2 = \frac{\|x\|^4}{4\|A^m x\|^2} \left(\frac{1}{\kappa^m} + \kappa^m \right)^2,
\end{aligned}$$

where $\kappa = \frac{\lambda_{\max}}{\lambda_{\min}}$ is the condition number of A. Therefore, the norm $\|A^{-m} x\|$ given by (3) can be bounded by

$$\|A^{-m} x\| \leq \frac{\|x\|^2}{2\|A^m x\|} \left(\frac{1}{\kappa^m} + \kappa^m \right). \tag{4}$$

Hence, we have

$$|x^T A^{-m} b| \leq \|A^{-m} x\| \cdot \|b\| = \frac{\|x\|^2}{2\|A^m x\|} \left(\frac{1}{\kappa^m} + \kappa^m \right) \|b\|.$$

UB2.

Due to the Cauchy–Schwarz inequality, it holds that

$$|x^T A^{-m} b| = |(x, A^{-m} b)| \leq \|x\| \cdot \|A^{-m} b\|.$$

Following a similar approach as above based on the Kantorovich inequality, we obtain

$$\|A^{-m} b\| \leq \frac{\|b\|^2}{2\|A^m b\|} \left(\frac{1}{\kappa^m} + \kappa^m \right).$$

So,

$$|x^T A^{-m} b| \leq \frac{\|x\| \cdot \|b\|^2}{2\|A^m b\|} \left(\frac{1}{\kappa^m} + \kappa^m \right).$$

UB3.

It holds that

$$\begin{aligned}
|x^T A^{-m} b| &= |(A^{-\frac{m}{2}} x, A^{-\frac{m}{2}} b)| \leq \|A^{-\frac{m}{2}} x\| \cdot \|A^{-\frac{m}{2}} b\| \\
&= \sqrt{(A^{-\frac{m}{2}} x, A^{-\frac{m}{2}} x)} \cdot \sqrt{(A^{-\frac{m}{2}} b, A^{-\frac{m}{2}} b)} = \sqrt{(x, A^{-m} x)} \cdot \sqrt{(b, A^{-m} b)}.
\end{aligned}$$

Applying the Kantorovich inequality to the matrix A^m in a similar way as above, we can immediately obtain the inequality

$$x^T A^{-m} x \le \frac{\|x\|^4}{4x^T A^m x}\left(\frac{1}{\kappa^{\frac{m}{2}}} + \kappa^{\frac{m}{2}}\right)^2.$$

So, we have

$$\begin{aligned} |x^T A^{-m} b| &\le \sqrt{\frac{\|x\|^4}{4x^T A^m x}\left(\frac{1}{\kappa^{\frac{m}{2}}} + \kappa^{\frac{m}{2}}\right)^2 \frac{\|b\|^4}{4b^T A^m b}\left(\frac{1}{\kappa^{\frac{m}{2}}} + \kappa^{\frac{m}{2}}\right)^2} \\ &= \frac{\|x\|^2\|b\|^2}{4\sqrt{x^T A^m x}\cdot\sqrt{b^T A^m b}}\left(\frac{1}{\kappa^{\frac{m}{2}}} + \kappa^{\frac{m}{2}}\right)^2. \end{aligned}$$

UB4.

Applying the Cauchy–Schwarz inequality, we obtain

$$|x^T A^{-m} b| = |(x, A^{-m} b)| \le \|x\| \cdot \|A^{-m} b\| \le \|x\| \frac{\|b\|}{\lambda_{\min}(A^m)} = \|x\| \frac{\|b\|}{\lambda_{\min}^m}.$$

UB5.

Since A is positive definite, as is A^q for any integer q, the angle between vectors v and $A^q v$ does not exceed $\pi/2$ for any v, i.e., $\measuredangle(v; A^q v) \le \frac{\pi}{2}$.

Taking $v = A^{-m}x$ and $q = p + m$, we obtain

$$\measuredangle(A^{-m}x; A^{p+m}A^{-m}x) \le \frac{\pi}{2} \quad \Rightarrow \quad \measuredangle(A^{-m}x; A^p x) \le \frac{\pi}{2}.$$

The assumption $\frac{(x, A^p x)}{(A^m x, A^p x)} < \alpha$ implies that

$$\begin{aligned} &(x, A^p x) - \alpha(A^m x, A^p x) < 0 \Rightarrow (x - \alpha A^m x, A^p x) < 0 \\ &\Rightarrow (-b, A^p x) < 0 \Rightarrow \measuredangle(A^p x; -b) \in \left(\frac{\pi}{2}, \pi\right]. \end{aligned}$$

Hence, we obtain

$$\measuredangle(A^{-m}x; -b) \ge \underbrace{\measuredangle(A^p x; -b)}_{\in(\frac{\pi}{2}, \pi]} - \underbrace{\measuredangle(A^{-m}x; A^p x)}_{\in[0, \frac{\pi}{2}]} \ge \measuredangle(A^p x; -b) - \frac{\pi}{2} > 0.$$

At the same time, the assumption $\alpha\|x\|^2 \le (x, A^{-m}x)$ implies

$$(x, \alpha x) \le (x, A^{-m}x) \Rightarrow (A^{-m}x, \alpha A^m x) \le (A^{-m}x, x) \Rightarrow (A^{-m}x, \underbrace{x - \alpha A^m x}_{-b}) \ge 0;$$

so, $\measuredangle(A^{-m}x; -b) \le \frac{\pi}{2}$. To summarize,

$$\frac{\pi}{2} \ge \measuredangle(A^{-m}x; -b) \ge \underbrace{\measuredangle(A^p x; -b)}_{\in(\frac{\pi}{2}, \pi]} - \frac{\pi}{2} > 0.$$

Consequently,

$$0 \le \cos\measuredangle(A^{-m}x; -b) \le \cos\left(\measuredangle(A^p x; -b) - \frac{\pi}{2}\right) = \sin\measuredangle(A^p x; -b).$$

So, we have

$$|(A^{-m}x, -b)| = \|A^{-m}x\| \cdot \|-b\| \cdot |\cos\measuredangle(A^{-m}x; -b)| \leq \|A^{-m}x\| \cdot \|b\| \cdot |\sin\measuredangle(A^{p}x, -b)|. \quad (5)$$

The norm $\|A^{-m}x\|$ can be bounded using the Kantorovich inequality, as shown in Relation (4). Regarding the factor $|\sin\measuredangle(A^{p}x, -b)|$, we have

$$|\sin(\measuredangle(A^p x; -b))| = \sqrt{1 - \cos^2\measuredangle(A^p x; -b)} = \sqrt{1 - \frac{(A^p x, -b)^2}{\|A^p x\|^2\|b\|^2}}$$
$$= \sqrt{1 - \frac{(A^p x, b)^2}{\|A^p x\|^2\|b\|^2}} = \frac{\sqrt{\|A^p x\|^2\|b\|^2 - (A^p x, b)^2}}{\|A^p x\| \cdot \|b\|}.$$

Therefore, the relation (5) can be reformulated as

$$|(A^{-m}x, b)| \leq \frac{\|x\|^2}{2\|A^m x\| \cdot \|A^p x\|}\left(\frac{1}{\kappa^m} + \kappa^m\right)\sqrt{\|A^p x\|^2\|b\|^2 - (A^p x, b)^2}.$$

□

3. Estimate of $x^T A^{-m} x$ by the Projection Method

Our goal is to find a number α such that $x^T A^{-m} x \approx \alpha\|x\|^2$ (cf. (1)). To that end, let us take a fixed $k \in \mathbb{N}_0 = \mathbb{N} \cup \{0\}$ and consider the following decomposition of x,

$$x = \alpha A^m x - b,$$

where $b \perp A^k x$. (That is, $\alpha A^m x$ is a projection of x onto $A^m x$ along the orthogonal complement of $A^k x$.) Then, we have

$$(x, A^k x) = (\alpha A^m x, A^k x) - (b, A^k x).$$

Using the assumption $b \perp A^k x$, we obtain

$$(x, A^k x) = \alpha(A^m x, A^k x),$$

and so

$$\alpha = \frac{(x, A^k x)}{(x, A^{m+k} x)}.$$

Hence, we obtain a family of estimates for $x^T A^{-m} x$ as follows:

$$(x, A^{-m}x) \approx \frac{(x, A^k x)}{(x, A^{m+k} x)}\|x\|^2 \qquad (k \in \mathbb{N}_0). \quad (6)$$

We denote these estimates by $est_{proj(k)}$, $k \in \mathbb{N}_0$. The computational implementation requires $\left\lceil \frac{m+k}{2} \right\rceil$ matrix-vector products (mvps).

Let us now explore the error corresponding to the above choice of α. We have

$$(x, A^{-m}x) = (\alpha A^m x, A^{-m}x) - (b, A^{-m}x);$$

therefore,

$$(x, A^{-m}x) = \alpha\|x\|^2 - (x, A^{-m}b).$$

Since $\alpha\|x\|^2$ is the estimate (see (1)), the error term is provided as $(x, A^{-m}b)$. Bounds on its absolute value can be found using Proposition 1 with

$$b = \alpha A^m x - x = \frac{(x, A^k x)}{(x, A^{m+k}x)} A^m x - x.$$

Remark 1. *Let us comment on the choice of the parameter k.*

- *Observe that upper bounds UB1 and UB4 from Proposition 1 are minimal for $k = m$. In this case, we have $b \perp A^m x$; thus, b has the smallest possible norm. Therefore, from the point of view of minimizing the upper bound on the error (more precisely, minimizing upper bounds UB1 and UB4), a convenient choice is $k = m$.*
- *However, if the goal is fast estimation, we can take $k = 0$ for even m and $k = 1$ for odd m, as these two choices provide $est_{proj(0)} = \frac{\|x\|^4}{\|A^{m/2}x\|^2}$ and $est_{proj(1)} = \frac{\|x\|^2(x,Ax)}{\|A^{(m+1)/2}x\|^2}$, respectively, which are both easy to evaluate.*

In general, for any choice of k, the error of the estimate can be assessed using Proposition 1.

4. Estimate of $x^T A^{-m} x$ Using the Minimization Method

The estimates that we present in this section stem from the upper bounds UB2 and UB3 for the absolute error $|(x, A^{-m}b)|$, which are derived in Proposition 1. Our goal is to reduce the absolute error by finding the value α that minimizes these bounds.

Plugging $b = \alpha A^m x - x$ in the explicit formulas for UB2 and UB3, we can easily check that the two upper bounds in question attain their minimal values if and only if α minimizes the function

$$f(\alpha) = \frac{\alpha^2\|A^m x\|^2 - 2\alpha(x, A^m x) + \|x\|^2}{\sqrt{\alpha^2(x, A^{3m+k}x) - 2\alpha(x, A^{2m+k}x) + (x, A^{m+k}x)}},$$

where $k = m$ corresponds to UB2 and $k = 0$ corresponds to UB3. By differentiating this expression with respect to α, we find that the upper bounds UB2 and UB3 are minimized at $\hat{\alpha}$, being the root of the equation

$$\begin{aligned}
&\|A^m x\|^2(x, A^{3m+k}x)\alpha^3 - 3\|A^m x\|^2(x, A^{2m+k}x)\alpha^2 + \\
&\quad + \Big(2\|A^m x\|^2(x, A^{m+k}x) + 2(x, A^m x)(x, A^{2m+k}x) - \|x\|^2(x, A^{3m+k}x)\Big)\alpha + \\
&\qquad + \|x\|^2(x, A^{2m+k}x) - 2(x, A^m x)(x, A^{m+k}x) = 0,
\end{aligned}$$

where, as before, the values $k = m$ and $k = 0$ correspond to UB2 and UB3, respectively. With this value $\hat{\alpha}$, we obtain the estimation of $x^T A^{-m} x$ as

$$est_{min} = \hat{\alpha}\|x\|^2.$$

For the sake of brevity, we adopt the notation est_{min1} for $k = 0$ and est_{min2} for $k = m$. The computational implementation requires $\left\lceil \frac{3m+k}{2} \right\rceil$ mvps.

5. The Heuristic Approach

Let us consider the quantity

$$R_m(x) = \frac{\|x\|^2\|A^m x\|^2}{(x, A^m x)^2}. \tag{7}$$

We refer to $R_m(x)$ as the generalized index of proximity.

Lemma 1. *Assume that $A \in \mathbb{R}^{n\times n}$ is a symmetric matrix. For any nonzero vector $x \in \mathbb{R}^n$, the value $R_m(x)$ satisfies $R_m(x) \geq 1$. The equality $R_m(x) = 1$ holds true if and only if x is an eigenvector of A.*

Proof. By the Cauchy–Schwarz inequality, we have $(x, A^m x)^2 \leq \|x\|^2\|A^m x\|^2$; hence, $R_m(x) \geq 1$. The equality $R_m(x) = 1$ is equivalent to the equality in the Cauchy–Schwarz inequality, which occurs if and only if the vector $A^m x$ is a scalar multiple of the vector x, in other words, when $A^m x = \alpha x$ for a certain $\alpha \in \mathbb{R}$. This is further equivalent to $Ax = \lambda x$ (with λ satisfying $\lambda^m = \alpha$) given the assumption that A is symmetric. □

As a result of Lemma 1, the equality

$$R_m(A^{-m/2}x)^{n_1} R_m(A^{m/2}x)^{n_2} = R_m(x)^{n_1+n_2},$$

where $n_1, n_2 \in \mathbb{Z}$, is identically true for any eigenvector of A (i.e., for any vector satisfying $R_m(x) = 1$), and becomes approximately true for vectors x with the property $R_m(x) \approx 1$.

Therefore, if $R_m(x) \approx 1$, we have

$$\begin{aligned}
&\frac{\|A^{-m/2}x\|^{2n_1}\|A^m A^{-m/2}x\|^{2n_1}}{(A^{-m/2}x, A^m A^{-m/2}x)^{2n_1}} \frac{\|A^{m/2}x\|^{2n_2}\|A^m A^{m/2}x\|^{2n_2}}{(A^{m/2}x, A^m A^{m/2}x)^{2n_2}} \approx \frac{\|x\|^{2(n_1+n_2)}\|A^m x\|^{2(n_1+n_2)}}{(x, A^m x)^{2(n_1+n_2)}} \\
\Rightarrow\quad &\frac{(x, A^{-m}x)^{n_1}\|A^{m/2}x\|^{2n_1}}{\|x\|^{4n_1}} \frac{\|A^{m/2}x\|^{2n_2}\|A^{3m/2}x\|^{2n_2}}{\|A^m x\|^{4n_2}} \approx \frac{\|x\|^{2(n_1+n_2)}\|A^m x\|^{2(n_1+n_2)}}{(x, A^m x)^{2(n_1+n_2)}} \\
\Rightarrow\quad &(x, A^{-m}x)^{n_1} \approx \frac{\|x\|^{6n_1+2n_2}\|A^m x\|^{2n_1+6n_2}}{(x, A^m x)^{3(n_1+n_2)}(x, A^{3m}x)^{n_2}} \\
\Rightarrow\quad &(x, A^{-m}x) \approx \sqrt[n_1]{\frac{\|x\|^{6n_1+2n_2}\|A^m x\|^{2n_1+6n_2}}{(x, A^m x)^{3(n_1+n_2)}(x, A^{3m}x)^{n_2}}}.
\end{aligned}$$

We refer to this estimate as est_h. If, in particular, $n_1 = 1$ and $n_2 = 0$, we denote the estimate by est_{h1}, and if $n_1 = n_2 = 1$, the corresponding estimate is denoted by est_{h2}. The computational implementation requires $\left\lceil \frac{3m}{2} \right\rceil$ mvps.

6. A Comparison with Other Methods

In this section, we briefly describe two methods that were proposed in the literature for estimating quadratic forms of the type $x^T f(A)x$, where $A \in \mathbb{R}^{n\times n}$, $x \in \mathbb{R}^n$, and f is a smooth function defined on the spectrum of A. The first method is an extrapolation procedure developed in [8] and the second one is based on Gaussian quadrature [5] (Chapter 7) and [6].

6.1. The Extrapolation Method

We adjust the family of estimates for $x^T f(A)x$ given in [8] (Proposition 2) by setting $f(t) = t^{-m}$, $m \in \mathbb{N}$. Hence, we directly obtain the estimating formula given in the following lemma.

Lemma 2. *Let $A \in \mathbb{R}^{n\times n}$ be a symmetric matrix. An extrapolation estimate for the quadratic form $x^T A^{-m}x$, $m \in \mathbb{N}$, is given by*

$$e_\nu = \rho^{-m\nu}\frac{\|x\|^{2(m+1)}}{(x, Ax)^m}, \quad \rho = \frac{\|x\|^2\|Ax\|^2}{(x, Ax)^2}, \quad \nu \in \mathbb{R}. \tag{8}$$

We refer to this estimation as $est_{extrap(\nu)}$. The computational implementation requires just one mvp.

Remark 2. *In the special case of $m = 1$, some of the proposed estimates are identified to the corresponding extrapolation estimates for specific choices of the family parameter ν. We have*

- *For $\nu = -1$, $est_{extrap(-1)} \equiv est_{h1}$.*
- *For $\nu = 0$, $est_{extrap(0)} \equiv est_{proj(0)}$.*
- *For $\nu = 1$, $est_{extrap(1)} \equiv est_{proj(1)}$.*

Notably, the extrapolation procedure proposes estimates for the quadratic form $x^T A^{-m} x$ and not bounds. The choice of the family parameter ν is arbitrary and no bounds for the absolute error of the estimates are provided.

6.2. Gaussian Techniques

We consider the spectral factorization of A, which allows us to express the matrix A as $A = \sum_{k=1}^{n} \lambda_k v_k v_k^T$, where $\lambda_k \in \mathbb{R}$ are the eigenvalues of A with corresponding eigenvectors v_k. Therefore, the quadratic form $x^T A^{-m} x$ can be written as

$$x^T A^{-m} x = \sum_{k=1}^{n} \lambda_k^{-m} (x, v_k)^2. \tag{9}$$

The Summation (9) can be considered a Riemann–Stieltjes integral of the form

$$\int_{\lambda_{min}}^{\lambda_{max}} \lambda^{-m} d\mu(\lambda),$$

where the measure $\mu(\lambda)$ is a piecewise constant function defined by

$$\mu(\lambda) = \begin{cases} 0, & \text{if } \lambda < \lambda_{min}, \\ \sum_{i=1}^{j} (x, v_i)^2, & \text{if } \lambda_j \leq \lambda < \lambda_{j+1}, \\ \sum_{i=1}^{p} (x, v_i)^2, & \text{if } \lambda_{max} \leq \lambda. \end{cases}$$

This Riemann–Stieltjes integral can be approximated using Gauss quadrature rules [5,6]. Hence, it is necessary to produce a sequence of orthogonal polynomials, which can be achieved by the Lanczos algorithm. The operation count for this procedure is dominated by the application of the Lanczos algorithm, which requires a cost of kn^2 matrix-vector products, where k is the number of Lanczos iterations. As the number of the iterations increases, the estimates increase in accuracy but the complexity and the execution time increase as well.

We refer to this estimation as to est_{Gauss}.

7. Application in Estimating $x^T (AA^T + \lambda I_n)^{-m} x$

In several applications, the appearance matrix has the form $B = AA^T + \lambda I_n$, $\lambda > 0$, which is a symmetric positive definite matrix. For instance, this type of matrix appears in specifying the regularization parameter in Tikhonov regularization. In this case, the estimation of the quadratic forms of the type $x^T B^{-m} x$ is required. The estimates derived in the previous sections involve positive powers of B, i.e., B^k, $k \in \mathbb{N}$. However, since the direct computation of the matrix powers B^k is not stable for every λ, our next goal was to develop an alternative approach to its evaluation. As we show below, the computation of B^k can be obviated.

Since the matrices AA^T and I_n commute, the binomial theorem applies,

$$B^m = (AA^T + \lambda I_n)^m = \sum_{j=0}^{m} \binom{m}{j} \lambda^j (AA^T)^{m-j}, \; m \in \mathbb{N},$$

and hence

$$B^m x = \sum_{j=0}^{m} \binom{m}{j} \lambda^j (AA^T)^{m-j} x, \ m \in \mathbb{N}.$$

The above representation of the vector $B^m x$ effectively allows us to avoid the computation of the powers of the matrix $B = AA^T + \lambda I_n$ that appear in the estimates of the quadratic form $x^T B^{-m} x$. The expressions of type $(AA^T)^{m-j}$ can be evaluated successively as follows:

$$A^T x, \quad AA^T x, \quad A^T AA^T x, \quad AA^T AA^T x, \quad \ldots$$

8. Numerical Examples

Here, we present several numerical examples that illustrate the performance of the derived estimates. All computations were performed using MATLAB (R2018a). Throughout the numerical examples, we denote by e_i the ith column of the identity matrix of appropriate order and 1_n as the nth vector with all elements equal to one.

Example 1. *Upper bounds for the absolute error.*

In this example, we consider the symmetric positive define matrix $A = B^T B \in \mathbb{R}^{1000 \times 1000}$, where B is the Parter matrix selected from the MATLAB gallery. The condition number of the matrix A is $\kappa = 17.8983$. We choose the vector $x \in \mathbb{R}^{1000}$ as the 100th column of the identity matrix, i.e., $x = e_{100}$. We estimate the quadratic form $x^T A^{-2} x$ whose exact value is 0.0127. In Table 1, we present the generated estimates following the proposed approach and the upper bounds for the corresponding absolute error, which are given in Proposition 1.

Table 1. Estimating $x^T A^{-2} x = 0.0127$, where $A = B^T B$, $B = Parter$, $x = e_{100}$.

	Estimated	**Upper Bounds on E_{abs}**				
	Value	**UB1**	**UB2**	**UB3**	**UB4**	**UB5**
$est_{proj(0)}$	0.0103	0.0541	0.1909	0.0690	0.1080	0.0540
$est_{proj(2)}$	0.0103	0.0540	0.1926	0.0692	0.1079	0.0540
est_{min1}	0.0106	0.0731	0.1029	0.0499	0.1460	0.0538
est_{min2}	0.0105	0.0701	0.1032	0.0497	0.1401	0.0538
est_{h1}	0.0103	0.0541	0.1872	0.0684	0.1082	0.0540
est_{h2}	0.0103	0.0543	0.1828	0.0677	0.1084	0.0540

Example 2. *Estimation of quadratic forms.*

We consider the Kac–Murdock–Szegö (KMS) matrix $A \in \mathbb{R}^{1000 \times 1000}$, which is symmetric positive-definite and Toeplitz. The elements A_{ij} of this matrix are $A_{ij} = r^{|i-j|}$, $i, j = 1, 2, \ldots, 1000$, $0 < r < 1$. We tested this matrix for $r = 0.2$ and the condition number of A is $\kappa = 2.25$. We estimated both the quadratic forms $x^T A^{-2} x = 1.2072$ and $x^T A^{-3} x = 296.8727$. The chosen vectors were $x = e_{1000} + 1/4 e_{120} \in \mathbb{R}^{1000}$ and $x = 1_n$. The results are provided in Tables 2 and 3. As we shown, the derived estimates are satisfactory in both cases.

Table 2. Estimating $x^T A^{-2} x = 1.2072$, where $A = KMS$, $x = e_{1000} + 1/4 e_{120}$.

$est_{proj(0)}$	$est_{proj(2)}$	est_{min1}	est_{min2}	est_{h1}	est_{h2}
1.0176	0.8636	1.0268	0.9910	1.1990	1.2335

Table 3. Estimating $x^T A^{-3} x = 296.8727$, where $A = KMS$, $x = 1_n$.

$est_{proj(0)}$	$est_{proj(3)}$	est_{min1}	est_{min2}	est_{h1}	est_{h2}
296.6203	296.5306	299.8469	297.7640	296.7100	296.7562

Example 3. *Estimation of the whole diagonal of the covariance matrices.*

In this example, we consider thecovariance matrices of order n, whose elements A_{ij} are given by

$$A_{ij} = \begin{cases} 1 + i^{\alpha}, & i = j \\ \dfrac{1}{|i-j|^{\beta}}, & i \neq j \end{cases}, \quad i = 1, 2, \ldots, n,$$

where $\alpha, \beta \in \mathbb{R}$ and $\beta \geq 1$ [9]. We estimated the whole diagonal of the inverse of covariance matrices through the derived estimates presented in this work. Moreover, we used the two approaches presented in Section 6, which were used in previous studies. We applied the Gauss quadrature using $k = 3$ Lanczos iterations. We chose the pair of values for the parameters $(\alpha, \beta) = (3, 1)$. We validated the quality of the generated estimates by computing the mean relative error (MRE) given by

$$MRE = \frac{1}{n} \sum_{i=1}^{n} \frac{|A_{ii}^{-1} - est(i)|}{|A_{ii}^{-1}|},$$

where $est(i)$ is the corresponding estimate for the diagonal element A_{ii}^{-1}. The results are recorded in Table 4. Specifically, we analyzed the performance of the proposed estimates in terms of the MRE and the execution time (in seconds).

Table 4. Mean relative errors and execution times for estimating the diagonal of the covariance matrices of order n with $(\alpha, \beta) = (3, 1)$.

n	Estimate	MRE	Time
1000	$est_{proj(0)} \equiv est_{extrap(0)}$	1.2688×10^{-4}	5.3683×10^{-4}
	$est_{proj(1)} \equiv est_{extrap(1)}$	4.3539×10^{-4}	5.4723×10^{-4}
	est_{min1}	2.9994×10^{-4}	2.3557×10^{-1}
	est_{min2}	3.0020×10^{-4}	2.1121×10^{-1}
	$est_{h1} \equiv est_{extrap(-1)}$	3.5996×10^{-4}	6.5678×10^{-4}
	est_{h2}	3.8761×10^{-3}	5.9529×10^{-2}
	est_{Gauss}	1.2687×10^{-4}	1.7068
3000	$est_{proj(0)} \equiv est_{extrap(0)}$	4.2294×10^{-5}	2.2339×10^{-3}
	$est_{proj(1)} \equiv est_{extrap(1)}$	1.4516×10^{-4}	2.2521×10^{-3}
	est_{min1}	1.0508×10^{-4}	1.2698
	est_{min2}	1.0528×10^{-4}	1.0726
	$est_{h1} \equiv est_{extrap(-1)}$	1.2004×10^{-4}	2.5384×10^{-3}
	est_{h2}	1.6973×10^{-3}	5.1289×10^{-1}
	est_{Gauss}	4.2294×10^{-5}	1.1647×10^{1}
5000	$est_{proj(0)} \equiv est_{extrap(0)}$	2.5377×10^{-5}	1.4881×10^{-2}
	$est_{proj(1)} \equiv est_{extrap(1)}$	8.7099×10^{-5}	1.4502×10^{-2}
	est_{min1}	6.6113×10^{-5}	1.2790×10^{1}
	est_{min2}	6.6256×10^{-5}	8.3479
	$est_{h1} \equiv est_{extrap(-1)}$	7.2027×10^{-5}	1.7101×10^{-2}
	est_{h2}	1.1532×10^{-3}	6.4850
	est_{Gauss}	2.5377×10^{-5}	2.0130×10^{2}

Example 4. *Network analysis.*

In this example, we tested the behavior of the proposed estimates in network analysis. Specifically, we estimated the whole diagonal of the resolvent matrix $(I_n - aA)^{-1}$, where A is the adjacency matrix of the network. We chose the parameter $a = 0.85/\lambda_{max}$. We considered three adjacency matrices of order $n = 4000$, which were selected by the CONTEST toolbox [10]. In Table 5, we provide the mean relative error for estimating the whole diagonal of the resolvent matrix. We also provide the execution time in seconds in the brackets in this table.

Table 5. Mean relative errors and execution times (seconds) for estimating the diagonal of the resolvent matrix.

Network	$est_{proj(0)}$	$est_{proj(1)}$	est_{min1}	est_{min2}	est_{h1}	est_{h2}
pref	8.770×10^{-3}	1.646×10^{-2}	3.008×10^{-3}	1.240×10^{-2}	9.218×10^{-4}	6.500×10^{-4}
	$[2.723 \times 10^{-4}]$	$[3.447 \times 10^{-4}]$	[5.091]	[4.105]	$[3.747 \times 10^{-4}]$	$[9.471 \times 10^{-2}]$
lock and key	3.590×10^{-2}	6.700×10^{-2}	1.540×10^{-2}	4.313×10^{-2}	3.620×10^{-3}	3.170×10^{-4}
	$[3.927 \times 10^{-4}]$	$[4.429 \times 10^{-4}]$	[6.754]	[4.884]	$[4.946 \times 10^{-4}]$	$[8.387 \times 10^{-1}]$
renga	7.173×10^{-2}	1.014×10^{-1}	2.875×10^{-2}	5.516×10^{-2}	4.110×10^{-2}	2.936×10^{-2}
	$[4.153 \times 10^{-4}]$	$[4.724 \times 10^{-4}]$	[4.597]	[4.059]	$[5.103 \times 10^{-4}]$	$[6.477 \times 10^{-2}]$

Example 5. *Solution of ill-posed problems via the GCV method.*

Let us consider the least-squares problem of the form $\min_{x \in \mathbb{R}^d} \|Ax - b\|^2$, where $A \in \mathbb{R}^{n \times d}$ and $b \in \mathbb{R}^n$. In ill-posed problems, the solution of the above minimization problem is not satisfactory and it is necessary to replace this problem with another one that is a penalized least-squares problem of the form

$$\min_{x \in \mathbb{R}^d} \{\|Ax - b\|^2 + \lambda \|x\|^2\}, \tag{10}$$

where $\lambda > 0$ is the regularization parameter. This is the popular Tikhonov regularization. The solution of (10) is $x_\lambda = (A^T A + \lambda I_d)^{-1} A^T b$. A major issue is the specification of the regularization parameter λ. This can be achieved by minimizing the GCV function. Following the expression of the GCV function $V(\lambda)$ in terms of quadratic forms presented in [11], we write

$$V(\lambda) = \frac{b^T B^{-2} b}{(Tr(B^{-1}))^2},$$

where $B = AA^T + \lambda I_n \in \mathbb{R}^{n \times n}$.

In this example, we considered three test problems of order n, which were selected from the Regularization Tools package [12]. In particular, we considered the Shaw, Tomo, and Baart problems. Each of these test problems generates a matrix A and a solution x. We computed the error-free vector b such that $b = Ax$. The perturbed data vector $b_{per} \in \mathbb{R}^p$ was computed by the formula $b_{per} = b + e \parallel b \parallel \frac{\sigma}{\sqrt{n}}$, where σ is a given noise level and $e \in \mathbb{R}^n$ is a Gaussian noise with mean zero and variance one. We estimated the GCV function using the estimate est_{h1} without computing the matrix B, but we used the relations for B^x given in Section 7. We found the minimum of the corresponding estimation over a grid of values for λ and we computed the solution x_λ. Concerning the grid of λ, we considered 100 equally spaced values in log-scale in the interval $[10^{-12}, 10]$.

In Figures 1–3, we plot the exact solution x of the problem and the estimated solution x_λ generated by Tikhonov regularization via the GCV function. Specifically, for each test problem, we depict two graphs. The left-hand-side graph corresponds to the determination of the regularization parameter via the estimated GCV using est_{h1}, and the right-hand-side graph concerns the exact computation of the GCV function. In Table 6, we list the characteristics of Figures 1–3. In particular, we provide the order n, the noise level σ, and the error norm of the derived solution x_λ of each test problem.

Table 6. Characteristics of Figures 1–3.

Test Problem (n, σ)	Method	$\| x - x_\lambda \|$
Shaw (200, 10^{-7})	estimation exact GCV	2.1885×10^{-1} 1.9049×10^{-1}
Tomo (100, 10^{-5})	estimation exact GCV	1.9188×10^{-2} 7.0236×10^{-2}
Baart (100, 10^{-7})	estimation exact GCV	5.9189×10^{-2} 5.9958×10^{-2}

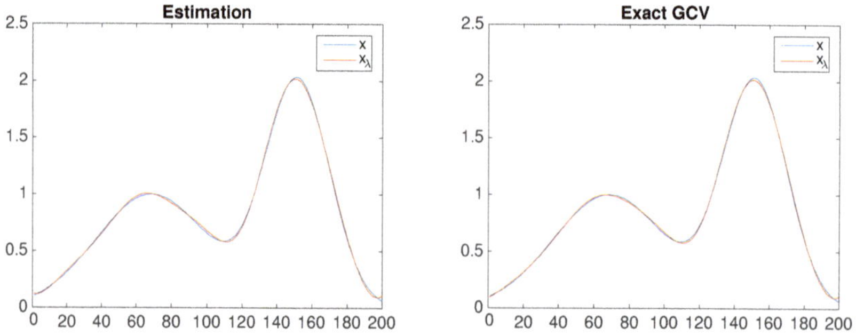

Figure 1. Solution of the Shaw test problem via an estimation of GCV (**left**) and the exact GCV (**right**).

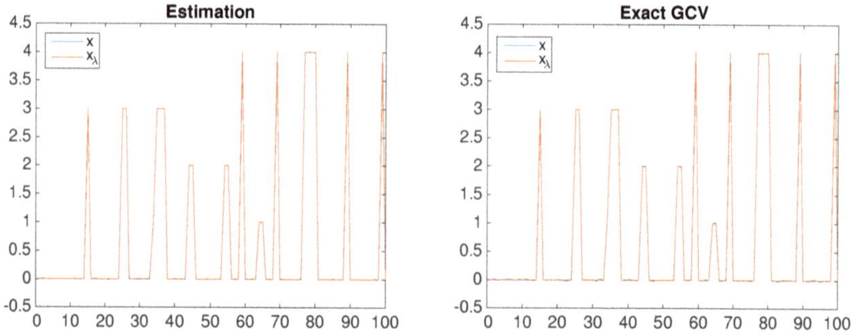

Figure 2. Solution of the Tomo test problem via an estimation of GCV (**left**) and the exact GCV (**right**).

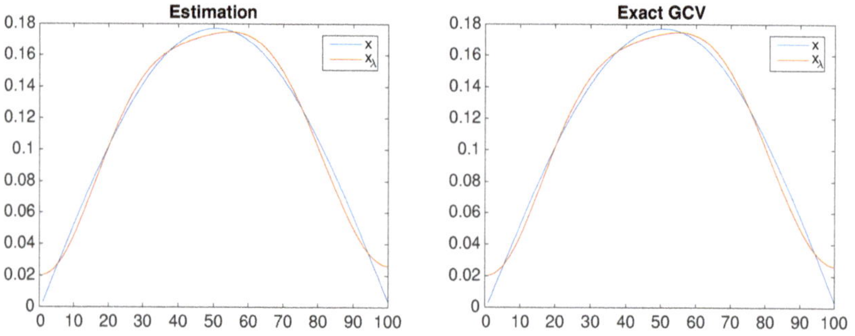

Figure 3. Solution of the Baart test problem via an estimation of GCV (**left**) and the exact GCV (**right**).

9. Conclusions

In this work, we proposed three different approaches for estimating the quadratic forms of the type $x^T A^{-m} x$, $m \in \mathbb{N}$. Specifically, we considered a projection method, a minimization approach, and a heuristic procedure. We also expressed upper bounds on the absolute error of the derived estimates; they allowed us to assess the precision of the results obtained by the aforementioned methods.

The proposed approaches provide efficient and fast estimates. Their efficiency was illustrated by numerical examples. Comparing the proposed estimates with the corresponding ones presented in the literature, we formed the following conclusions.

- The projection method improves the results of the extrapolation procedure by providing bounds on the absolute error.
- Although the estimates based on the Gauss quadrature are accurate, they require more time and more mvps than the proposed approaches as the number of the Lanczos iterations increases. The methods shown in the present paper are thus convenient especially in situations when a fast estimation of moderate accuracy is sought.

Author Contributions: Conceptualization, M.M., P.R., and O.T.; methodology, M.M., P.R., and O.T.; software, A.P. and P.R.; validation, M.M., P.R., and O.T.; formal analysis, A.P. and P.R.; investigation, M.M., A.P., P.R., and O.T.; data curation, A.P. and P.R.; writing—original draft preparation, M.M., P.R., and O.T.; writing—review and editing, M.M., P.R., and O.T.; visualization, A.P. and P.R.; supervision, M.M.; project administration, M.M. All authors have read and agreed to the published version of the manuscript.

Funding: This research received no external funding.

Institutional Review Board Statement: Not applicable.

Informed Consent Statement: Not applicable.

Acknowledgments: We thank the reviewers of the paper for the valuable remarks. This paper is dedicated to Constantin M. Petridi.

Conflicts of Interest: The authors declare no conflict of interest.

References

1. Fika, P.; Mitrouli, M.; Turek, O. On the estimation of $x^T A^{-1} x$ for symmetric matrices. **2020**, submitted.
2. Fan, J.; Liao, Y.; Liu, H. An overview on the estimation of large covariance and precision matrices. *Econom. J.* **2016**, *19*, C1–C32. [CrossRef]
3. Tang, J.; Saad, Y. A probing method for computing the diagonal of a matrix inverse. *Numer. Linear Algebra Appl.* **2012**, *19*, 485–501. [CrossRef]
4. Benzi, M.; Klymko, C. Total Communicability as a centrality measure. *J. Complex Netw.* **2013**, *1*, 124–149. [CrossRef]
5. Golub, G.H.; Meurant, G. *Matrices, Moments and Quadrature with Applications*; Princeton University Press: Princeton, NJ, USA, 2010.
6. Bai, Z.; Fahey, M.; Golub, G. Some large-scale matrix computation problems. *J. Comput. Appl. Math.* **1996**, *74*, 71–89. [CrossRef]
7. Fika, P.; Mitrouli, M.; Roupa, P. Estimates for the bilinear form $x^T A^{-1} y$ with applications to linear algebra problems. *Electron. Trans. Numer. Anal.* **2014**, *43*, 70–89.
8. Fika, P.; Mitrouli, M. Estimation of the bilinear form $y^* f(A) x$ for Hermitian matrices. *Linear Algebra Appl.* **2016**, *502*, 140–158. [CrossRef]
9. Bekas, C.; Curioni, A.; Fedulova, I. Low-cost data uncertainty quantification. *Concurr. Comput. Pract. Exp.* **2012**, *24*, 908–920. [CrossRef]
10. Taylor, A.; Higham, D.J. CONTEST: Toolbox Files and Documentation. Available online: http://www.mathstat.strath.ac.uk/research/groups/numerical_analysis/contest/toolbox (accessed on 15 April 2021).
11. Reichel, L.; Rodriguez, G.; Seatzu, S. Error estimates for large-scale ill-posed problems. *Numer. Algorithms* **2009**, *51*, 341–361. [CrossRef]
12. Hansen, P.C. Regularization Tools Version 4.0 for MATLAB 7.3. *Numer. Algorithms* **2007**, *46*, 189–194. [CrossRef]

mathematics MDPI

Article

A Multidimensional Principal Component Analysis via the C-Product Golub–Kahan–SVD for Classification and Face Recognition †

Mustapha Hached [1,‡], Khalide Jbilou [2,‡], Christos Koukouvinos [3,‡], Marilena Mitrouli [4,*,‡]

1 University of Lille, CNRS, UMR 8524—Laboratoire Paul Painlevé, F-59000 Lille, France; mustapha.hached@univ-lille.fr
2 Laboratoire LMPA, 50 rue F. Buisson, ULCO, 62228 Calais, France; jbilou@univ-littoral.fr
3 Department of Mathematics, National Technical University of Athens, Zografou, 15773 Athens, Greece; ckoukouv@math.ntua.gr
4 Department of Mathematics, National and Kapodistrian University of Athens Panepistimiopolis, 15784 Athens, Greece
* Correspondence: mmitroul@math.uoa.gr
† This paper is dedicated to Mr Constantin M. Petridi.
‡ These authors contributed equally to this work.

Abstract: Face recognition and identification are very important applications in machine learning. Due to the increasing amount of available data, traditional approaches based on matricization and matrix PCA methods can be difficult to implement. Moreover, the tensorial approaches are a natural choice, due to the mere structure of the databases, for example in the case of color images. Nevertheless, even though various authors proposed factorization strategies for tensors, the size of the considered tensors can pose some serious issues. Indeed, the most demanding part of the computational effort in recognition or identification problems resides in the training process. When only a few features are needed to construct the projection space, there is no need to compute a SVD on the whole data. Two versions of the tensor Golub–Kahan algorithm are considered in this manuscript, as an alternative to the classical use of the tensor SVD which is based on truncated strategies. In this paper, we consider the Tensor Tubal Golub–Kahan Principal Component Analysis method which purpose it to extract the main features of images using the tensor singular value decomposition (SVD) based on the tensor cosine product that uses the discrete cosine transform. This approach is applied for classification and face recognition and numerical tests show its effectiveness.

Keywords: cosine product; Golub–Kahan algorithm; Krylov subspaces; PCA; SVD; tensors

Citation: Hached, M.; Jbilou, K.; Koukouvinos, C.; Mitrouli, M. A Multidimensional Principal Component Analysis via the C-Product Golub–Kahan–SVD for Classification and Face Recognition. *Mathematics* **2021**, *9*, 1249. https://doi.org/10.3390/math9111249

Academic Editor: Luca Gemignani

Received: 11 May 2021
Accepted: 25 May 2021
Published: 29 May 2021

Publisher's Note: MDPI stays neutral with regard to jurisdictional claims in published maps and institutional affiliations.

1. Introduction

An important challenge in the last few years was the extraction of the main information in large datasets, measurements, observations that appear in signal and hyperspectral image processing, data mining, machine learning. Due to the increasing volume of data required by these applications, approximative low-rank matrix and tensor factorizations play a fundamental role in extracting latent components. The idea is to replace the initial large and maybe noisy and ill conditioned large scale original data by a lower dimensional approximate representation obtained via a matrix or multi-way array factorization or decomposition. Principal Components Analysis is a widely used technique for image recognition or identification. In the matrix case, it involves the computation of eigenvalues or singular decompositions. In the tensor case, even though various factorization techniques have been developed over the last decades (high-order SVD (HOSVD), Candecomp–Parafac (CP) and Tucker decomposition), the recent tensor SVDs (t-SVD and c-SVD), based on the use of the tensor t-product or c-products offer a matrix-like framework for third-order tensors, see [1–15] for more details on recent work related to tensors and applications. In the present work, we consider third order tensors that could be defined as three dimensional arrays of data. As our study is based on the cosine transform product, we limit this work to three-order tensors.

For a given 3-mode tensor $\mathcal{X} \in \mathbb{R}^{n_1 \times n_2 \times n_3}$, we denote by x_{i_1,i_2,i_3} the element (i_1, i_2, i_3) of the tensor $\mathcal{X}$. A fiber is defined by fixing all the indexes except one. An element $c \in \mathbb{R}^{1\times 1\times n}$ is called a tubal-scalar or simply tube of length n. For more details refer to [1,2].

2. Definitions and Notations

2.1. Discrete Cosine Transformation

In this subsection we recall some definitions and properties of the discrete cosine transformation and the c-product of tensors. During recent years, many advances were made in order to establish a rigorous framework enabling the treatment of problems for which the data is stored in three-way tensors without having to resort to matricization [1,8]. One of the most important feature of such a framework is the definition of a tensor-tensor product as the t-product, based on the Fast Fourier Transform . For applications as image treatment, the tensor-tensor product based on the Discrete Cosine Transformation (DCT) has shown to be an interesting alternative to FFT. We now give some basic facts on the DCT and its associated tensor-tensor product. The DCT of a vector $v \in \mathcal{R}^n$ is defined by

$$\tilde{v} = C_n v s. \in \mathcal{R}^n, \tag{1}$$

where C_n is the $n \times n$ discrete cosine transform matrix with entries

$$(C_n)_{ij} = \sqrt{\frac{2-\delta_{i1}}{n}} \cos\left(\frac{(i-1)(2j-1)\pi}{2n}\right) \quad 1 \le i,j \le n$$

with δ_{ij} is the Kronecker delta; see p. 150 in [16] for more details. It is known that the matrix C_n is orthogonal, i.e., $C_n^T C_n = C_n C_n^T = I_n$; see [17]. Furthermore, for any vector $v \in \mathbb{R}^n$, the matrix vector multiplication $C_n v$ can be computed in $O(nlog(n))$ operations. Moreover, Reference [17] have shown that a certain class of Toeplitz-plus-Hankel matrices can be diagonalized by C_n. More precisely, we have

$$C_n \, \mathtt{th}(v) \, C_n^{-1} = \mathrm{Diag}(\tilde{v}), \tag{2}$$

where

$$\mathtt{th}(v) = \underbrace{\begin{pmatrix} v_1 & v_2 & \dots & v_n \\ v_2 & v_1 & \dots & v_3 \\ \vdots & \vdots & \dots & \vdots \\ v_n & v_{n-1} & \dots & v_1 \end{pmatrix}}_{\text{Toeplitz}} + \underbrace{\begin{pmatrix} v_2 & \dots & v_n & 0 \\ \vdots & \iddots & \iddots & v_n \\ v_n & 0 & \dots & \vdots \\ 0 & v_n & \dots & v_2 \end{pmatrix}}_{\text{Hankel}}$$

and $\mathrm{Diag}(\tilde{v})$ is the diagonal matrix whose i-th diagonal element is $(\tilde{v})_i$.

2.2. Definitions and Properties of the Cosine Product

In this subsection, we briefly review some concepts and notations, which play a central role for the elaboration of the tensor global iterative methods based on the c-product; see [18] for more details on the c-product.

Let $\mathcal{A} \in \mathbb{R}^{n_1 \times n_2 \times n_3}$ be a real valued third-order tensor, then the operations mat and its inverse ten are defined by

$$\mathtt{mat}(\mathcal{A}) = \underbrace{\begin{pmatrix} A_1 & A_2 & \dots & A_n \\ A_2 & A_1 & \dots & A_3 \\ \vdots & \vdots & \dots & \vdots \\ A_n & A_{n-1} & \dots & A_1 \end{pmatrix}}_{\text{Block Toeplitz}} + \underbrace{\begin{pmatrix} A_2 & \dots & A_n & 0 \\ \vdots & ⋰ & ⋰ & A_n \\ A_n & 0 & \dots & \vdots \\ 0 & A_n & \dots & A_2 \end{pmatrix}}_{\text{Block Hankel}} \in \mathcal{R}^{n_1 n_3 \times n_2 n_3}$$

and the inverse operation denoted by ten is simply defined by

$$\mathtt{ten}(\mathtt{mat}(\mathcal{A})) = \mathcal{A}.$$

Let us denote $\widetilde{\mathcal{A}}$ the tensor obtained by applying the DCT on all the tubes of the tensor $\mathcal{A}$. This operation and its inverse are implemented in the Matlab by the commands dct and idct as

$$\widetilde{\mathcal{A}} = \mathtt{dct}(\mathcal{A}, [\,], 3), \text{ and } \mathtt{idct}(\widetilde{\mathcal{A}}, [\,], 3) = \mathcal{A},$$

where idct denotes the Inverse Discrete Cosine Transform.

Remark 1. *Notice that the tensor $\widetilde{\mathcal{A}}$ can be computed by using the 3-mode product defined in [2] as follows:*

$$\widetilde{\mathcal{A}} = \mathcal{A} \times_3 M$$

where M is the $n_3 \times n_3$ invertible matrix given by

$$M = W^{-1} C_{n_3} (I + Z)$$

where C_{n_3} denote de $n_3 \times n_3$ Discrete Cosine Transform DCT matrix, $W = \mathrm{diag}(C_{n_3}(:,1))$ is the diagonal matrix made of the first column of the DCT matrix, Z is $n_3 \times n_3$ circulant upshift matrix which can be computed in MATLAB using $W = \mathrm{diag}(\mathrm{ones}(n_3 - 1, 1), 1)$ and I the $n_3 \times n_3$ identity matrix; see [18] for more details.

Let $\mathbf{A}$ be the matrix

$$\mathbf{A} = \begin{pmatrix} A^{(1)} & & & \\ & A^{(2)} & & \\ & & \ddots & \\ & & & A^{(n_3)} \end{pmatrix} \in \mathbb{R}^{n_3 n_1 \times n_3 n_2} \quad (3)$$

where the matrices $A^{(i)}$'s are the frontal slices of the tensor $\widetilde{\mathcal{A}}$. The block matrix $\mathtt{mat}(\mathcal{A})$ can also be block diagonalized by using the DCT matrix as follows

$$(C_{n_3} \otimes I_{n_1})\, \mathtt{mat}(\mathcal{A})\, (C_{n_3}^T \otimes I_{n_2}) = \mathbf{A} \quad (4)$$

Definition 1. *The c-product of two tensors $\mathcal{A} \in \mathbb{R}^{n_1 \times n_2 \times n_3}$ and $\mathcal{B} \in \mathbb{R}^{n_2 \times m \times n_3}$ is the $n_1 \times m \times n_3$ tensor defined by:*

$$\mathcal{A} \star_c \mathcal{B} = \mathtt{ten}(\mathtt{mat}(\mathcal{A})\mathtt{mat}(\mathcal{B})).$$

Notice that from Equation (3), we can show that the product $\mathcal{C} = \mathcal{A} \star_c \mathcal{B}$ is equivalent to $\mathbf{C} = \mathbf{A}\,\mathbf{B}$. Algorithm 1 allows us to compute, in an efficient way, the c-product of the tensors $\mathcal{A}$ and $\mathcal{B}$, see [18].

Algorithm 1 Computing the c-product.

Inputs: $\mathcal{A} \in \mathbb{R}^{n_1 \times n_2 \times n_3}$ and $\mathcal{B} \in \mathbb{R}^{n_2 \times m \times n_3}$
Output: $\mathcal{C} = \mathcal{A} \star_c \mathcal{B} \in \mathbb{R}^{n_1 \times m \times n_3}$

1. Compute $\widetilde{\mathcal{A}} = \mathtt{dct}(\mathcal{A}, [\,], 3)$ and $\widetilde{\mathcal{B}} = \mathtt{dct}(\mathcal{B}, [\,], 3)$.
2. Compute each frontal slices of $\widetilde{\mathcal{C}}$ by

$$C^{(i)} = A^{(i)} B^{(i)}$$

3. Compute $\mathcal{C} = \mathtt{idct}(\widetilde{\mathcal{C}}, [\,], 3)$.

Next, give some definitions and remarks on the c-product and related topics.

Definition 2. *The identity tensor $\mathcal{I}_{n_1 n_1 n_3}$ is the tensor such that each frontal slice of $\widetilde{\mathcal{I}}_{n_1 n_1 n_3}$ is the identity matrix $I_{n_1 n_1}$.*

An $n_1 \times n_1 \times n_3$ tensor $\mathcal{A}$ is said to be invertible if there exists a tensor $\mathcal{B}$ of order $n_1 \times n_1 \times n_3$ such that

$$\mathcal{A} \star_c \mathcal{B} = \mathcal{I}_{n_1 n_1 n_3} \qquad \text{and} \qquad \mathcal{B} \star_c \mathcal{A} = \mathcal{I}_{n_1 n_1 n_3}.$$

In that case, we denote $\mathcal{B} = \mathcal{A}^{-1}$. It is clear that $\mathcal{A}$ is invertible if and only if $\mathtt{mat}(\mathcal{A})$ is invertible. The inner scalar product is defined by

$$\langle \mathcal{A}, \mathcal{B} \rangle = \sum_{i_1=1}^{n_1} \sum_{i_2=1}^{n_2} \sum_{i_3=1}^{n_3} a_{i_1 i_2 i_3} b_{i_1 i_2 i_3}$$

and its corresponding norm is given by $\|\mathcal{A}\|_F = \sqrt{\langle \mathcal{A}, \mathcal{A} \rangle}$.
An $n_1 \times n_1 \times n_3$ tensor $\mathcal{Q}$ is said to be orthogonal if $\mathcal{Q}^T \star_c \mathcal{Q} = \mathcal{Q} \star_c \mathcal{Q}^T = \mathcal{I}_{n_1 n_1 n_3}$.

Definition 3 ([1]). *A tensor is called f-diagonal if its frontal slices are diagonal matrices. It is called upper triangular if all its frontal slices are upper triangular.*

Next we recall the Tensor Singular Value Decomposition of a tensor (Algorithm 2); more details can be found in [19].

Theorem 1. *Let $\mathcal{A}$ be an $n_1 \times n_2 \times n_3$ real-valued tensor. Then $\mathcal{A}$ can be factored as follows*

$$\mathcal{A} = \mathcal{U} \star_c \mathcal{S} \star_c \mathcal{V}^T, \tag{5}$$

where $\mathcal{U}$ and $\mathcal{V}$ are orthogonal tensors of order (n_1, n_1, n_3) and (n_2, n_2, n_3), respectively, and $\mathcal{S}$ is an f-diagonal tensor of order $(n_1 \times n_2 \times n_3)$. This factorization is called Tensor Singular Value Decomposition (c-SVD) of the tensor $\mathcal{A}$.

Algorithm 2 The Tensor SVD (c-SVD).

Input: $\mathcal{A} \in \mathbb{R}^{n_1 \times n_2 \times n_3}$ **Output:** $\mathcal{U}$, $\mathcal{V}$ and $\mathcal{S}$.

1. Compute $\widetilde{\mathcal{A}} = \mathtt{dct}(\mathcal{A}, [], 3)$.
2. Compute each frontal slices of $\widetilde{\mathcal{U}}$, $\widetilde{\mathcal{V}}$ and $\widetilde{\mathcal{S}}$ from $\widetilde{\mathcal{A}}$ as follows
   (a) for $i = 1, \ldots, n_3$

$$[\widetilde{\mathcal{U}}^{(i)}, \widetilde{\mathcal{S}}^{(i)}, \widetilde{\mathcal{V}}^{(i)}] = svd(\widetilde{\mathcal{A}}^{(i)})$$

   (b) End for
3. Compute $\mathcal{U} = \mathtt{idct}(\widetilde{\mathcal{U}}, [\,], 3)$, $\mathcal{S} = \mathtt{idct}(\widetilde{\mathcal{S}}, [\,], 3)$ and $\mathcal{V} = \mathtt{idct}(\widetilde{\mathcal{V}}, [\,], 3)$.

Remark 2. *As for the t-product [19], we can show that if* $\mathcal{A} = \mathcal{U} \star_c \mathcal{S} \star_c \mathcal{V}^T$ *is a c-SVD of the tensor* $\mathcal{A}$*, then we have*

$$\sum_{k=1}^{n_3} A_k = \left(\sum_{k=1}^{n_3} U_k\right)\left(\sum_{k=1}^{n_3} S_k\right)\left(\sum_{k=1}^{n_3} V_k^T\right), \tag{6}$$

where A_k*,* U_k*,* S_k *and* V_k *are the frontal slices of the tensors* $\mathcal{A}$*,* $\mathcal{U}$*,* $\mathcal{S}$ *and* $\mathcal{V}$*, respectively, and*

$$\mathcal{A} = \sum_{i=1}^{\min(n_1,n_2)} \mathcal{U}(:,i,:) \star_c \mathcal{S}(i,i,:) \star_c \mathcal{V}(:,i,:)^T. \tag{7}$$

Theorem 2. *Let* $\mathcal{A} = \mathcal{U} \star_c \mathcal{S} \star_c \mathcal{V}^T$ *given by (5), and define for* $k \leq min(n_1, n_2)$ *the tensor*

$$\mathcal{A}_k = \sum_{i=1}^{k} \mathcal{U}(:,i,:) \star_c \mathcal{S}(i,i,:) \star_c \mathcal{V}(:,i,:)^T. \tag{8}$$

Then

$$\mathcal{A}_k = arg \min_{\mathcal{X} \in \mathcal{M}} \|\mathcal{A}_k - \mathcal{A}\|_F, \tag{9}$$

where $\mathcal{M} = \{\mathcal{X} \star_c \mathcal{Y};\ \mathcal{X} \in \mathcal{R}^{n_1 \times k \times n_3},\ \mathcal{Y} \in \mathcal{R}^{k \times n_2 \times n_3}\}$.

Note that when $n_3 = 1$ this theorem reduces to the well known Eckart–Young theorem for matrices [20].

Definition 4 (The tensor tubal-rank). *Let* $\mathcal{A}$ *be an* $n_1 \times n_2 \times n_3$ *be a tensor and consider its c-SVD* $\mathcal{A} = \mathcal{U} \star_c \mathcal{S} \star_c \mathcal{V}^T$*. The tensor tubal rank of* $\mathcal{A}$*, denoted as* $rank_t(\mathcal{A})$ *is defined to be the number of non-zero tubes of the f-diagonal tensor* $\mathcal{S}$*, i.e.,*

$$\mathrm{rank}_t(\mathcal{A}) = \#\{i, \mathcal{S}(i,i,:) \neq 0\}.$$

Definition 5. *The multi-rank of the tensor* $\mathcal{A}$ *is a vector* $p \in \mathbb{R}^{n_3}$ *with the i-th element equal to the rank of the i-th frontal slice of* $\widetilde{\mathcal{A}} = \texttt{fft}(\mathcal{A}, [], 3)$*, i.e.,*

$$p(i) = rank(A^{(i)}),\ i = 1, \ldots, n_3.$$

The well known QR matrix decomposition can also be extended to the tensor case; see [19].

Theorem 3. *Let* $\mathcal{A}$ *be a real-valued tensor of order* $n_1 \times n_2 \times n_3$*. Then* $\mathcal{A}$ *can be factored as follows*

$$\mathcal{A} = \mathcal{Q} \star_c \mathcal{R}, \tag{10}$$

where $\mathcal{Q}$ *is an* $n_1 \times n_1 \times n_3$ *orthogonal tensor and* $\mathcal{R}$ *is an* $n_1 \times n_1 \times n_3$ *f-upper triangular tensor.*

3. Tensor Principal Component Analysis for Face Recognition

Principle Component Analysis (PCA) is a widely used technique in image classification and face recognition. Many approaches involve a conversion of color images to grayscale in order to reduce the training cost. Nevertheless, for some applications, color an is important feature and tensor based approaches offer the possibility to take it into account. Moreover, especially in the case of facial recognition, it allows the treatment of enriched databases including for instance additional biometric information. However, one has to bear in mind that the computational cost is an important issue as the volume of data can be very large. We first recall some background facts on the matrix based approach.

3.1. The Matrix Case

One of the simplest and most effective PCA approaches used in face recognition systems is the so-called eigenface approach. This approach transforms faces into a small set of essential characteristics, eigenfaces, which are the main components of the initial set of learning images (training set). Recognition is done by projecting a test image in the eigenface subspace, after which the person is classified by comparing its position in eigenface space with the position of known individuals. The advantage of this approach over other face recognition strategies resides in its simplicity, speed and insensitivity to small or gradual changes on the face.

The process is defined as follows: Consider a set of training faces $I_1, I_2, \ldots, I_p$. All the face images have the same size: $n \times m$. Each face I_i is transformed into a vector x_i using the operation vec: $x_i = vec(I_i)$. These vectors are columns of the $nm \times p$ matrix

$$X = [x_1, \ldots, x_p].$$

We compute the average image $\mu = \frac{1}{p}\sum_{i=1}^{p} x_i$. Set $\bar{x}_i = x_i - \mu$ and consider the new matrices

$$\bar{X} = [\bar{x}_1, \ldots, \bar{x}_p], \text{ and } C = \bar{X}\bar{X}^T.$$

Notice that the $nm \times nm$ covariance matrix $C = \bar{X}\bar{X}^T$ can be very large. Therefore, the computation of the nm eigenvalues and the corresponding eigenvectors (eigenfaces) can be very difficult. To circumvent this issue, we instead consider the smaller $p \times p$ matrix $L = \bar{X}^T\bar{X}$.

Let v_i be an eigenvector of L then $Lv_i = \bar{X}^T\bar{X}v_i = \lambda_i v_i$ and

$$\bar{X}Lv_i = \bar{X}\bar{X}^T\bar{X}v_i = \lambda_i\bar{X}v_i,$$

which shows that $\bar{X}v_i$ is an eigenvector of the covariance matrix $C = \bar{X}\bar{X}^T$.

The p eigenvectors of $L = \bar{X}^T\bar{X}$ are then used to find the p eigenvectors $u_i = \bar{X}v_i$ of C that form the eigenface space. We keep only k eigenvectors corresponding to the largest k eigenvalues (eigenfaces corresponding to small eigenvalues can be omitted, as they explain only a small part of characteristic features of the faces.)

The next step consists of projecting each image of the training sample onto the eigenface space spanned by the orthogonal vectors $u_1, \ldots, u_k$:

$$\mathcal{U}_k = span\{u_1, \ldots, u_k\}, \text{ with } U_k = [u_1, \ldots, u_k]$$

The matrix $U_k U_k^T$ is an orthogonal projector onto the subspace $\mathcal{U}_k$. A face image can be projected onto this face space as $y_i = U_k^T(x_i - \mu)$.

We now give the steps of an image classification process based on this approach:

Let $x = vec(I)$ be a test vector-image and project it onto the face space to get $y = U_k^T(x - \mu)$. Notice that the reconstructed image is given by

$$x^r = \widetilde{U}_k y + \mu.$$

Compute the Euclidean distance

$$\epsilon_i = \|y - y_i\|, \; i = 1, \ldots, k.$$

A face is classified as belonging to the class l when the minimum l is below some chosen threshold θ Set

$$\theta = \frac{1}{2}\max_{i,j} \|y_i - y_j\|, \; i,j = 1, \ldots, k,$$

and let ϵ be the distance between the original test image x and its reconstructed image x^r: $\epsilon = \|x - x^r\|$. Then

- If $\epsilon \geq \theta$, then the input image is not even a face image and not recognized.
- If $\epsilon < \theta$ and $\epsilon_i \geq \theta$ for all i then the input image is a face image but it is an unknown image face.
- If $\epsilon < \theta$ and $\epsilon_i < \theta$ for all i then the input images are the individual face images associated with the class vector x_i.

We now give some basic facts on the relation between the singular value decomposition (SVD) and PCA in this context:

Consider the Singular Value Decomposition of the matrix A as

$$\bar{X} = U\Sigma V^T = \sum_{i=1}^{p} \sigma_i u_i v_i^T$$

where U and V are orthonormal matrices of sizes nm and p, respectively. The singular values σ_i are the square roots of the eigenvalues of the matrix $L = \bar{X}^T\bar{X}$, the u_i's are the left vectors and the $v_i^{\prime}s$ are the right vectors. We have

$$L = \bar{X}^T\bar{X} = V\Delta V^T; \;\; \Delta = diag(\sigma_1^2, \ldots, \sigma_p^2)$$

which is is the eigendecomposition of the matrix L and

$$C = \bar{X}\bar{X}^T = UDU^T; \; D = diag(\sigma_1^2, \ldots, \sigma_p^2, 0, \ldots, 0).$$

In the PCA method, the projected eigenface space is then generated by the first $u_1, \ldots, u_k$ columns of the unitary matrix U derived from the SVD decomposition of the matrix $\bar{X}$.

As only a small number k of the largest singular values are needed in PCA, we can use the well known Golub–Kahan algorithm to compute these wanted singular values and the corresponding singular vectors to define the projected subspace.

In the next section, we explain how the SVD based PCA can be extended to tensors and propose an algorithm for facial recognition in this context.

4. The Tensor Golub–Kahan Method

As explained in the previous section, it is important to take into account the potentially large size of datasets, especially for the training process. The idea of extending the matrix Golub–Kahan bidiagonalization algorithm to the tensor context has been explored in the recent years for large and sparse tensors [21]. In [1], the authors established the foundations of a remarkable theoretical framework for tensor decompositions in association with the tensor-tensor t- or c-products, allowing to generalize the main notions of linear algebra to tensors.

4.1. The Tensor C-Global Golub–Kahan Algorithm

Let $\mathcal{A} \in \mathbb{R}^{n_1 \times n_2 \times n_3}$ be a tensor ans $s \geq 1$ an integer. The Tensor c-global Golub–Kahan bidiagonalization algorithm (associated to the c-product) is described in Algorithm 3.

Algorithm 3 The Tensor Global Golub–Kahan algorithm (TGGKA).

1. Choose a tensor $\mathcal{V}_1 \in \mathbb{R}^{n_2 \times s \times n_3}$ such that $\|\mathcal{V}_1\|_F = 1$ and set $\beta_0 = 0$.
2. For $i = 1, 2, \ldots, k$
   (a) $\mathcal{U}_i = \mathcal{A} \star_c \mathcal{V}_i - \beta_{i-1}\mathcal{U}_{i-1}$,
   (b) $\alpha_i = \|\mathcal{U}_i\|_F$,
   (c) $\mathcal{U}_i = \mathcal{U}_i / \alpha_i$,
   (d) $\mathcal{V}_{i+1} = \mathcal{A}^T \star_c \mathcal{U}_i - \alpha_i \mathcal{V}_i$,
   (e) $\beta_i = \|\mathcal{V}_{i+1}\|_F$.
   (f) $\mathcal{V}_{i+1} = \mathcal{V}_{i+1} / \beta_i$.

   End

Let C_k be the $k \times k$ upper bidiagonal matrix defined by

$$C_k = \begin{bmatrix} \alpha_1 & \beta_1 & & & \\ & \alpha_2 & \beta_2 & & \\ & & \ddots & \ddots & \\ & & & \alpha_{k-1} & \beta_{k-1} \\ & & & & \alpha_k \end{bmatrix}. \tag{11}$$

Let $\mathbb{V}_k$ and $\mathcal{A} \star_c \mathbb{V}_k$ be the $(n_2 \times (sk) \times p)$ and $(n_1 \times (sk) \times n_3)$ tensors with frontal slices $\mathcal{V}_1, \ldots, \mathcal{V}_k$ and $\mathcal{A} \star_c \mathcal{V}_1, \ldots, \mathcal{A} \star_c \mathcal{V}_k$, respectively, and let $\mathbb{U}_k$ and $\mathcal{A}^T \star_c \mathbb{U}_k$ be the $(n_1 \times (sk) \times n_3)$ and $(n_2 \times (sk) \times n_3)$ tensors with frontal slices $\mathcal{U}_1, \ldots, \mathcal{U}_k$ and $\mathcal{A}^T \star_c \mathcal{U}_1, \ldots, \mathcal{A}^T \star_c \mathcal{U}_k$, respectively. We set

$$\mathbb{V}_k := [\mathcal{V}_1, \ldots, \mathcal{V}_k], \quad \text{and} \quad \mathcal{A} \star_c \mathbb{V}_k := [\mathcal{A} \star_c \mathcal{V}_1, \ldots, \mathcal{A} \star_c \mathcal{V}_k], \tag{12}$$

$$\mathbb{U}_k := [\mathcal{U}_1, \ldots, \mathcal{U}_k], \quad \text{and} \quad \mathcal{A}^T \star_c \mathbb{U}_k := [\mathcal{A}^T \star_c \mathcal{U}_1, \ldots, \mathcal{A}^T \star_c \mathcal{U}_k], \tag{13}$$

with

$$\widetilde{C}_k^T = \begin{bmatrix} C_k^T \\ \beta_k e_k^T \end{bmatrix} \in \mathbb{R}^{(k+1) \times k}, \; e_k^T = (0, 0, \ldots, 0, 1)^T.$$

Then, we have the following results [13].

Proposition 1. *The tensors produced by the tensor c-global Golub–Kahan algorithm satisfy the following relations*

$$\mathcal{A} \star_c \mathbb{V}_k = \mathbb{U}_k \circledast C_k, \tag{14}$$

$$\mathcal{A}^T \star_c \mathbb{U}_k = \mathbb{V}_{k+1} \circledast \widetilde{C}_k^T \tag{15}$$

$$= \mathbb{V}_k \circledast C_k^T + \beta_k [\mathcal{O}_{n \times s \times p}, \ldots, \mathcal{O}_{n_1 \times s \times n_3}, \mathcal{V}_{k+1}], \tag{16}$$

where the product $\circledast$ is defined by:

$$\mathbb{U}_k \circledast y = \sum_{j=1}^{k} y_j \mathcal{V}_j, \; y = (y_1, \ldots, y_m)^T \in \mathbb{R}^k.$$

We set the following notation:

$$\mathbb{U}_k \circledast C_k = \left[\mathbb{U}_k \circledast C_k^1, \ldots, \mathcal{U}_k \circledast C_k^k\right],$$

where C_k^i is the i-th column of the matrix C_k.

We note that since the matrix C_k is bidiagonal, $T_k = C_k^T C_k$ is symmetric and tridiagonal and then Algorithm computes the same information as tensor global Lanczos algorithm applied to the symmetric matrix $A^* \star_c A$.

4.2. Tensor Tubal Golub–Kahan Bidiagonalisation Algorithm

First, we introduce some new products that will be useful in this section.

Definition 6 ([13]). *Let* $\mathbf{a} \in \mathbb{R}^{1\times 1\times n_3}$ *and* $\mathcal{B} \in \mathbb{R}^{n_1\times n_2\times n_3}$*, the tube fiber tensor product* $(\mathbf{a} \circledast \mathcal{B})$ *is an* $(n_1 \times n_2 \times n_3)$ *tensor defined by*

$$\mathbf{a} \circledast \mathcal{B} = \begin{pmatrix} \mathbf{a} \star_c b(1,1,:) & \dots & \mathbf{a} \star_c b(1,n_2,:) \\ \vdots & \ddots & \vdots \\ \mathbf{a} \star_c b(n_1,1,:) & \dots & \mathbf{a} \star_c b(n_1,n_2,:) \end{pmatrix}$$

Definition 7 ([13]). *Let* $\mathcal{A} \in \mathbb{R}^{n_1\times m_1\times n_3}$, $\mathcal{B} \in \mathbb{R}^{n_1\times m_2\times n_3}$, $\mathcal{C} \in \mathbb{R}^{n_2\times m_1\times n_3}$ *and* $\mathcal{D} \in \mathbb{R}^{n_2\times m_2\times n_3}$ *be tensors. The block tensor*

$$\begin{bmatrix} \mathcal{A} & \mathcal{B} \\ \mathcal{C} & \mathcal{D} \end{bmatrix} \in \mathbb{R}^{(n_1+n_2)\times(m_1+m_2)\times n_3}$$

is defined by compositing the frontal slices of the four tensors.

Definition 8. *Let* $\mathcal{A} = [\mathcal{A}_1,\dots,\mathcal{A}_{n_2}] \in \mathbb{R}^{n_1\times n_2\times n_3}$ *where* $\mathcal{A}_i \in \mathbb{R}^{n_1\times 1\times n_3}$ *, we denoted by* `TVect(` $\mathcal{A}$ `)` *the* ***tensor vectorization*** *operator:* $\mathbb{R}^{n_1\times n_2\times n_3} \mapsto \mathbb{R}^{n_1 n_2\times 1\times n_3}$ *obtained by superposing the laterals slices* $\mathcal{A}_i$ *of* $\mathcal{A}$*, for* $i = 1,\dots,n_2$*. In others words, for a tensor* $\mathcal{A} = [\mathcal{A}_1,\dots,\mathcal{A}_{n_2}] \in \mathbb{R}^{n_1\times n_2\times n_3}$ *where* $\mathcal{A}_i \in \mathbb{R}^{n_1\times 1\times n_3}$ *, we have :*

$$\texttt{TVect}(\mathcal{A}) = \begin{pmatrix} \mathcal{A}_1 \\ \mathcal{A}_2 \\ \vdots \\ \mathcal{A}_{n_2} \end{pmatrix} \in \mathbb{R}^{n_1 n_2\times 1\times n_3}$$

Remark 3. *The* `TVect` *operator transform a given tensor on lateral slice. Its easy to see that when we take* $p = 1$*, the* `TVect` *operator coincides with the operation vec which transform the matrix on vector.*

Proposition 2. *Let* $\mathcal{A}$ *be a tensor of size* $\mathbb{R}^{n_1\times n_2\times n_3}$ *, we have*

$$\|\mathcal{A}\|_F = \|\texttt{TVec}(\mathcal{A})\|_F$$

Definition 9. *Let* $\mathcal{A} = [\mathcal{A}_1,\dots,\mathcal{A}_{n_2}] \in \mathbb{R}^{n_1\times n_2\times n_3}$ *where* $\mathcal{A}_i \in \mathbb{R}^{n_1\times 1\times n_3}$*. We define the range space of* $\mathcal{A}$ *denoted by* $\texttt{Range}(\mathcal{A})$ *as the c-linear span of the lateral slices of* $\mathcal{A}$

$$\texttt{Range}(\mathcal{A}) = \left\{\mathcal{A}_1 \star_c a(1,1,:) + \dots + \mathcal{A}_{n_2} \star_c a(n_2,n_2,:) | a(i,i,:) \in \mathbb{R}^{1\times 1\times n_3}\right\} \quad (17)$$

Definition 10 ([14]). *Let* $\mathcal{A} \in \mathbb{R}^{n_1\times n_2\times n_3}$ *and* $\mathcal{B} \in \mathbb{R}^{m_1\times m_2\times n_3}$*, the* ***c-Kronecker product*** $\mathcal{A} \odot \mathcal{B}$ *of* $\mathcal{A}$ *and* $\mathcal{B}$ *is the* $n_1 m_1 \times n_2 m_2 \times n_3$ *tensor in which the i-th frontal slice of their transformed tensor* $(\widetilde{\mathcal{A} \odot \mathcal{B}})$ *is given by:*

$$(\widetilde{\mathcal{A} \odot \mathcal{B}})_i = (A^{(i)} \otimes B^{(i)}), \;\; i = 1,\dots,n_3$$

where $A^{(i)}$ *and* $B^{(i)}$ *are the i-th frontal slices of the tensors* $\widetilde{\mathcal{A}} = \texttt{dct}(\mathcal{A},[\,],3)$ *and* $\widetilde{\mathcal{B}} = \texttt{dct}(\mathcal{B},[\,],3)$*, respectively.*

We introduce now a normalization algorithm allowing us to decompose the non-zero tensor $\mathcal{C} \in \mathbb{R}^{n_1\times n_2\times n_3}$, such that:

$$\mathcal{C} = \mathbf{a} \circledast \mathcal{Q}, \text{ with } \langle \mathcal{Q}, \mathcal{Q} \rangle = \mathbf{e},$$

where $\mathbf{a}$ is an invertible tube fiber of size $\mathbf{a} \in \mathbb{R}^{1\times 1\times n_3}$ and $\mathcal{Q} \in \mathbb{R}^{n_1\times n_2\times n_3}$ and $\mathbf{e}$ is the tube fiber $\mathbf{e} \in \mathbb{R}^{1\times 1\times n_3}$ defined by $\texttt{unfold}(\mathbf{e}) = (1,0,0\ldots,0)^T$.

This procedure is described in Algorithm 4.

Algorithm 4 Normalization algorithm (Normalize).

1. **Input.** $\mathcal{A} \in \mathbb{R}^{n_1\times n_2\times n_3}$ and a tolerance $tol > 0$.
2. **Output.** The tensor $\mathcal{Q}$ and the tube fiber $\mathbf{a}$.
3. Set $\widetilde{\mathcal{Q}} = \texttt{dct}(\mathcal{A}, [], 3)$
   (a) For $j = 1, \ldots, n_3$
      i. $a_j = ||\widetilde{\mathcal{Q}}^{(j)}||_F$
      ii. if $a_j > tol$, $\widetilde{\mathcal{Q}}^{(j)} = \dfrac{\widetilde{\mathcal{Q}}^{(j)}}{a_j}$
      iii. else $\widetilde{\mathcal{Q}}_j = \text{rand}(n_1, n_2)$; $a_j = ||\widetilde{\mathcal{Q}}^{(j)}||_F$
      $\widetilde{\mathcal{Q}}^{(j)} = \dfrac{\widetilde{\mathcal{Q}}^{(j)}}{a_j}$; $a_j = 0$,
   (b) End
4. $\mathcal{Q} = \texttt{idct}(\widetilde{\mathcal{Q}}, [], 3)$, $\mathbf{a} = \texttt{idct}(\mathbf{a}, [], 3)$
5. End

Next, we give the Tensor Tube Global Golub–Kahan (TTGGKA) algorithm, seeEllchi1. Let $\mathcal{A} \in \mathbb{R}^{n_1\times n_2\times n_3}$ be a tensor and let $s \geq 1$ be an integer. The Tensor Tube Global Golub–Kahan bidiagonalization process is described in Algorithm 5.

Algorithm 5 The Tensor Tube Global Golub–Kahan algorithm (TTGGKA).

1. Choose a tensor $\mathcal{V}_1 \in \mathbb{R}^{n_2\times s\times n_3}$ such that $\langle \mathcal{V}_1, \mathcal{V}_1 \rangle = \mathbf{e}$ and set $\mathbf{b}_0 = 0$.
2. For $i = 1, 2, \ldots, k$
   (a) $\mathcal{U}_i = \mathcal{A} \star_c \mathcal{V}_i - \mathbf{b}_{i-1} \circledast \mathcal{U}_{i-1}$,
   (b) $[\mathcal{U}_i, \mathbf{a}_i] = Normalize(\mathcal{U}_i)$.
   (c) $\mathcal{V}_{i+1} = \mathcal{A}^T \star_c \mathcal{U}_i - \mathbf{a}_i \circledast \mathcal{V}_i$,
   (d) $[\mathcal{V}_{i+1}, \mathbf{b}_i] = Normalize(\mathcal{V}_{i+1})$.
   End

Let $\mathcal{C}_k$ be the $k \times k \times n_3$ upper bidiagonal tensor (each frontal slice of $\mathcal{C}_k$ is a bidiagonal matrix) and $\widetilde{\mathcal{C}}_k$ the $k \times (k+1) \times n_3$ defined by

$$\mathcal{C}_k = \begin{bmatrix} \mathbf{a}_1 & \mathbf{b}_1 & & & \\ & \mathbf{a}_2 & \mathbf{b}_2 & & \\ & & \ddots & \ddots & \\ & & & \mathbf{a}_{k-1} & \mathbf{b}_{k-1} \\ & & & & \mathbf{a}_k \end{bmatrix}, \text{ and } \widetilde{\mathcal{C}}_k = \begin{bmatrix} \mathbf{a}_1 & \mathbf{b}_1 & & & & \\ & \mathbf{a}_2 & \mathbf{b}_2 & & & \\ & & \ddots & \ddots & & \\ & & & \mathbf{a}_{k-1} & \mathbf{b}_{k-1} & \\ & & & & \mathbf{a}_k & \mathbf{b}_k \end{bmatrix}. \quad (18)$$

Let $\mathbb{V}_k$ and $\mathcal{A} \star_c \mathbb{V}_k$ be the $(n_2 \times (sk) \times n_3)$ and $(n_1 \times (sk) \times n_3)$ tensors with frontal slices $\mathcal{V}_1, \ldots, \mathcal{V}_k$ and $\mathcal{A} \star_c \mathcal{V}_1, \ldots, \mathcal{A} \star_c \mathcal{V}_k$, respectively, and let $\mathbb{U}_k$ and $\mathcal{A}^T \star_c \mathbb{U}_k$ be the $(n_1 \times (sk) \times n_3)$ and $(n_2 \times (sk) \times n_3)$ tensors with frontal slices $\mathcal{U}_1, \ldots, \mathcal{U}_k$ and $\mathcal{A}^T \star_c \mathcal{U}_1, \ldots, \mathcal{A}^T \star_c \mathcal{U}_k$, respectively. We set

$$\mathbb{V}_k := [\mathcal{V}_1, \ldots, \mathcal{V}_k], \quad \text{and} \quad \mathcal{A} \star_c \mathbb{V}_k := [\mathcal{A} \star_c \mathcal{V}_1, \ldots, \mathcal{A} \star_c \mathcal{V}_k], \quad (19)$$

$$\mathbb{U}_k := [\mathcal{U}_1, \ldots, \mathcal{U}_k], \quad \text{and} \quad \mathcal{A}^T \star_c \mathbb{U}_k := [\mathcal{A}^T \star_c \mathcal{U}_1, \ldots, \mathcal{A}^T \star_c \mathcal{U}_k], \quad (20)$$

Then, we have the following results.

Proposition 3. *The tensors produced by the tensor TTGGKA algorithm satisfy the following relations*

$$\begin{aligned} \mathcal{A} \star_c \mathbb{V}_k &= \mathbb{U}_k \star_c (\mathcal{C}_k \odot \mathcal{I}_{ssn_3}), & (21)\\ \mathcal{A}^T \star_c \mathbb{U}_k &= \mathbb{V}_{k+1} \star_c (\widetilde{\mathcal{C}}_k^T \odot \mathcal{I}_{ssn_3}) & (22)\\ &= \mathbb{V}_k \star_c (\mathcal{C}_k^T \odot \mathcal{I}_{ssp}) + \mathcal{V}_{k+1} \star_c ((\mathbf{b}_k \star_c \mathbf{e}_{1,k,:}) \odot \mathcal{I}_{ssn_3}), & (23)\end{aligned}$$

where $\mathbf{e}_{1,k,:} \in \mathbb{R}^{1\times k\times n_3}$ *with* 1 *in the* $(1,k,1)$ *position and zeros in the other positions,* $\mathcal{I}_{ssn_3} \in \mathbb{R}^{s\times s\times n_3}$ *the identity tensor and* $\mathbf{b}_k$ *is the fiber tube in the* $(k, k+1, :)$ *position of the tensor* $\widetilde{\mathcal{C}}_k$.

5. The Tensor Tubal PCA Method

In this section, we describe a tensor-SVD based PCA method for order 3 tensors which naturally arise in problems involving images such as facial recognition. As for the matrix case, we consider a set of N training images, each of one being encoded as $n_1 \times n_2 \times n_3$ real tensors $\mathcal{I}_i, 1 \le i \le N$. In the case of RGB images, each frontal slice would contain the encoding for each color layer ($n_3 = 3$) but in order to be able to store additional features, the case $n_3 > 3$ could be contemplated.

Let us consider one training image $\mathcal{I}_{i_0}$. Each one of the n_3 frontal slices $I_{i_0}^{(j)}$ of $\mathcal{I}_{i_0}$ is resized into a column vector $vec(I_{i_0}^{(j)})$ of length $L = n_1 \times n_2$ and we form a $L \times 1 \times n_3$ tensor $\mathcal{X}_{i_0}$ defined by $\mathcal{X}_{i_0}(:,:,j) = vec(I_{i_0}^{(j)})$. Applying this procedure to each training image, we obtain N tensors $\mathcal{X}_i$ of size $L \times 1 \times n_3$. The average image tensor is defined as $\bar{\mathcal{X}} = \frac{1}{N}\sum_{i=1}^{N} \mathcal{X}_i$ and we define the $L \times N \times n_3$ training tensor $\mathcal{X} = [\bar{\mathcal{X}}_1, \ldots, \bar{\mathcal{X}}_N]$, where $\bar{\mathcal{X}}_i = \mathcal{X}_i - \bar{\mathcal{X}}$.

Let us now consider the c-SVD decomposition $\mathcal{X} = \mathcal{U} *_c \mathcal{S} *_c \mathcal{V}^T$ of $\mathcal{X}$, where $\mathcal{U}$ and $\mathcal{V}$ are orthogonal tensors of size $L \times L \times n_3$ and $N \times N \times n_3$, respectively, and S is a f-diagonal tensor of size $L \times N \times n_3$.

In the matrix context, it is known that just a few singular values suffice to capture the main features of an image, therefore, applying this idea to each one of the three color layers, an RGB image can be approximated by a low tubal rank tensor. Let us consider an image tensor $\mathcal{S} \in \mathbb{R}^{n_1\times n_2\times n_3}$ and its c-SVD decomposition $\mathcal{S} = \mathcal{U} \star_c \mathcal{S} \star_c \mathcal{V}^T$. Choosing an integer r such as $r \le \min(n_1, n_2)$, we can approximate $\mathcal{S}$ by the r tubal rank tensor

$$\mathcal{S}_r \approx \sum_{i=1}^{r} \mathcal{U}(:,i,:) *_c \mathcal{S}(i,i,:) *_c \mathcal{V}(:,i,:)^T.$$

In Figure 1, we represented a 512×512 RGB image and the images obtained for various truncation indices. On the left part, we plotted the singular values of one color layer of the RGB tensor (the exact same behaviour is observed on the two other layers). The rapid decrease of the singular values explain the good quality of compressed images even for small truncation indices.

Applying this idea to our problem, we want to be able to obtain truncated tensor SVDs of the training tensor $\mathcal{X}$, without needing to compute the whole c-SVD. After k iterations of the TTGGKA algorithm (for the case $s = 1$), we obtain three tensors $\mathbb{U}_k \in \mathbb{R}^{n_1\times k\times n_3}$, $\mathbb{V}_{k+1} \in \mathbb{R}^{n_2\times (k+1)\times n_3}$ and $\widetilde{\mathcal{C}}_k \in \mathbb{R}^{(k\times (k+1)\times n_3}$ as defined in Equation (21) such as

$$\mathcal{A}^T \star_c \mathbb{U}_k = \mathbb{V}_{k+1} \star_c \widetilde{\mathcal{C}}_k^T.$$

Let $\widetilde{\mathcal{C}}_k = \Phi \star_c \Sigma \star_c \Psi$ the c-SVD of $\widetilde{\mathcal{C}}_k$, noticing that $\widetilde{\mathcal{C}}_k \in \mathbb{R}^{k\times (k+1)\times n_3}$ is much smaller than $\bar{\mathcal{X}}$. Then first tubal singular values and the left tubal singular tensors of $\bar{\mathcal{X}}$ are given by $\Sigma(i,i,:)$ and $\mathcal{U}_k \star_c \Phi(:,i,:)$, respectively, for $i \le k$, see [1] for more details.

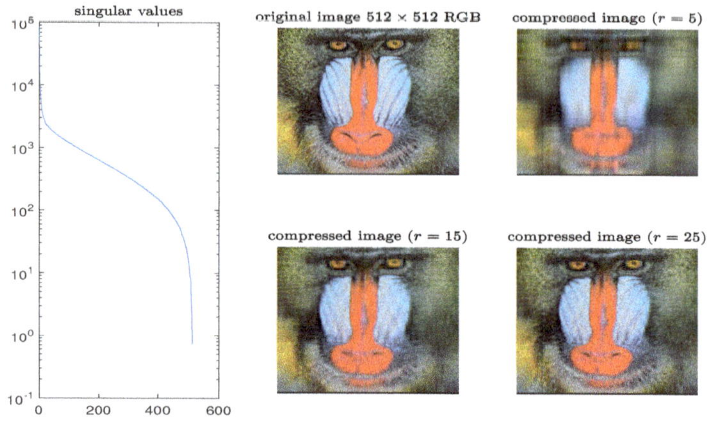

Figure 1. Image compression.

In order to illustrate the ability to approximate the first singular elements of a tensor using the TTGGKA algorithm, we considered a $900 \times 900 \times 3$ real tensor $\mathcal{A}$ which frontal slices were matrices generated by a finite difference discretization method of differential operators. On Figure 2, we displayed the error on the first diagonal coefficient of the first frontal $\mathcal{S}(1,1,1)$ in function of the number of iteration of the Tensor Tube Golub–Kahan algorithm, where $\mathcal{A} = \mathcal{U} \star_c \mathcal{S} \star_c \mathcal{V}^T$ is the c-SVD of $\mathcal{A}$.

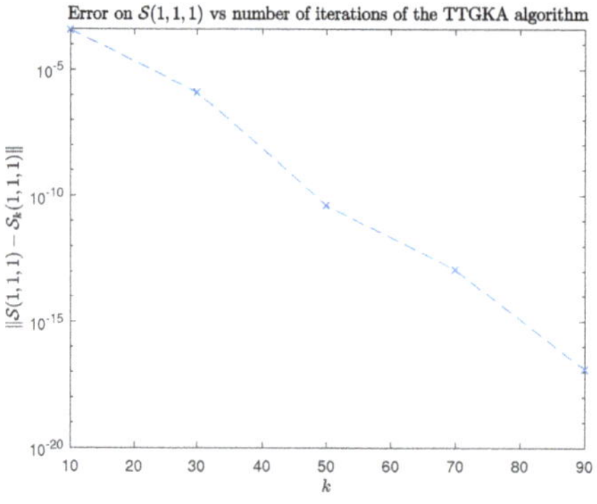

Figure 2. $\|\Sigma(1,1,1) - \mathcal{S}(1,1,1)\|$ *vs.* number of TTGGKA iteration k.

In Table 1, we reported on the errors on the tensor Frobenius norms of the singular tubes in function of the number k of the Tensor Tube Golub–Kahan algorithm.

Table 1. $\|\mathcal{S}(i,i,:) - \Sigma(i,i,:)\|_F$ *vs* k.

	$k = 10$	$k = 30$	$k = 50$	$k = 70$
$\mathcal{S}(1,1,:)$	3.6×10^{-4}	1.3×10^{-5}	5.1×10^{-11}	4.8×10^{-17}
$\mathcal{S}(2,2,:)$	2.0×10^{-3}	1.6×10^{-6}	5.2×10^{-7}	3.1×10^{-8}
$\mathcal{S}(3,3,:)$	4.9×10^{-3}	5.9×10^{-4}	2.3×10^{-4}	5.6×10^{-8}
$\mathcal{S}(4,4,:)$	8.4×10^{-3}	8.8×10^{-4}	1.5×10^{-4}	1.0×10^{-8}
$\mathcal{S}(5,5,:)$	1.4×10^{-2}	1.3×10^{-3}	2.7×10^{-4}	1.1×10^{-8}

The same behaviour was observed on all the other frontal slices. This example illustrate the ability of the TTGKA algorithm for approximating the largest singular tubes.

The projection space is generated by the lateral slices of the tensor $\mathcal{P} = \mathbb{U}_k \star_c \Phi(:, 1:k, :) \in \mathbb{R}^{n_1 \times i \times n_3}$ derived from the TTGGKA algorithm and the c-SVD decomposition of the bidiagonal tensor $\widetilde{\mathcal{C}}_k$, i.e., the c-linear span of first k lateral slices of $\mathcal{P}$, see [1,19] for more details.

The steps of the Tensor Tubal PCA algorithm for face recognition which finds the closest image in the training database for a given image $\mathcal{I}_0$ are summarized in Algorithm 6:

Algorithm 6 The Tensor Tubal PCA algorithm (TTPCA).

1. **Inputs** Training Image tensor $\mathcal{X}$ (N images), mean image tensor $\bar{\mathcal{X}}$,Test image $\mathcal{I}_0$, index of truncation r, k=number of iterations of the TTGGKA algorithm ($k \geq r$).
2. **Output** Closest image in the Training database.
3. Run k iterations of the TTGGKA algorithm to obtain tensors $\mathbb{U}_k$ and $\widehat{\mathcal{C}}_k$
4. Compute $[\Phi, \Sigma, \Psi]$ =c-SVD($\widetilde{\mathcal{C}}_k$)
5. Compute the projection tensor $\mathcal{P}_r = [\mathcal{P}_r(:, 1, :), \ldots, \mathcal{P}_r(:, r, :)]$, where $\mathcal{P}_r(:, i, :) = \mathbb{U}_k \star_c \Phi(:, i, :) \in \mathbb{R}^{n_1 \times 1 \times n_3}$
6. Compute the projected Training tensor $\hat{\mathcal{X}}_r = \mathcal{P}_r^T \star_c \mathcal{X}$ and projected centred test image $\hat{\mathcal{I}}_r = \mathcal{P}_r^T \star_c (\mathcal{I} - \bar{\mathcal{X}})$
7. Find $i = \arg\min_{i=1,..,N} \|\hat{\mathcal{I}}_r - \hat{\mathcal{X}}_r(:, i, :)\|_F$

In the next section, we consider image identification problems on various databases.

6. Numerical Tests

In this section, we consider three examples of image identification. In the case of grayscale images, the global version of Golub–Kahan was used to compute the dominant singular values in order to perform a PCA on the data. For the two other situations, we used the Tensor Tubal PCA (TTPCA) method based on the Tube Global Golub–Kahan (TTGGKA) algorithm in order to perform facial recognition on RGB images. The tests were performed with Matlab 2019a, on an Intel i5 laptop with 16 Go of memory. We considered various truncation indices r for which the recognition rates were computed. We also reported the CPU time for the training process.

6.1. Example 1

In this example, we considered the MNIST database of handwritten digits [22]. The database contains two subsets of 28×28 grayscale images (60,000 training images and 10,000 test images). A sample is shown in Figure 3. Each image was vectorized as a vector of length $28 \times 28 = 784$ and, following the process described in Section 3.1, we formed the training and the test matrices of sizes $784 \times 60{,}000$ and $784 \times 10{,}000$, respectively.

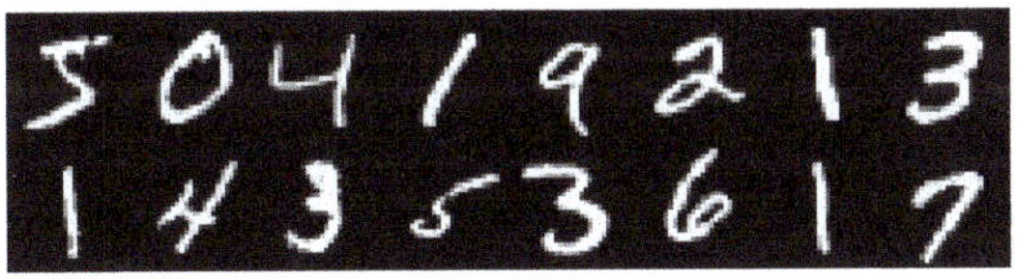

Figure 3. First 16 images of MNIST training subset.

Both matrices were centred by substracting the mean training image and the Golub–Kahan algorithm was used to generate an approximation of r dominant singular values s_i and left singular vectors u_i, $i = 1, \ldots, r$.

Let us denote $\mathcal{U}_r$ the subspace spanned by the columns of $U_r = [u_1, \ldots, u_r]$. Let t be a test image and $\hat{t}_r = U_r^T t$ its projection onto $\mathcal{U}_r$. The closest image in the training dataset is determined by computing

$$i = \arg \min_{i=1,..,60{,}000} \|\hat{t}_r - \hat{X}_r(:, i)\|,$$

where $\hat{X}_r = \mathcal{U}_r^T X$.

For various truncation indices r, we tested each image of the test subset and computed the recognition rate (i.e., a test is successful if the digit is correctly identified). The results are plotted on Figure 4 and show that a good level of accuracy is obtained with only a few approximate singular values. Due to the large size of the training matrix, it validates the interest of computing only a few singular values with the Golub–Kahan algorithm.

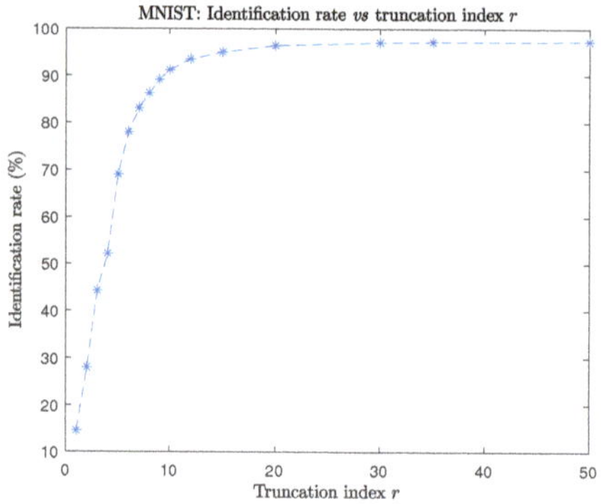

Figure 4. Identification rates for different truncation indices r.

6.2. Example 2

In this example, we used the Georgia Tech database GTDB_ crop [23], which contains 750 face images of 50 persons in different illumination conditions, facial expression and face orientation, as shown in Figure 5. The RGB JPEG images were resized to $100 \times 100 \times 3$ tensors.

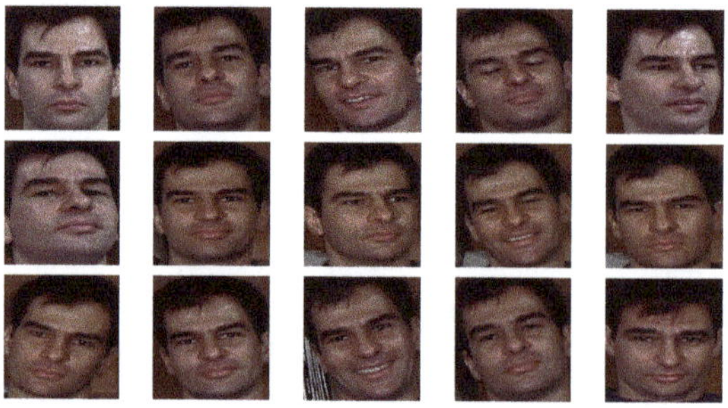

Figure 5. Fifteen pictures of one individual in the database.

Each image file is coded as a $100 \times 100 \times 3$ tensor and transformed into a $10{,}000 \times 1 \times 3$ tensor as explained in the previous section. We built the training and test tensors as follows: from 15 pictures of each person in the database, five pictures were randomly chosen and stored in the test folder and the 10 remaining pictures were used for the train tensor. Hence, the database was partitioned into two subsets containing 250 and 500 items, respectively, at each iteration of the simulation.

We applied the TTGGKA based Algoritm 6 for various truncation indices. In Figure 6, we represented a test image (top left position), the closest image in the database (top right), the mean image of the training database (bottom left) and the eigenface associated to the test image (bottom right).

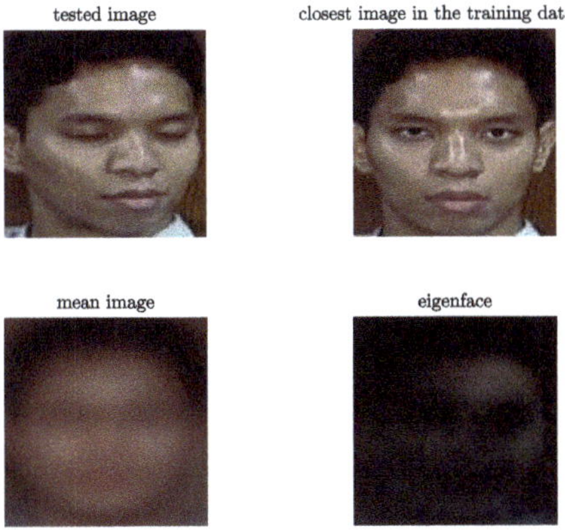

Figure 6. Test image, closest image, mean image and eigenface.

In order compute the rate of recognition, we ran 100 simulations, obtained the number of successes (i.e., a test is successful if the person is correctly identified) and reported the best identification rates, in function of the truncation index r in Figure 7.

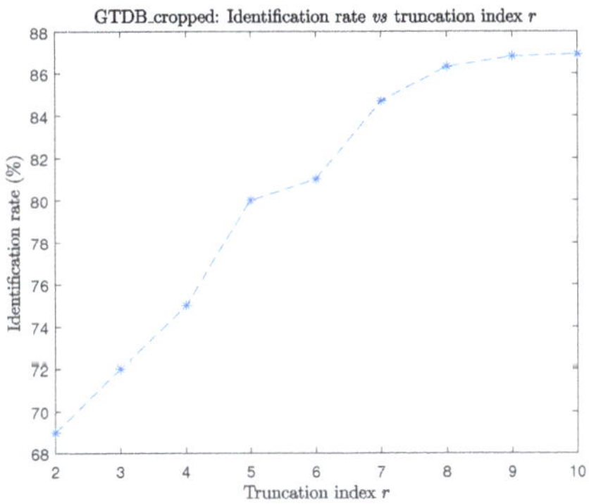

Figure 7. Identification rates for different truncation indices r.

The results match the performances observed in the literature [24] for this database and it confirms that the use of a Golub–Kahan strategy is interesting especially because, in terms of training, the Tube Tensor PCA algorithm required only 5 s instead of 25 s when using a c-SVD.

6.3. *Example 3*

In the second example, we used the larger AR face database (cropped version) (Face crops) [9], which contains 2600 bitmap pictures of human faces (50 males and 50 females, 26 pictures per person), with different expressions, lightning conditions, facial expressions and face orientation. The bitmap pictures were resized to 100×100 Jpeg images. The same protocol as for Example 1 was followed: we partitioned the set of images in two subsets. Out of 26 pictures, 6 pictures were randomly chosen as test images and the remaining 20 were put into the training folder. The training process took 24 s while it would have taken 81.5 s if using a c-SVD. An example of test image, the closest match in the dataset, the mean image and its associated eigenface are shown in Figure 8.

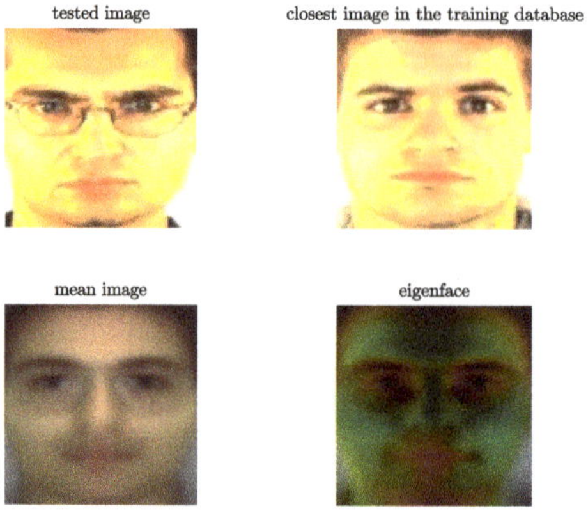

Figure 8. Test image, closest image, mean image and eigenface.

We applied our approach (TTPCA) to the 10,000 × 2000 × 3 training tensor $\mathcal{X}$ and plotted the recognition rate as a function of the truncation index in Figure 9.

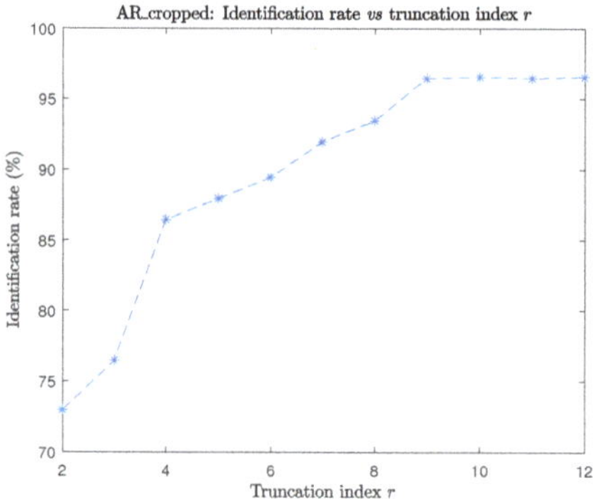

Figure 9. Identification rates for different truncation indices r.

For all examples, it is worth noticing that, as expected in face identification problems, only a few of the first largest singular elements suffice to capture the main features of an image. Therefore, the Golub–Kahan based strategies such as the TTPCA method are an interesting choice.

7. Conclusions

In this manuscript, we focused on two types of Golub–Kahan factorizations. We used the recent advances in the field of tensor factorization and showed that this approach is efficient for image identification. The main feature of this approach resides in the ability of the Global Golub–Kahan algorithms to approximate the dominant singular elements of a training matrix or tensor without needing to compute the SVD. This is particularly important as the matrices and tensors involved in this type of application can be very large. Moreover, in the case for which color has to be taken into account, this approach do not involve a conversion to grayscale, which can be very important for some applications. In a future work, we would like to study the feasability of implementing the promising randomized PCA approaches in the Golub–Kahan tensor algorithm in order to improve the training process computational cost in the case of very large datasets.

Author Contributions: Conceptualization, M.H., K.J., C.K. and M.M.; methodology, M.H. and K.J.; software, M.H.; validation, M.H., K.J., C.K. and M.M.; writing—original draft preparation, M.H., K.J., C.K. and M.M.; writing—review and editing, M.H., K.J., C.K. and M.M.; visualization, M.H., K.J., C.K. and M.M.; supervision, K.J.; project administration, M.H. and K.J. All authors have read and agreed to the published version of the manuscript.

Funding: This research received no external funding.

Institutional Review Board Statement: Not applicable.

Informed Consent Statement: Not applicable.

Data Availability Statement: Not applicable.

Acknowledgments: Mustapha Hached acknowledges support from the Labex CEMPI (ANR-11-LABX-0007-01).

Conflicts of Interest: The authors declare no conflict of interest.

References

1. Kilmer, M.E.; Braman, K.; Hao, N.; Hoover, R.C. Third-order tensors as operators on matrices: A theoretical and computational framework with applications in imaging. *SIAM J. Matrix Anal. Appl.* **2013**, *34*, 148–172.
2. Kolda, T.G.; Bader, B.W. Tensor Decompositions and Applications. *SIAM Rev.* **2009**, *3*, 455–500. [CrossRef]
3. Zhang, J.; Saibaba, A.K.; Kilmer, M.E.; Aeron, S. A randomized tensor singular value decomposition based on the t-product. *Numer Linear Algebra Appl.* **2018**, *25*, e2179. [CrossRef]
4. Cai, S.; Luo, Q.; Yang, M.; Li, W.; Xiao, M. Tensor robust principal component analysis via non-convex low rank approximation. *Appl. Sci.* **2019**, *9*, 1411. [CrossRef]
5. Kong, H.; Xie, X.; Lin, Z. t-Schatten-*p* norm for low-rank tensor recovery. *IEEE J. Sel. Top. Signal Process.* **2018**, *12*, 1405–1419. [CrossRef]
6. Lin, Z.; Chen, M.; Ma, Y. The augmented Lagrange multiplier method for exact recovery of corrupted low-rank matrices. *arXiv* **2010**, arXiv:1009.5055.
7. Kang, Z.; Peng, C.; Cheng, Q. Robust PCA via nonconvex rank approximation. In Proceedings of the 2015 IEEE International Conference on Data Mining, Atlantic City, NJ, USA, 14–17 November 2015.
8. Lu, C.; Feng, J.; Chen, Y.; Liu, W.; Lin, Z.; Yan, S. Tensor Robust Principal Component Analysis with a New Tensor Nuclear Norm. *IEEE Anal. Mach. Intell.* **2020**, *42*, 925–938. [CrossRef] [PubMed]
9. Martinez, A.M.; Kak, A.C. PCA versus LDA. *IEEE Trans. Pattern Anal. Mach. Intell.* **2001**, *23*, 228–233. [CrossRef]
10. Guide, M.E.; Ichi, A.E.; Jbilou, K.; Sadaka, R. Tensor Krylov subspace methods via the T-product for color image processing. *arXiv* **2020**, arXiv:2006.07133.
11. Brazell, M.; Navasca, N.L.C.; Tamon, C. Solving Multilinear Systems Via Tensor Inversion. *SIAM J. Matrix Anal. Appl.* **2013**, *34*, 542–570. [CrossRef]
12. Beik, F.P.A.; Jbilou, K.; Najafi-Kalyani, M.; Reichel, L. Golub–Kahan bidiagonalization for ill-conditioned tensor equations with applications. *Numer. Algorithms* **2020**, *84*, 1535–1563. [CrossRef]
13. Ichi, A.E.; Jbilou, K.; Sadaka, R. On some tensor tubal-Krylov subspace methods via the T-product. *arXiv* **2020**, arXiv:2010.14063.
14. Guide, M.E.; Ichi, A.E.; Jbilou, K. Discrete cosine transform LSQR and GMRES methods for multidimensional ill-posed problems. *arXiv* **2020**, arXiv:2103.11847.
15. Vasilescu, M.A.O.; Terzopoulos, D. Multilinear image analysis for facial recognition. In Proceedings of the Object Recognition Supported by User Interaction for Service Robots, Quebec City, QC, Canada, 11–15 August 2002; pp. 511–514.
16. Jain, A. *Fundamentals of Digital Image Processing*; Prentice–Hall: Englewood Cliffs, NJ, USA, 1989.
17. Ng, M.K.; Chan, R.H.; Tang, W. A fast algorithm for deblurring models with Neumann boundary conditions. *SIAM J. Sci. Comput.* **1999**, *21*, 851–866. [CrossRef]
18. Kernfeld, E.; Kilmer, M.; Aeron, S. Tensor-tensor products with invertible linear transforms. *Linear Algebra Appl.* **2015**, *485*, 545–570. [CrossRef]
19. Kilmer, M.E.; Martin, C.D. Factorization strategies for third-order tensors. *Linear Algebra Appl.* **2011**, *435*, 641–658. [CrossRef]
20. Golub, G.H.; Van Loan, C.F. *Matrix Computations*, 3rd ed.; Johns Hopkins University Press: Baltimore, MD, USA, 1996.
21. Savas, B.; Eldén, L. Krylov-type methods for tensor computations I. *Linear Algebra Appl.* **2013**, *438*, 891–918. [CrossRef]
22. Lecun, Y.; Cortes, C.; Curges, C. The MNIST Database. Available online: http://yann.lecun.com/exdb/mnist/ (accessed on 22 February 2021).
23. Nefian, A.V. Georgia Tech Face Database. Available online: http://www.anefian.com/research/face_reco.htm (accessed on 22 February 2021).
24. Wang, S.; Sun, M.; Chen, Y.; Pang, E.; Zhou, C. STPCA: Sparse tensor Principal Component Analysis for feature extraction. In Proceedings of the 21st International Conference on Pattern Recognition (ICPR2012), Tsukuba, Japan, 11–15 November 2012; pp. 2278–2281.

mathematics

MDPI

Article

Sensitivity of the Solution to Nonsymmetric Differential Matrix Riccati Equation

Vera Angelova [1,†], Mustapha Hached [2,*,†] and Khalide Jbilou [3,†]

1 Department of Intelligent Systems, Institute of Information and Communication Technologies, Bulgarian Academy of Sciences, Akad. G. Bonchev, Bl. 2, 1113 Sofia, Bulgaria; vera.angelova@iict.bas.bg
2 Université de Lille, CNRS, UMR 8524-Laboratoire Paul Painlevé, F-59000 Lille, France
3 Laboratoire LMPA, 50 Rue F. Buisson, ULCO Calais, CEDEX, 62228 Calais, France; jbilou@univ-littoral.fr
* Correspondence: mustapha.hached@univ-lille.fr
† These authors contributed equally to this work.

Abstract: Nonsymmetric differential matrix Riccati equations arise in many problems related to science and engineering. This work is focusing on the sensitivity of the solution to perturbations in the matrix coefficients and the initial condition. Two approaches of nonlocal perturbation analysis of the symmetric differential Riccati equation are extended to the nonsymmetric case. Applying the techniques of Fréchet derivatives, Lyapunov majorants and fixed-point principle, two perturbation bounds are derived: the first one is based on the integral form of the solution and the second one considers the equivalent solution to the initial value problem of the associated differential system. The first bound is derived for the nonsymmetric differential Riccati equation in its general form. The perturbation bound based on the sensitivity analysis of the associated linear differential system is formulated for the low-dimensional approximate solution to the large-scale nonsymmetric differential Riccati equation. The two bounds exploit the existing sensitivity estimates for the matrix exponential and are alternative.

Keywords: non-linear matrix equations; perturbation bounds; Lyapunov majorants; fixed-point principle; nonsymmetric differential matrix Riccati equation

MSC: 15A24

Citation: Angelova, V.; Hached, M.; Jbilou, K. Sensitivity of the Solution to Nonsymmetric Differential Matrix Riccati Equation. *Mathematics* **2021**, *9*, 855. https://doi.org/10.3390/math9080855

Academic Editor: Luca Gemignani

Received: 1 March 2021
Accepted: 10 April 2021
Published: 14 April 2021

1. Introduction and Notations

In the present paper, we consider the nonsymmetric differential matrix Riccati equation /NDRE/

$$\begin{aligned} \dot{X}(t) &= -AX(t) - X(t)D + X(t)SX(t) + Q, \\ X(0) &= X_0. \end{aligned} \tag{1}$$

where the solution $X(t)$ is a $n \times p$ real matrix and $A \in \mathbb{R}^{n\times n}$, $D \in \mathbb{R}^{p\times p}$, $Q \in \mathbb{R}^{n\times p}$ and $S \in \mathbb{R}^{p\times n}$ are the coefficient matrices and $X_0 \in \mathbb{R}^{n\times p}$ is a given initial value.

We assume that the matrix

$$\mathcal{H} = \begin{bmatrix} D & -S \\ -Q & A \end{bmatrix} \in \mathbb{R}^{p+n\times p+n}$$

is a nonsingular M-matrix, or an irreducible singular M-matrix. (Recall that a real square matrix A is said M-matrix if $A = sI - B$ with $B \geq 0$ and $s \geq r(B)$, where $r(.)$ denotes the spectral radius. If $s > r(B)$, the M-matrix A is nonsingular.) As a consequence, [1], A and D are both nonsingular M-matrices and can be decomposed as $A = A_1 - A_2$ and

$D = D_1 - D_2$, where A_2, D_2 are positive and A_1, D_1 are nonsingular M-matrices. The NDRE (1) can then be formulated as

$$\begin{aligned} \dot{X}(t) + X(t)D_1 + A_1X(t) &= A_2X(t) + X(t)D_2 + X(t)SX(t) + Q \\ X(0) &= X_0. \end{aligned}$$

The solution of NDRE (1) is given by the implicit formula [2]

$$\begin{aligned} X(t) &= e^{-tA_1}X_0e^{-tD_1} + \int_0^t e^{-(t-\tau)A_1}Qe^{-(t-\tau)D_1}d\tau \\ &+ \int_0^t e^{-(t-\tau)A_1}(X(\tau)SX(\tau) + A_2X(\tau) + X(\tau)D_2)e^{-(t-\tau)D_1}d\tau. \end{aligned} \tag{2}$$

Let us now consider a nonsingular solution X^* to the nonsymmetric algebraic Riccati equation

$$-AX - XD + XSX + Q = 0.$$

In [1], it is proved that if $\mathcal{H}$ is assumed to be a nonsingular M-matrix, then the NDRE (1) has a global solution $X(t)$, provided that the initial value X_0 satisfies the condition $0 \leq X_0 \leq X^*$, where for every matrices A, $B \in \mathbb{R}^{m\times n}$, we write $A \leq B$ if $a_{ij} \leq b_{ij}$ for all $i \in \{1,\ldots,m\}$ and $j \in \{1,\ldots,n\}$.

Nonsymmetric differential Riccati equations are related to linear boundary value problems arising in game and control theory, oscillation criterion problems for second order differential systems, variational calculus and theory of transport processes [3]. NDRE are an intermediate step in problems from singular perturbations and control theory when linear transformations are applied to reduce high-order systems to lower order or to partially decomposed systems. The properties of nonsymmetric differential Riccati equations determine the existence of the optimal open-loop strategies in Nash and Stackelberg control in game theory [4]. NDRE are induced via invariant embedding and interpretation formula from an "angularly shifted" transport model in the slab geometry [2]. Of mathematical interest, nonsymmetric differential Riccati equation describes the local coordinates of the restriction to a subset of the Lagrangian Grassmannian manifold. The most important results for NDRE are generalized in [5]. Fital and Guo, in [1], prove that for a suitable initial value X_0, the initial value problem (1) has a nonnegative solution $X(t)$, which converges to the stable equilibrium of (1). A closed formula, in terms of exponential of data matrices, for the general solution of (1), when S is invertible, is proposed in [6]. An analytical review of existing numerical methods to find the minimal nonnegative solution to low-dimensional NDRE (1) is given in [7], where the approximate low-dimensional solution to the large-scale case with low-dimensional right hand side is obtained after projecting (1) to low-dimensional differential equation by applying the extended block Arnoldi process.

The numerically computed solution contains errors, as a result of truncation of infinite series, round-off errors due to the finite precision machine arithmetic, error of stopping iteration procedures, etc. The computed perturbed solution can be represented as the exact solution of a slightly perturbed problem, simulating the effect of the errors mentioned above by equivalent perturbations in the data matrices. To estimate the actual error in the computed solution, it is important to find a bound of the error in the computed solution in terms of the perturbations in the data. Perturbation analysis of the nonsymmetric algebraic Riccati equation is given in [8], normwise, mixed and componentwise condition numbers, as well as residual bounds are proposed in [9–11]. To the best of our knowledge, the sensitivity and the conditioning of the NDRE are not yet analyzed.This work has two goals. First, we study the sensitivity of the solution $X(t)$ to (1) to perturbations in the matrix coefficients A, D, Q, S, X_0. It is done by adapting the bounds established for the symmetric differential Riccati equation, obtained by [12,13] to the nonsymmetric Riccati equation, which show good upper sensitivity. The perturbation bounds are very important for interpreting a numerically computed solution. The second objective is to apply the derived nonlocal perturbation bound to estimate the error of approximation in the solution when solving large-scale nonsymmetric differential Riccati equations by Krylov-type methods.

The paper is organized as follows: In Section 2, nonlocal sensitivity analysis of the nonsymmetric differential matrix Riccati Equation (1) is presented. An effective perturbation bound is proposed. In Section 3, an alternative perturbation bound based on the sensitivity analysis of the associated differential system is derived and then applied for estimating the error of approximation of the low-dimensional approximate solution. The bounds exploit existing sensitivity estimates of the matrix exponential. Numerical examples are presented in Section 4 to illustrate the theoretical results established in this work.

Throughout the paper, the following notations are used: $\mathbb{R}^{m\times n}$ denotes the space on $m\times n$ real matrices, $\|.\|$ is the spectral norm $\|M\| = [\lambda_{\max}(M^\top M)]^{1/2}$, where $\lambda_{\max}(N)$ is the maximum eigenvalue of the symmetric matrix N, $\|.\|_F$ is the Frobenius norm, $A^\top$ is the transpose of the matrix $A \in \mathbb{R}^{m\times n}$, I_n is the $n\times n$ unit matrix, and the symbol $:=$ stands for "equal by definition".

2. Nonlocal Perturbation Bound of NDRE

In this section, we will extend the approach proposed in [12] to the nonsymmetric differential Riccati Equation (1).

Let us denote by $\mathcal{Z} := (A, D, Q, S, X_0)$ the collection of matrix coefficients and by $\Delta\mathcal{Z} := (\Delta Z, \Delta D, \Delta Q, \Delta S, \Delta X_0)$ the collection of equivalent perturbations in the data. The perturbation $\Delta Z \in \Delta\mathcal{Z}$ is continuous with $\|\Delta Z\| \approx \texttt{macheps}\,\phi(n)\|Z\|$, where $\phi(n)$ is a low-order polynomial in n and macheps is the round-off unit of the machine arithmetic. If some of the matrix coefficients are not perturbed, then the corresponding perturbations are assumed to be zero. The perturbed nonsymmetric differential matrix Riccati equation, obtained from (1) by replacing the nominal values $Z \in \mathcal{Z}$ by $Z + \Delta Z$, $(\Delta Z \in \Delta\mathcal{Z})$ is given by

$$
\begin{aligned}
(X(t) + \Delta X(t))' &= -(A + \Delta A)(X(t) + \Delta X(t)) \\
&\quad -(X(t) + \Delta X(t))(D + \Delta D) \\
&\quad +(X(t) + \Delta X(t))(S + \Delta S)(X(t) + \Delta X(t)) + Q + \Delta Q, \\
X(0) + \Delta X(0) &= X_0 + \Delta X_0,
\end{aligned} \tag{3}
$$

where $X(t) + \Delta X(t)$ is the solution to the perturbed nonsymmetric differential matrix Riccati Equation (3). For sufficiently small perturbations $\Delta Z \in \Delta\mathcal{Z}$ in the data $Z \in \mathcal{Z}$, the solution $X(t) + \Delta X(t)$ to the perturbed Equation (3) exists and depends continuously on the elements of the perturbations ΔZ in the data Z. Let $\delta := [\delta_A; \delta_D; \delta_Q; \delta_S; \delta_{X_0}] \in \mathbb{R}^5_+$ be the perturbation vector, where $\delta_Z := \|\Delta Z\|$ for $\Delta Z \in \Delta\mathcal{Z}$.

Our aims in this section, are to extend the results obtained in [12] for the symmetric differential matrix Riccati equation to the nonsymmetric case (1) and to give a bound for the perturbations in the solution $\|\Delta X(t)\| \le f(\delta, t)$ as a function of the perturbation vector δ.

From (3), taking into account (1), we can write the perturbation of the solution as

$$
\begin{aligned}
\Delta\dot{X}(t) &= -A_c(t)\Delta X(t) - \Delta X(t) D_c(t) + \mathcal{M}(t, \Delta X(t)), \\
\Delta X(0) &= \Delta X_0,
\end{aligned} \tag{4}
$$

where $A_c(t) := A - X(t)S$, $D_c(t) := D - SX(t)$ are the closed-loop matrices and $\mathcal{M}(t, P)$ is the operator

$$
\mathcal{M}(t, P) := \mathcal{M}_1(t, P) + \mathcal{M}_2(t, P), \tag{5}
$$

defined for some matrix $P \in \mathbb{R}^{n\times p}$, with

$$
\begin{aligned}
\mathcal{M}_1(t, P) &:= X(t)\Delta S X(t) - \Delta A X(t) - X(t)\Delta D + \Delta Q, \\
\mathcal{M}_2(t, P) &:= -(\Delta A - X(t)\Delta S)P - P(\Delta D - \Delta S X(t)) + P(S + \Delta S)P
\end{aligned} \tag{6}
$$

and spectral norm

$$\begin{aligned}\|\mathcal{M}(t,P)\| \;\le\; & \|X(t)\|^2\delta_S + \|X(t)\|(\delta_A+\delta_D)+\delta_Q \\ & +\|P\|(\delta_A+2\|X(t)\|\delta_S+\delta_D)+\|P\|^2(\|S\|+\delta_S).\end{aligned} \tag{7}$$

From (4), we can state the following nonlocal perturbation bound:

Theorem 1. *Let $\Delta X(t)$ be the perturbation in a solution $X(t)$ to Equation (1), solved by a numerically stable algorithm in finite precision arithmetic according to the perturbation vector $\delta := (\delta_A, \delta_D, \delta_Q, \delta_S, \delta_{X_0})$. Let us define the set Ω_t*

$$\Omega_t := \left\{\delta \ge 0,\; a_1(\delta) + 2\sqrt{a_0(\delta)a_2(\delta)} \le 1\right\} \in \mathbb{R}^5_+, \tag{8}$$

where

$$\begin{aligned} a_0(\delta) &:= \nu(\|S\|+\delta_S), \\ a_1(\delta) &:= \nu(\delta_A + 2\|X(t)\|\delta_S + \delta_D), \\ a_2(\delta) &:= \nu\delta_Q + \nu\|X(t)\|(\delta_A+\delta_D) + \nu\|X(t)\|^2\delta_S + \beta\delta_{X_0}, \end{aligned} \tag{9}$$

with

$$\beta = \max\{\|\Phi_{A_c}(0,t)\|\,\|\Phi_{D_c}(0,t)\| : t \in T\}, \tag{10}$$

$$\nu = \max\left\{\int_0^t \|\Phi_{A_c}(\tau,t)\|\,\|\Phi_{D_c}(\tau,t)\|\,d\tau : t \in T\right\}, \tag{11}$$

and $\Phi_P(t,t_0) = e^{(t-t_0)P}$ is the fundamental matrix of equation $\dot\eta(t) = P\eta(t)$ for some real matrix P.

If δ satisfies the inclusion

$$\delta \in \Omega_t, \tag{12}$$

for Ω_t given in (8), then the norm of the perturbation $\Delta X(t)$ is bounded by the nonlocal perturbation bound

$$\|\Delta X(t)\| \le f(\delta,t) := \frac{2a_2(\delta)}{1-a_1(\delta)+\sqrt{(1-a_1(\delta))^2-4a_0(\delta)a_2(\delta)}}. \tag{13}$$

Proof. Premultiplying and postmultiplying the differential Equation (4) by the factors $e^{-(t-\tau)A_c(\tau)}$ and $e^{-(t-\tau)D_c(\tau)}$ respectively, and integrating with respect to τ from 0 to t, we obtain the equivalent integral form of the initial value problem (4) [2]:

$$\begin{aligned}\Delta X(t) \;=\; & e^{-tA_c(t)}\Delta X_0 e^{-tD_c(t)} \\ & + \int_0^t e^{-(t-\tau)A_c(\tau)}\mathcal{M}(\tau,\Delta X(\tau))e^{-(t-\tau)D_c(\tau)}\delta\tau.\end{aligned} \tag{14}$$

According to its definition, $\Phi_P(t,t_0)$ satisfies

$$\dot\Phi_P(t) = \Phi_P(t)P(t),\; \Phi_P(t,t) = \Phi(t-t) = \Phi(0) = I, \text{ for } t \in T. \tag{15}$$

Equation (14) can be stated as

$$\Delta X(t) = \Pi(\Delta X)(t), \tag{16}$$

where the operator Π is defined as

$$\Pi(\Delta X)(t) \;:=\; \Phi_{A_c}(0,t)\Delta X_0 \Phi_{D_c}(0,t) \;+\int_0^t \Phi_{A_c}(\tau,t)\mathcal{M}(\tau,\Delta X(\tau))\Phi_{D_c}(\tau,t)d\tau.$$

The spectral norm of the operator $\Pi(P)(t)$ in terms of (7), (9)–(11) is

$$\|\Pi(P)(t) \le \beta\delta_{X_0} + \nu\|\mathcal{M}(t,P)\|, \tag{17}$$

and the second order polynomial

$$h(\|\Delta X(t)\|,\delta) := a_0(\delta)\|\Delta X(t)\|^2 + a_1(\delta)\|\Delta X(t)\| + a_2(\delta), \tag{18}$$

with $a_i(\delta), i = 0,1,2,$ defined in (9) via (10), (11) is a Lyapunov majorant for the operator $\Pi(.)$ such that

$$\|\Pi(\Delta X)(t)\| \le h(\|\Delta X(t)\|,\delta). \tag{19}$$

In a similar way, for two arbitrary matrices $V(t), W(t) \in \mathbb{R}^{n\times p}$ with $\|V(t)\|, \|W(t)\| \le \|\Delta X(t)\|$, we get

$$\begin{aligned} \|\Pi(V)(t) - \Pi(W)(t)\| &\le \frac{\partial h(\theta,\delta)}{\partial\theta}\|V(t) - W(t)\| \\ &= (a_1(\delta) + 2a_0(\delta)\theta)\|V(t) - W(t)\|, \end{aligned} \tag{20}$$

where $\theta := \max\{\|V(t)\|, \|W(t)\|\}$. If inequalities (17) and (20) hold and for any positive number ρ such as

$$h(\rho,\delta) \le \rho, \quad h'(\rho,\delta) = \frac{\partial h(\rho,\delta)}{\partial\rho} < 1, \tag{21}$$

then the operator $\Pi(.)$ is a contraction on the ball $M_\rho := \{\|V(t)\| \in \mathbb{R}^{n\times p} : \|V(t)\| \le \rho\}$. According to the fixed-point principle[14], the operator Equation (16) admits a solution $\Delta X(t) \in M_\rho$ such that for

$$\delta \in \Omega_t := \left\{\delta \in \mathbb{R}^5_+,\; a_1(\delta) + 2\sqrt{a_0(\delta)a_2(\delta)} \le 1\right\} \in \mathbb{R}^5_+,$$

we have

$$\|\Delta X(t)\| \le \frac{2a_2(\delta)}{1 - a_1(\delta) + \sqrt{(1-a_1(\delta))^2 - 4a_0(\delta)a_2(\delta)}},$$

which concludes the proof. □

The perturbation bound formulated in Theorem 1 is a nonlocal sensitivity bound. The inclusion (12), (8) guarantees that there exists a solution $X(t) + \Delta X(t)$ of the perturbed Equation (3) for which the bound (13) holds.

Let $\alpha = \max\{\delta_A, \delta_D, \delta_Q, \delta_S, \delta_{X_0}\}$. Then (9) and (8) yield

$$a_0(\alpha) \;=\; \nu(\|S\| + \alpha),\; a_1(\alpha) = 2\alpha\nu\sigma,\; a_2(\alpha) = \alpha(\nu\sigma^2 + \beta),$$

and

$$\Omega_t \;=\; \left\{\alpha < \left(-\kappa + \sqrt{\kappa^2 + \beta/\nu}\right)/2\beta\right\},$$

with $\sigma := 1 + \|X(t)\|$ and $\kappa := \sigma + \|S\|(\beta + \nu\sigma^2)$. The estimate (13) becomes

$$\|\Delta X(t)\| \leq \frac{1 - 2\alpha\nu\sigma - \sqrt{1 - 4\alpha\nu(\kappa + \alpha\beta)}}{2\nu(\|S\| + \alpha)}.$$

The assumption for $\mathcal{H}$ to be a nonsingular M-matrix implies that the closed loop-matrices $A_c(t) = A - X(t)S$ and $D_c(t) = D - SX(t)$ are nonsingular M-matrices too [15]. This allows us, to facilitate the computation of the terms ν and β, to derive computable bounds for the spectral norm of the fundamental matrices $\Phi_{A_c}(0,t)$ and $\Phi_{D_c}(0,t)$

$$\begin{aligned} \|\Phi_{A_c}(0,t)\| &\leq e^{-\int_0^t \lambda(\tau)d\tau}; \\ \|\Phi_{D_c}(0,t)\| &\leq e^{-\int_0^t \xi(\tau)d\tau}, \end{aligned} \tag{22}$$

based on the logarithmic norms

$$\lambda(t) \;=\; 0,5\,\lambda_{\max}(\left[A_c(t) + A_c(t)^\top\right]);\; \xi(t) = 0,5\,\xi_{\max}(\left[D_c(t) + D_c(t)^\top\right])$$

of the closed-loop matrices $A_c(t) = A - X(t)S$ and $D_c(t) = D - SX(t)$, respectively.

3. Sensitivity of Low-Dimensional Approximate Solutions to Large-Scale NDRE

For large NDRE with low-rank matrix Q, decomposed as $Q = FG^\top$ with $F \in \mathbb{R}^{n\times s}$, $G \in \mathbb{R}^{p\times s}$ and $s << n$, we proposed in [7] to project the problem (1) onto extended Krylov subspace $\mathbb{K}_m(A,F)$ and $\mathbb{K}_m(D,G)$ applying the Extended block Arnoldi algorithm and to obtain the approximate solution

$$X_m(t) = \mathcal{V}_m Y_m(t) \mathcal{W}_m^\top \in \mathbb{R}^{n\times p}, \tag{23}$$

where Y_m solves the projected low-dimensional NDRE

$$\begin{aligned} \dot{Y}_m(t) &= -\mathcal{T}_m^A Y_m(t) - Y_m(t)\mathcal{T}_m^D + Y_m(t) S_m Y_m(t) + F_m G_m^\top, \\ Y_m(0) &= Y_0 = \mathcal{V}_m^\top X_0 \mathcal{W}_m \in \mathbb{R}^{2ms\times 2ms}, \end{aligned} \tag{24}$$

instead of the exact solution to (1). Here $S_m = \mathcal{W}_m^\top S \mathcal{V}_m \in \mathbb{R}^{2ms\times 2ms}$, $F_m = \mathcal{V}_m^\top F \in \mathbb{R}^{2ms\times s}$, $G_m = \mathcal{W}_m^\top G \in \mathbb{R}^{2ms\times s}$ and the block Hessenberg matrices $\mathcal{T}_m^A = \mathcal{V}_m^\top A \mathcal{V}_m^\top \in \mathbb{R}^{2ms\times 2ms}$ and $\mathcal{T}_m^D = \mathcal{W}_m^\top D \mathcal{W}_m \in \mathbb{R}^{2ms\times 2ms}$ are obtained after transformation by the orthonormal matrices $\mathcal{V}_m = \left[\begin{array}{ccc} V_1, & \ldots, & V_m \end{array}\right] \in \mathbb{R}^{n\times 2ms}$ and $\mathcal{W}_m = \left[\begin{array}{ccc} W_1, & \ldots, & W_m \end{array}\right] \in \mathbb{R}^{p\times 2ms}$ composed of the orthonormal bases $\{V_1,\ldots,V_m\}$, $(V_i \in \mathbb{R}^{n\times 2s}, i = 1,\ldots.m)$ and $\{W_1,\ldots,W_m\}$, $(W_i \in \mathbb{R}^{p\times 2s}, i = 1,\ldots.m)$. The orthonormal bases are generated after applying the Extended block Arnoldi algorithm to the pairs (A,F) and (D,G); see [7] for more details.

The classical theory of Radon (see, e.g., [5]) states that any solution $Y_m(t)$ of the low-dimensional NDRE (24) is locally equivalent to a solution of the initial value problem

$$\dot{\Psi}(t) \;=\; \mathcal{H}_m(t)\Psi(t), \;\; \Psi(0) := \left[\begin{array}{c} I \\ Y_0 \end{array}\right] \in \mathbb{R}^{4ms\times 2ms}, \tag{25}$$

where $\mathcal{H}_m = \mathcal{U}_m^\top \mathcal{H} \mathcal{U}_m := \left[\begin{array}{cc} \mathcal{T}_m^D & -S_m \\ F_m G_m^\top & -\mathcal{T}_m^A \end{array}\right] \in \mathbb{R}^{4ms\times 4ms}$, with $\mathcal{H} := \left[\begin{array}{cc} D & -S \\ FG^\top & -A \end{array}\right]$ and $\mathcal{U}_m := \left[\begin{array}{cc} \mathcal{W}_m & 0 \\ 0 & \mathcal{V}_m \end{array}\right], \mathcal{U}_m^\top \mathcal{U}_m = I.$

The solution of (25) is

$$\begin{aligned} \Psi(t) &:= \left[\begin{array}{c} Y_{1,m}(t) \\ Y_{2,m}(t) \end{array}\right] = e^{t\mathcal{H}_m}\Psi(0) := \left[\begin{array}{cc} \Psi_{11}(t) & \Psi_{12}(t), \\ \Psi_{21}(t) & \Psi_{22}(t) \end{array}\right]\Psi(0), \\ &= \left[\begin{array}{c} \Psi_{11}(t) + \Psi_{12}(t)Y_0 \\ \Psi_{21}(t) + \Psi_{22}(t)Y_0 \end{array}\right]. \end{aligned} \tag{26}$$

If the matrix $Y_{1,m}(t)$ is nonsingular, the solution $Y_m(t)$ of the projected low-order nonsymmetric differential Riccati Equation (24) is represented as [16]

$$Y_m(t) = Y_{2,m}(t)Y_{1,m}^{-1}(t) = (\Psi_{21}(t) + \Psi_{22}(t)Y_0)(\Psi_{11}(t) + \Psi_{12}(t)Y_0)^{-1}. \quad (27)$$

To estimate the sensitivity of the problem (24), we consider the strategies proposed in [13]. We represent the calculated perturbed solution to (24) with collection of data coefficients $\mathcal{Z}_m = (\mathcal{T}_m^A,\ \mathcal{T}_m^D, S_m, F_m, G_m, Y_0)$ as the exact solution to a slightly perturbed problem with collection of data coefficients $\mathcal{Z}_m + \Delta\mathcal{Z}_m$. The data perturbation $\Delta Z_m \in \Delta\mathcal{Z}_m$ $:= (\Delta\mathcal{T}_m^A,\ \Delta\mathcal{T}_m^D, \Delta S_m, \Delta F_m, \Delta G_m, \Delta Y_0)$ with $\|\Delta Z\| \leq \delta_Z$, $\delta_Z \approx \mathtt{macheps}\,\phi(n)\|Z\|$, reflects the effect of round-off errors and approximation errors in the computed solution to (24).

The perturbed projected low-dimensional NDRE is

$$\begin{aligned}
(Y_m(t) + \Delta Y_m(t))' &= -(\mathcal{T}_m^A + \Delta\mathcal{T}_m^A)(Y_m(t) + \Delta Y_m(t)) \\
&\quad -(Y_m(t) + \Delta Y_m(t))(\mathcal{T}_m^D + \Delta\mathcal{T}_m^D) \\
&\quad +(Y_m(t) + \Delta Y_m(t))(S_m + \Delta S_m)(Y_m(t) + \Delta Y_m(t)) \\
&\quad +(F_m + \Delta F_m)(G_m + \Delta G_m)^\top, \\
Y_m(0) + \Delta Y_m(0) &= Y_0 + \Delta Y_0.
\end{aligned} \quad (28)$$

The equivalent to (28) initial value problem is

$$\begin{aligned}
(\Psi(t) + \Delta\Psi(t))' &:= (\mathcal{H}_m(t) + \Delta\mathcal{H}_m(t))(\Psi(t) + \Delta\Psi(t)), \\
\Psi(0) + \Delta\Psi(0) &:= \begin{bmatrix} Y_{1,m}(0) \\ Y_{2,m}(0) \end{bmatrix} + \begin{bmatrix} \Delta Y_{1,m}(0) \\ \Delta Y_{2,m}(0) \end{bmatrix},
\end{aligned} \quad (29)$$

where

$$\begin{aligned}
\Delta\mathcal{H}_m &:= \begin{bmatrix} \Delta\mathcal{T}_m^D & -\Delta S_m \\ \Delta F_m G_m^\top + F_m \Delta G_m^\top + \Delta F_m \Delta G_m^\top & -\Delta\mathcal{T}_m^A \end{bmatrix} \\
\text{and}\Delta\Psi(t) &= \begin{bmatrix} \Delta Y_{1,m}(t) \\ \Delta Y_{2,m}(t) \end{bmatrix} := \begin{bmatrix} \Delta\Psi_{11}(t) & \Delta\Psi_{12}(t) \\ \Delta\Psi_{21}(t) & \Delta\Psi_{22}(t) \end{bmatrix}.
\end{aligned}$$

The perturbations $\Delta\Psi_{11}(t)$, $\Delta\Psi_{12}(t)$, $\Delta\Psi_{21}(t)$, $\Delta\Psi_{22}(t)$ are analytical functions of the data perturbations $\Delta Z_m \in \Delta\mathcal{Z}_m$ and reflect the errors in the solution $\Psi(t) + \Delta\Psi(t)$ to the perturbed linear differential system

$$\begin{aligned}
\Psi(t) + \Delta\Psi(t) &= e^{t(\mathcal{H}_m + \Delta\mathcal{H}_m)}(\Psi(0) + \Delta\Psi(0)), \\
&= \begin{bmatrix} Y_{1,m}(t) \\ Y_{2,m}(t) \end{bmatrix} + \begin{bmatrix} \Delta Y_{1,m}(t) \\ \Delta Y_{2,m}(t) \end{bmatrix}, \\
&:= \begin{bmatrix} \Psi_{11}(t) + \Delta\Psi_{11}(t) & \Psi_{12}(t) + \Delta\Psi_{12}(t), \\ \Psi_{21}(t) + \Delta\Psi_{21}(t) & \Psi_{22}(t) + \Delta\Psi_{22}(t) \end{bmatrix}(\Psi(0) + \Delta\Psi(0)).
\end{aligned} \quad (30)$$

According to (26) and (30), the perturbation $\Delta\Psi(t)$ is

$$\begin{aligned}
\Delta\Psi(t) &= e^{t(\mathcal{H}_m + \Delta\mathcal{H}_m)}(\Psi(0) + \Delta\Psi(0)) - e^{t\mathcal{H}_m}\Psi(0) \\
&= \begin{bmatrix} \Delta Y_{1,m}(t) \\ \Delta Y_{2,m}(t) \end{bmatrix} = \begin{bmatrix} \Delta\Psi_{11}(t) + \Delta\Psi_{12}(t)Y_0 + (\Psi_{12}(t) + \Delta\Psi_{12}(t))\Delta Y_0, \\ \Delta\Psi_{21}(t) + \Delta\Psi_{21}(t)Y_0 + (\Psi_{22}(t) + \Delta\Psi_{22}(t))\Delta Y_0 \end{bmatrix}.
\end{aligned} \quad (31)$$

If the matrix

$$Y_{1,m}(t) + \Delta Y_{1,m}(t) := \Psi_{11}(t) + \Delta\Psi_{11}(t) + (\Psi_{12}(t) + \Delta\Psi_{12}(t))(Y_0 + \Delta Y_0)$$

is invertible, then the solution

$$Y_m(t) + \Delta Y_m(t) = (Y_{2,m}(t) + \Delta Y_{2,m}(t))(Y_{1,m}(t) + \Delta Y_{1,m}(t))^{-1}, \quad (32)$$

with $\Delta Y_{1,m}(t)$ and $\Delta Y_{2,m}(t)$ given in (31) to the perturbed projected low-dimensional Equation (28) exists.

The perturbation bound of the solution $Y_m(t)$ to the NDRE (24) consists of finding an interval $T : [0, t^*)$ such that for each $t \in T$, the matrix $Y_{1,m}(t) + \Delta Y_{1,m}(t)$ is invertible and then the perturbed solution $Y_m(t) + \Delta Y_m(t)$ given by (32) exists, as well as to derive a normwise bound in terms of spectral norm for the error $\Delta Y_m(t)$ in the solution $Y_m(t) + \Delta Y_m(t)$ (32) as a function of the equivalent perturbations ΔZ_m in the data coefficients Z_m.

We formulate the following perturbation bound of the solution to the projected low-dimensional NDRE (24).

Theorem 2. *Let us denote*

$$\begin{aligned} \omega_1(t,\delta_m) &:= \|\Psi_{12}(t)\|\delta_{Y_0} + \sqrt{\operatorname{rank}(\Delta\Psi(t))}(1+\|Y_0\|+\delta_{Y_0})\|\Delta\Psi(t)\|, \\ \omega_2(t,\delta_m) &:= \sqrt{\operatorname{rank}(\Delta\Psi(t))}(1+\|Y_0\|+\delta_{Y_0})\|\Delta\Psi(t)\| + \|\Psi_{22}(t)\|\delta_{Y_0}, \end{aligned} \tag{33}$$

for Y_0, $\Psi_{1,i}(t)$, $i = 1,2$, $\Psi_{22}(t)$ and $\Delta\Psi(t)$ as defined in (25), (26) and (29) respectively.

For $t \in [0,\ t^*)$, where

$$t^* = \sup\Big\{t \in T : \omega_1(t,\delta_m)\|Y_{1,m}(t)^{-1}\| < 1\Big\}, \tag{34}$$

$Y_{1,m}(t)$ as stated in (26) and $\delta_m := \left[\begin{array}{cccccc} \delta_{T_m^A} & \delta_{T_m^D} & \delta_{F_m} & \delta_{G_m} & \delta_{S_m} & \delta_{Y_0} \end{array}\right]^\top$, the spectral norm of the perturbation $\Delta Y_m(t)$ in the calculated solution $Y_m(t)$ to (24) satisfies the inequality

$$\|\Delta Y_m(t)\| \le f_m(t,\delta_m) := \frac{(\omega_2(t,\delta_m) + \omega_1(t,\delta_m)\|Y_m(t)\|)\|Y_{1,m}^{-1}(t)\|}{1-\omega_1(t,\delta_m)\|Y_{1,m}^{-1}(t)\|}. \tag{35}$$

Proof. The initial value of problem (25) is $\Psi(0) = \begin{bmatrix} I \\ Y_0 \end{bmatrix}$. Then, according to (26) $\Psi_{11}(0) = I_n$, $\Psi_{12}(0) = 0$. The matrix $Y_{1,m}(0) = \Psi_{11}(0) + \Psi_{12}(0)Y_0 = I_n$ is invertible and its inverse is $Y_{1,m}(0)^{-1} = (\Psi_{11}(0) + \Psi_{12}(0)Y_0)^{-1} = I_n$. Denote by $\sigma_1(t) \ge \sigma_2(t) \ge \cdots \ge \sigma_n(t) \ge 0$ the singular values of the matrix $\Psi_{11}(t)$. Then the interval $T = [0,\ t^*)$ can be chosen from

$$t^* \ := \ \sup\{t : \|\Delta Y_{1,m}(t)\| + \|\Psi_{12}(t)\|\|Y_0\| < \sigma_n(t)\}. \tag{36}$$

From (32) and taking into account (27), the perturbation $\Delta Y_m(t)$ in the solution to the projected low-dimensional NDRE satisfies

$$\begin{aligned} \Delta Y_m(t) &= (Y_{2,m} + \Delta Y_{2,m}(t))(Y_{1,m}(t) + \Delta Y_{1,m}(t))^{-1} - Y_{2,m}(t)Y_{1,m}^{-1}(t) \\ &= (\Delta Y_{2,m}(t) - Y_m(t)\Delta Y_{1,m}(t))(Y_{1,m}(t) + \Delta Y_{1,m}(t))^{-1}. \end{aligned} \tag{37}$$

Applying the property $\left\|(I_n + X^{-1}Y)^{-1}\right\| \le \frac{1}{1-\|X^{-1}\|\|Y\|}$, which is valid for any matrices $X, Y \in \mathbb{R}^{n\times n}$, with existing inverse X^{-1} and $\|X^{-1}\|\|Y\| \le 1$ [17], from (37), we obtain

$$\begin{aligned} \|\Delta Y_m(t)\| \ &\le \ (\|\Delta Y_{2,m}(t)\| + \|Y_m(t)\|\|\Delta Y_{1,m}(t)\|) \times \\ &\quad \times \frac{\|Y_{1,m}^{-1}(t)\|}{1-\|Y_{1,m}^{-1}(t)\|\|\Delta Y_{1,m}(t)\|} \end{aligned} \tag{38}$$

provided that

$$\|Y_{1,m}^{-1}(t)\|\|\Delta Y_{1,m}(t)\| < 1.$$

Using the fact that for any matrix $M = [M_{ij}] \in \mathbb{R}^{2ms\times 2ms}$, we have

$$\|M_{ij}\|_F < \|M\|_F < \sqrt{\text{rank}(M)}\|M\|_2,$$

the norms of the perturbations $\Delta Y_{1,m}(t)$ and $\Delta Y_{2,m}(t)$ can be estimated by

$$\begin{aligned}\|\Delta Y_{1,m}(t)\| &\le \|\Delta\Psi_{11}(t)\|_F + \|\Psi_{12}(t)\|\delta_{Y_0} + \|\Delta\Psi_{12}(t)\|_F(\|Y_0\| + \delta_{Y_0} \\ &\le \|\|\Psi_{12}(t)\|\delta_{Y_0} + (1 + \|Y_0\| + \delta_{Y_0})\|\Delta\Psi(t)\|_F \\ &\le \|\Psi_{12}(t)\|\delta_{Y_0} + \sqrt{\text{rank}(\Delta\Psi(t))}(1 + \|Y_0\| + \delta_{Y_0})\|\Delta\Psi(t)\| \\ &\le \omega_1(t,\delta_m),\end{aligned} \tag{39}$$

and

$$\begin{aligned}\|\Delta Y_{2,m}(t)\| &\le \sqrt{\text{rank}(\Delta\Psi(t))}(1 + \|Y_0\| + \delta_{Y_0})\|\Delta\Psi(t)\| + \|\Psi_{22}(t)\|\delta_{Y_0} \\ &\le \omega_2(t,\delta_m).\end{aligned} \tag{40}$$

Replacing $\|\Delta Y_{1,m}(t)\|$ and $\|\Delta Y_{2,m}(t)\|$ in (38) by $\omega_1(t,\delta_m)$ and $\omega_2(t,\delta_m)$ from (39), (40), we prove the non-local bound $\|\Delta Y_m(t)\| \le f_m(t,\delta_m)$ as stated in (35).

Finally, the expression $\|\Delta Y_{1,m}(t)\| + \|\Psi_{12}(t)\|\|Y_0\| < \sigma_n(t)$ from (36) in view of (39), becomes $\omega_1(t,\delta_m) < \|Y_{1,m}(t)\|$. Then, since $Y_{1,m}(0) = I_n$ and $\omega_1(t,0) = 0$, the interval

$$t^* = \sup\left\{t \in T : \omega_1(t,\delta_m)\|Y_{1,m}(t)^{-1}\| < 1\right\}$$

from (34) is correctly defined, which achieves the proof. □

In order to represent the norm $\|\Delta\Psi(t)\|$ of the perturbation $\Delta\Psi(t)$ in terms of ω_1 and ω_2 by the norms of the perturbations in the data matrices $\mathcal{T}_m^A, \mathcal{T}_m^D, F_m, G_m, S_m$ and Y_0, we consider the perturbed differential Equation (29). We have

$$\Delta\Psi(t) = \int_0^t e^{\mathcal{H}_m(t-\tau)}\Delta\mathcal{H}_m e^{(\mathcal{H}_m+\Delta\mathcal{H}_m)\tau}d\tau.$$

Then, taking the spectral norm, we have

$$\begin{aligned}\|\Delta\Psi(t)\| &\le \delta_{\mathcal{H}_m}\int_0^t \|e^{\mathcal{H}_m(t-\tau)}\|\|e^{(\mathcal{H}_m+\Delta\mathcal{H}_m)\tau}\|d\tau \\ &\le \delta_{\mathcal{H}_m}\int_0^t g(t-\tau)(\|\Delta\Psi(\tau)\| + g(\tau))d\tau,\end{aligned}$$

where $\delta_{\mathcal{H}_m} := \|\Delta\mathcal{H}_m\| < \delta_m$ and $g(t)$ is an upper bound for $\|e^{\mathcal{H}_m(t)}\|$, i.e., $\|e^{\mathcal{H}_m(t)}\| \le g(t)$. Some bounds for the matrix exponential $e^{\mathcal{H}_m(t)}$ based on Jordan and Schur matrix decompositions, logarithmic norm and power series are summarized in [18]:

$$g(t) = c_0 e^{\varrho t}\sum_{k=0}^{p-1}(\varpi t)^k/k!, \tag{41}$$

with constants c_0, ϱ, ϖ and p, listed in Table 1.

Here $\mu(\mathcal{H}_m(t)) = \lambda_{\max}(\mathcal{H}_m(t) + \mathcal{H}_m(t)^\top)/2)$; $\varsigma \geq 1$ is the dimension of the maximum block in the Jordan canonical form $J = Y^{-1}\mathcal{H}_m(t)Y$ of $\mathcal{H}_m(t)$, where the matrix Y is chosen so as the condition number $\mathrm{cond}(Y) = \|Y\|\|Y^{-1}\|$ to be minimized; $d_\varsigma = \cos\left(\frac{\pi}{\varsigma+1}\right)$; $\alpha(\mathcal{H}_m(t))$ is the spectral abscissa of $\mathcal{H}_m(t)$, i.e., the maximum real part of the eigenvalues of $\mathcal{H}_m(t)$; $T = U^H\mathcal{H}_m(t)U = \Lambda + \mathcal{N}$ is the Schur decomposition of $\mathcal{H}_m(t)$ with unitary matrix U, chosen so as $\varpi = \|\mathcal{N}\|$ to be minimized, diagonal matrix Λ and $\mathcal{N}$ - strictly upper triangular matrix with index of nilpotency $l = \min\{s : \mathcal{N}^s = 0\}$.

Table 1. Values of the constants in the matrix exponential bounds.

	Jordan (1)	Jordan (2)	Schur	Log Norm	Power Series
c_0	$\mathrm{cond}(Y)$	$\mathrm{cond}(Y)$	1	1	1
ϱ	$\alpha(\mathcal{H}_m(t))$	$\alpha(\mathcal{H}_m(t)) + d_\varsigma$	$\alpha(\mathcal{H}_m(t))$	$\mu(\mathcal{H}_m(t))$	$\|\mathcal{H}_m(t)\|$
ϖ	1	0	ϖ	0	0
p	m	-	l	-	-

The results stated in Theorem 2 can be used to formulate a perturbation bound for the solution $X(t)$ to the large-scale NDRE (1).

Theorem 3. *Let a large-scale NDRE (1) for which the constant matrix coefficient Q is low-rank and can decomposed as $Q = FG^\top$ with $F \in \mathbb{R}^{n\times s}$, $G \in \mathbb{R}^{p\times s}$, ($s << n$) be projected onto a pair of extended Krylov subspaces $\mathbb{K}_m(A, F)$ and $\mathbb{K}_m(D, G)$. Let $X_m(t) = \mathcal{V}_m Y_m(t)\mathcal{W}_m^\top \in \mathbb{R}^{n\times p}$ be its approximate solution as stated in (23), obtained by applying the Extended block Arnoldi algorithm to the projected low-dimensional NDRE*

$$\begin{aligned} \dot{Y}_m(t) &= -\mathcal{T}_m^A Y_m(t) - Y_m(t)\mathcal{T}_m^D + Y_m(t)S_m Y_m(t) + F_m G_m^\top, \\ Y_m(0) &= Y_0 = \mathcal{V}_m^\top X_0 \mathcal{W}_m \in \mathbb{R}^{2ms\times 2ms}. \end{aligned}$$

with solution $Y_m(t)$ and perturbation bound $\|\Delta Y_m(t)\| \leq f_m(t, \delta_m)$ (35) as defined in Theorem 2. A perturbation bound in terms of spectral norm for the approximate solution $X(t)$ to (1) is given by

$$\|\Delta X(t)\| \leq f_m(t, \delta_m) := \frac{(\omega_2(t, \delta_m) + \omega_1(t, \delta_m)\|Y_m(t)\|)\|Y_{1,m}^{-1}(t)\|}{1 - \omega_1(t, \delta_m)\|Y_{1,m}^{-1}(t)\|}, \tag{42}$$

for $t \in [0,\ t^*)$, with t^* as defined in (34) and $Y_{1,m}(t)$ stated in (26), $\omega_1(t, \delta_m)$, $\omega(t, \delta_m)$ stated in (33), $\delta_m := \left[\begin{array}{cccccc} \delta_{\mathcal{T}_m^A} & \delta_{\mathcal{T}_m^D} & \delta_{F_m} & \delta_{G_m} & \delta_{S_m} & \delta_{Y_0} \end{array}\right]^\top.$

Proof. The proof follows directly from the definition (23) of the approximate solution $Y_m(t)$ and the preservation of the spectral norm by unitary matrices. □

Next, we apply the preceding results to estimate the approximation error $\mathcal{E}_m = X(t) - X_m(t)$ of the approximate solution $X_m(t)$ to the projected low-dimensional NDRE versus the exact solution to (1) from Theorem (4), which was already established by the authors in [19].

Theorem 4. *[Theorem 4. form [19]] Let X_m be the approximate solution given by (23). Then we have*

$$\begin{aligned} \dot{X}_m(t) &= -(A - \Delta_m^A)\, X_m(t) - X_m(t)\,(D - \Delta_m^D) + X_m(t)S\, X_m(t) + FG^T, \\ R_m(t) &= \Delta_m^A X_m(t) + X_m(t)\Delta_m^D, \text{ and} \\ \dot{\mathcal{E}}_m(t) &= -(A - X_m(t)S)\mathcal{E}_m(t) - \mathcal{E}_m(t)(D - SX_m(t)) + \mathcal{E}_m(t)S\mathcal{E}_m(t) \\ &\quad -\Delta_m^A X_m(t) - X_m(t)\Delta_m^D. \end{aligned}$$

where $\Delta_m^A = V_{m+1}T_{m+1,m}^A V_m^T$, $\Delta_m^D = W_m T_{m+1,m}^D W_m^T$, $\mathcal{E}_m(t) = X(t) - X_m(t)$ *and* $X(t)$ *is an exact solution* $X(t)$ *of* (1).

Let us rewrite the NDRE associated with the error $\mathcal{E}_m(t)$

$$\begin{aligned} \dot{\mathcal{E}}_m(t) &= -(A - X_m(t)S)\mathcal{E}_m(t) - \mathcal{E}_m(t)(D - SX_m(t)) + \mathcal{E}_m(t)S\mathcal{E}_m(t) \\ &\quad -\Delta_m^A X_m(t) - X_m(t)\Delta_m^D \end{aligned} \tag{43}$$

in the equivalent form

$$\dot{\mathcal{E}}_m(t) = -A_{c,m}(t)\mathcal{E}_m(t) - \mathcal{E}_m(t)D_{c,m}(t) + \mathcal{M}_m(t, \mathcal{E}_m(t)), \tag{44}$$

where $A_{c,m}(t) = A - X_m(t)S$, $D_{c,m}(t) = D - SX_m(t)$, $\mathcal{M}(t, \mathcal{E}_m) := \mathcal{M}_{1,m}(t, \mathcal{E}_m) + \mathcal{M}_{2,m}(t, \mathcal{E}_m)$ with

$$\mathcal{M}_{1,m}(t, \mathcal{E}_m(t)) := -\Delta_m^A \mathcal{E}_m(t) - \mathcal{E}_m(t)\Delta_m^D; \quad \mathcal{M}_{2,m}(t, \mathcal{E}_m(t)) := \mathcal{E}_m(t)S\mathcal{E}_m(t). \tag{45}$$

Here $\Delta_m^A = V_{m+1}T_{m+1,n}^A V_,^\top$, $\Delta_m^D = W_m T_{m+1,n}^D W_{m+1}^\top$. As the unitary matrices V_m and W_m have unit spectral norm, we have $\|\Delta_m^A\| = \|T_{m+1,n}^A\|$ and $\|\Delta_m^D\| = \|T_{m+1,n}^D\|$. We notice that the fact that the term $T_{m+1,n}$ tends normwisely to 0 as m increases implies that the spectral norm of Δ_m^A, Δ_m^D decreases towards 0. This allows us to consider Δ_m^A, Δ_m^D as equivalent data perturbations, and Equation (43) as an equation of the perturbation in the solution. Equation (43) is equivalent to the NDRE (4) of the perturbation $\Delta X(t)$ in the perturbed NDRE (2). This allows us to apply the technique of the nonlocal perturbation analysis of the NDRE, based on the integral solution to the NDRE and the statements of Theorem 1 to formulate a bound for the error $\mathcal{E}_m(t)$.

Theorem 5. *For* Δ_m^D, Δ_m^D, *satisfying* $\delta := [\ \|\Delta_m^A\| \quad \|\Delta_m^D\|\ ]^\top \in \Omega_{t,m} := \{a_0(\delta)a_2(\delta) \le 0.25\}$, *the spectral norm of the error* $\mathcal{E}_m(t)$, *solution to the NDRE* (43), *is bounded by*

$$\|\mathcal{E}_m(t)\| \le f(\delta, t) = \frac{2a_2(\delta)}{1 + \sqrt{1 - 4a_0(\delta)a_2(\delta)}}, \tag{46}$$

where

$$a_0(\delta) = \nu\|S\|; \quad a_2 = \nu\|X_m(t)\|\left(\|\Delta_m^A\| + \|\Delta_m^D\|\right) + \beta\|\mathcal{E}_m(0)\|,$$

for $\nu = \max\left\{\int_0^t \|\Phi_{A_{c,m}}(\tau, t)\|\|\Phi_{D_{c,m}}(\tau, t)\|\,d\tau, t \in T\right\}$, $\beta = \max\{\|\Phi_{A_{c,m}}(0, t)\|\|\Phi_{D_{c,m}}(0, t)\|\}$ *and* $\Phi_Z(t, t_0) = e^{(t-t_0)Z}$ *being the fundamental matrix of equation* $\dot{\eta}(t) = Z\eta(t)$.

Proof. Comparing $\mathcal{M}_{1,m}(t, \mathcal{E}_m(t))$, $\mathcal{M}_{2,m}(t, \mathcal{E}_m(t))$ (45) to $\mathcal{M}_1(t, P)$, $\mathcal{M}_2(t, P)$ (6), for the coefficients $a_i(\delta)$ (9) we obtain

$$a_0(\delta) = \nu\|S\|; \quad a_1(\delta) = 0; \quad a_2(\delta) = \nu\|X_m(t)\|(\|\Delta_m^A\| + \|\Delta_m^D\|) + \beta\|\mathcal{E}_m(0)\|.$$

Replacing the coefficients $a_i(\delta)$, $i = 0, 1, 2$ in the inequality of the set $\Omega_{t,m}$ (8) and the bound $f(\delta, t)$ (13) we obtain

$$2\sqrt{a_0(\delta)a_2(\delta)} \le 1, \text{ or } a_1(\delta)a_2(\delta) \le 0.25.$$

Then the existence condition of the bound becomes

$$\delta := \left[\; \|\Delta_m^A\| \quad \|\Delta_m^D\| \; \right]^\top \in \Omega_{t,m} := \{a_0(\delta)a_2(\delta) \leq 0.25\},$$

and we obtain the bound

$$f(\delta, t) = \frac{2a_2(\delta)}{1 + \sqrt{1 - 4a_0(\delta)a_2(\delta)}}.$$

□

4. Numerical Examples

To illustrate the effectiveness of the bounds proposed in Theorems 1 and 2, we consider nonsymmetric differential matrix Riccati equations of type (1) on a time interval $T = [0, 1]$, for different matrix coefficients and for several sizes. The experimental tests are performed with Matlab R2020a on an Intel processor laptop equipped with 16GB of RAM. The reference solutions $X(t)$ to the NDRE (1) and $X(t) + \Delta X(t)$ to the perturbed NDRE (3) are computed by the backward differential formula - BDF1-Newton method, see [19] for more details.

Example 1. *Consider the NDRE (1), constructed according to the rules given in [15]. This scheme is used in [10] to analyze the effectiveness of mixed and componentwise condition numbers, and in [11], to illustrate the validity of a condition number and backward errors of nonsymmetric algebraic Riccati equation.*

The matrix coefficients of the NDRE (1) are:

$$\begin{aligned} A &= W(n+1:2n, n+1:2n) + \alpha I; \quad D = W(1:n, 1:n) + \alpha I, \\ S &= -W(1:n, n+1:2n); \quad Q = -W(n+1:2n, 1:n), \end{aligned}$$

where W is a singular M-matrix with nonzero elements: $W = \mathrm{diag}(Re) - R$, with $R - a2n \times 2n$ nonzero random matrix and $e = \left[\; 1, \; 1, \; \ldots, \; 1 \; \right]^\top \in \mathbb{R}^{2n}$. The time interval $T = \left[\; 0, \; 1 \; \right]$ is chosen. For $\alpha \geq 0$ the existence of a positive definite solution to (1) is guaranteed.

Experiment 1. *In [10], an equation of size $n = 3$ is considered and the perturbations are chosen as:*

$$\begin{aligned} \Delta A &= \begin{bmatrix} -0.3 & 0.2 & 0.1 \\ 0.1 & -0.2 & 0.3 \\ 0.1 & 0.1 & -0.3 \end{bmatrix} * 10^{-j}; \quad \Delta D = \begin{bmatrix} 0.1 & -0.2 & 0.3 \\ 0 & 0.1 & 0.2 \\ -0.2 & 0.3 & 0.1 \end{bmatrix} * 10^{-j} \\ \Delta S &= \begin{bmatrix} 0.2 & -0.1 & 0.3 \\ -0.1 & 0.2 & 0.3 \\ -0.1 & 0.1 & -0.3 \end{bmatrix} * 10^{-j}; \quad \Delta Q = \begin{bmatrix} -0.2 & -0.3 & 0.1 \\ 0.1 & -0.1 & 0.1 \\ -0.1 & 0.1 & 0.2 \end{bmatrix} * 10^{-j}, \\ &\text{for } j = 12, 11, 10, 9, 8, 7, \ldots, 2. \end{aligned}$$

The results, obtained for the estimated value - the relative perturbation $\rho_1(t) = \dfrac{\|\Delta X(t)\|}{\|X(t)\|}$ and the estimate—the relative bound $\rho_2(t) = \dfrac{f(t)}{\|X(t)\|}$, with $f(t) = f(\delta, t)$ given by (8)–(13) for $j = 12, 10, 8, 6, 4, 2$ and $\alpha = 0$ are listed in Table 2.

Table 2. Relative perturbation $\rho_1(t) = \dfrac{\|\Delta X(t)\|}{\|X(t)\|}$ and bound $\rho_2(t) = \dfrac{f(t)}{\|X(t)\|}$.

			$\alpha = 0$		
	$t = 0.2$	$t = 0.4$	$t = 0.6$	$t = 0.8$	$t = 1$
			$j = 12$		
$\rho_1(t)$	2.57×10^{-13}	2.46×10^{-13}	2.40×10^{-13}	2.37×10^{-13}	2.36×10^{-13}
$\rho_2(t)$	2.97×10^{-12}	1.75×10^{-12}	1.36×10^{-12}	1.16×10^{-12}	1.05×10^{-12}
			$j = 10$		
$\rho_1(t)$	2.58×10^{-11}	2.46×10^{-11}	2.40×10^{-11}	2.37×10^{-11}	2.36×10^{-11}
$\rho_2(t)$	2.97×10^{-10}	1.75×10^{-10}	1.36×10^{-10}	1.16×10^{-10}	1.05×10^{-10}
			$j = 8$		
$\rho_1(t)$	2.58×10^{-09}	2.46×10^{-09}	2.40×10^{-09}	2.37×10^{-09}	2.36×10^{-09}
$\rho_2(t)$	2.97×10^{-08}	1.75×10^{-08}	1.36×10^{-08}	1.16×10^{-08}	1.05×10^{-08}
			$j = 6$		
$\rho_1(t)$	2.58×10^{-07}	2.46×10^{-07}	2.40×10^{-07}	2.37×10^{-07}	2.36×10^{-07}
$\rho_2(t)$	2.97×10^{-06}	1.75×10^{-06}	1.36×10^{-06}	1.16×10^{-06}	1.05×10^{-06}
			$j = 4$		
$\rho_1(t)$	2.58×10^{-05}	2.46×10^{-05}	2.40×10^{-05}	2.37×10^{-05}	2.36×10^{-05}
$\rho_2(t)$	2.97×10^{-04}	1.75×10^{-04}	1.36×10^{-04}	1.16×10^{-04}	1.05×10^{-04}
			$j = 2$		
$\rho_1(t)$	2.58×10^{-03}	2.46×10^{-03}	2.40×10^{-03}	2.37×10^{-03}	2.36×10^{-03}
$\rho_2(t)$	3.01×10^{-02}	1.77×10^{-02}	1.38×10^{-02}	1.18×10^{-02}	1.06×10^{-02}

Example 1: Experiment 1, bound $f(t) = f(\delta, t)$, (8)–(13), Theorem 1, $\alpha = 0$, $j = 12, 10, 8, 6, 4, 2$, $t = 0.2$ to 1.

Table 3 reports on the obtained results for the bound (8)–(13) from Theorem (1) for the case $\alpha = 5$.

Table 3. Relative perturbation $\rho_1(t) = \dfrac{\|\Delta X(t)\|}{\|X(t)\|}$ and bound $\rho_2(t) = \dfrac{f(t)}{\|X(t)\|}$.

			$\alpha = 5$		
	$t = 0.2$	$t = 0.4$	$t = 0.6$	$t = 0.8$	$t = 1$
			$j = 12$		
$\rho_1(t)$	1.74×10^{-13}	1.60×10^{-13}	1.56×10^{-13}	1.58×10^{-13}	1.64×10^{-13}
$\rho_2(t)$	2.37×10^{-12}	1.48×10^{-12}	1.19×10^{-12}	1.05×10^{-12}	9.63×10^{-13}
			$j = 10$		
$\rho_1(t)$	1.72×10^{-11}	1.60×10^{-11}	1.56×10^{-11}	1.58×10^{-11}	1.63×10^{-11}
$\rho_2(t)$	2.37×10^{-10}	1.48×10^{-10}	1.19×10^{-10}	1.05×10^{-10}	9.63×10^{-11}
			$j = 8$		
$\rho_1(t)$	1.73×10^{-09}	1.60×10^{-09}	1.56×10^{-09}	1.58×10^{-09}	1.64×10^{-09}
$\rho_2(t)$	2.37×10^{-08}	1.48×10^{-08}	1.19×10^{-08}	1.05×10^{-08}	9.65×10^{-09}
			$j = 6$		
$\rho_1(t)$	1.73×10^{-07}	1.59×10^{-07}	1.56×10^{-07}	1.58×10^{-07}	1.64×10^{-07}
$\rho_2(t)$	2.37×10^{-06}	1.48×10^{-06}	1.19×10^{-06}	1.05×10^{-06}	9.63×10^{-07}
			$j = 4$		
$\rho_1(t)$	1.73×10^{-05}	1.59×10^{-05}	1.56×10^{-05}	$2.1.58 \times 10^{-05}$	1.63×10^{-05}
$\rho_2(t)$	2.37×10^{-04}	1.48×10^{-04}	1.19×10^{-04}	1.05×10^{-04}	9.63×10^{-05}
			$j = 2$		
$\rho_1(t)$	1.74×10^{-03}	1.59×10^{-03}	1.56×10^{-03}	1.58×10^{-03}	1.64×10^{-03}
$\rho_2(t)$	2.40×10^{-02}	1.50×10^{-02}	1.21×10^{-02}	1.06×10^{-02}	9.77×10^{-03}

Example 1: Experiment 1, bound $f(t) = f(\delta, t)$, (8)–(13), Theorem 1, $\alpha = 5$, $j = 12, 10, 8, 6, 4, 2$, $t = 0.2$ to 1.

As it is seen, the estimate based on the perturbation bound $f(\delta, t)$ *from (8)–(13) is quite sharp.*

The same experimental statement is used to test the accuracy of the estimate (34) and (35) from Theorem 2. The results obtained for $j = 12, 10, 8, 6, 4, 2$ are listed in Table 4 for $\alpha = 0$ and in Table 5 for $\alpha = 5$. Comparing the results for the bound (34) and (35) to these for the bound (8)–(13) given in Tables 2 and 3, it is seen that the two bounds are of the same size of the domain of validity. The bound (8)–(13) from Theorem 1 is superior to the bound (34) and (35) from Theorem 2 with respect of closeness to the estimated quantity. However, the bound (34) and (35) from Theorem 2 has the advantage that it is not related with the solution of the NDRE and hence with problems of divergence of the numerical procedure.

Table 4. Relative perturbation $\rho_1(t) = \frac{\|\Delta X(t)\|}{\|X(t)\|}$ and bound $\rho_2(t) = \frac{f(t)}{\|X(t)\|}$.

$\alpha = 0$					
	$t = 0.2$	$t = 0.4$	$t = 0.6$	$t = 0.8$	$t = 1$
$j = 12$					
$\rho_1(t)$	2.17×10^{-13}	2.11×10^{-13}	2.09×10^{-13}	2.11×10^{-13}	2.16×10^{-13}
$\rho_2(t)$	1.01×10^{-12}	1.82×10^{-12}	3.23×10^{-12}	5.63×10^{-12}	9.80×10^{-12}
$j = 10$					
$\rho_1(t)$	2.17×10^{-11}	2.11×10^{-11}	2.10×10^{-11}	2.12×10^{-11}	2.17×10^{-11}
$\rho_2(t)$	1.01×10^{-10}	1.82×10^{-10}	3.22×10^{-10}	5.63×10^{-10}	9.80×10^{-10}
$j = 8$					
$\rho_1(t)$	2.17×10^{-09}	2.11×10^{-09}	2.11×10^{-09}	2.12×10^{-09}	2.16×10^{-09}
$\rho_2(t)$	1.01×10^{-08}	1.82×10^{-08}	3.22×10^{-08}	5.63×10^{-08}	9.80×10^{-08}
$j = 6$					
$\rho_1(t)$	2.17×10^{-07}	2.11×10^{-07}	2.11×10^{-07}	2.12×10^{-07}	2.16×10^{-07}
$\rho_2(t)$	1.01×10^{-06}	1.82×10^{-06}	3.22×10^{-06}	5.63×10^{-06}	9.80×10^{-06}
$j = 4$					
$\rho_1(t)$	2.17–05	2.52×10^{-05}	2.42×10^{-05}	2.36×10^{-05}	2.31×10^{-05}
$\rho_2(t)$	1.01×10^{-04}	1.82×10^{-04}	3.22×10^{-04}	5.64×10^{-04}	9.80×10^{-04}
$j = 2$					
$\rho_1(t)$	2.68×10^{-03}	2.52×10^{-03}	2.43×10^{-03}	2.36×10^{-03}	2.32×10^{-03}
$\rho_2(t)$	1.01×10^{-02}	1.83×10^{-02}	3.26×10^{-02}	5.75×10^{-02}	1.02×10^{-01}

Example 1: Experiment 1, bound $f(t)= f_m(t, \delta_m)$ from (34) and (35),Theorem 2, $\alpha = 0$, $j = 12, 10, 8, 6, 4, 2$, $t = 0.2$ to 1.

Table 5. Relative perturbation $\rho_1(t) = \frac{\|\Delta X(t)\|}{\|X(t)\|}$ and bound $\rho_2(t) = \frac{f(t)}{\|X(t)\|}$.

$\alpha = 5$					
	$t = 0.2$	$t = 0.4$	$t = 0.6$	$t = 0.8$	$t = 1$
$j = 12$					
$\rho_1(t)$	2.68×10^{-13}	2.53×10^{-13}	2.43×10^{-13}	2.36×10^{-13}	2.31×10^{-13}
$\rho_2(t)$	1.21×10^{-12}	2.07×10^{-12}	3.49×10^{-12}	5.84×10^{-12}	9.76×10^{-12}
$j = 10$					
$\rho_1(t)$	2.68×10^{-11}	2.52×10^{-11}	2.42×10^{-11}	2.36×10^{-11}	2.31×10^{-11}
$\rho_2(t)$	1.21×10^{-10}	2.07×10^{-10}	3.49×10^{-10}	5.85×10^{-10}	9.74×10^{-10}
$j = 8$					
$\rho_1(t)$	2.68×10^{-09}	2.52×10^{-09}	2.42×10^{-09}	2.36×10^{-09}	2.31×10^{-09}
$\rho_2(t)$	1.21×10^{-08}	2.07×10^{-08}	3.49×10^{-08}	5.85×10^{-08}	9.74×10^{-08}
$j = 6$					
$\rho_1(t)$	2.68×10^{-07}	2.52×10^{-07}	2.43×10^{-07}	2.36×10^{-07}	2.31×10^{-07}
$\rho_2(t)$	1.21×10^{-06}	2.07×10^{-06}	3.49×10^{-06}	5.85×10^{-06}	9.74×10^{-06}
$j = 4$					
$\rho_1(t)$	2.68–05	2.52×10^{-05}	2.42×10^{-05}	2.36×10^{-05}	2.31×10^{-05}
$\rho_2(t)$	1.21×10^{-04}	2.07×10^{-04}	3.49×10^{-04}	5.85×10^{-04}	9.75×10^{-04}
$j = 2$					
$\rho_1(t)$	2.68×10^{-03}	2.52×10^{-03}	2.43×10^{-03}	2.36×10^{-03}	2.32×10^{-03}
$\rho_2(t)$	1.21×10^{-02}	2.08×10^{-02}	3.53×10^{-02}	5.96×10^{-02}	1.01×10^{-01}

Example 1: Experiment 1, bound $f(t)= f_m(t, \delta_m)$, (34) and (35), Theorem 2, $\alpha = 5$, $j = 12, 10, 8, 6, 4, 2$, $t = 0.2$ to 1.

Experiment 2. *The size n of the matrices* $A, D, S, Q \in \mathbb{R}^{n \times n}$ *varies from 5 to 50. The perturbations are randomly generated following the scheme* $\Delta Z = (rand(size(Z))/\|Z\|) * 10^{-j}$ *for* $Z = A, D, S, Q$ *and* $j = 12$. *The average values over 30 trials for the relative perturbation* $\rho_1(t) = \frac{\|\Delta X(t)\|}{\|X(t)\|}$ *and the bound* $\rho_2(t) = \frac{f(t)}{\|X(t)\|}$, $f(t) = f(\delta, t)$ *from (8)–(13), for* $t = 0.2, 0.4, 0.6$ *and* 0.8 *are displayed in Figure 1 for* $\alpha = 0$.

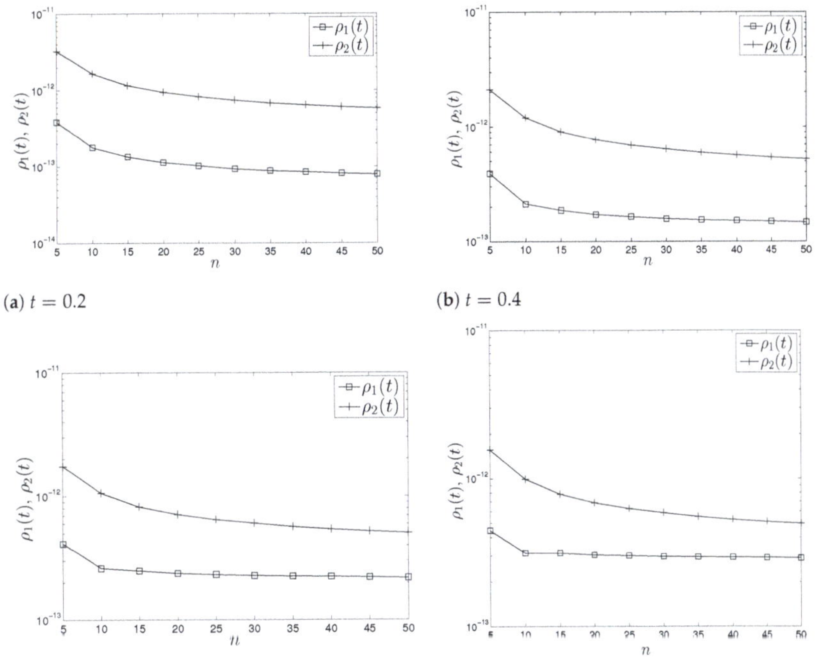

(**a**) $t = 0.2$ (**b**) $t = 0.4$

(**c**) $t = 0.6$ (**d**) $t = 0.8$

Figure 1. Example 2, experiment 2, bound $f(t) = f(\delta, t)$, (8)–(13) from Theorem 1, $\alpha = 0$, $j = 12$, $t = 0.2$ to 0.8 and n from 5 to 50.

It appears in Figure 1 that for $\alpha = 0$ *and j from* 10 *to* 4, *the bound* $\rho_2(t)$ *remains of the order of the estimated value* $\rho_1(t)$.

The average values over 30 trials for the relative perturbation $\rho_1(t) = \frac{\|\Delta X(t)\|}{\|X(t\|}$ *and the bound* $\rho_2(t) = \frac{f(t)}{\|X(t)\|}$, $f(t) = f(\delta, t)$ *from (8)–(13) for* $t = 0.2, 0.4, 0.6$ *and* 0.8 *are displayed in Figure 2 for* $\alpha = 5$.

The results for the perturbation bound $f(\delta, t)$, *(8)–(13) from Theorem 1, visualized on Figures 1 and 2 demonstrate that the perturbation bound* $f(\delta, t)$, *(8)–(13) is an effective upper perturbation bound of* $X(t)$ *in a large range of the size n of the NDRE (1) (n varies from 5 to 50). With the increasing of the dimension n of Equation (1), the accuracy of the estimate improves.*

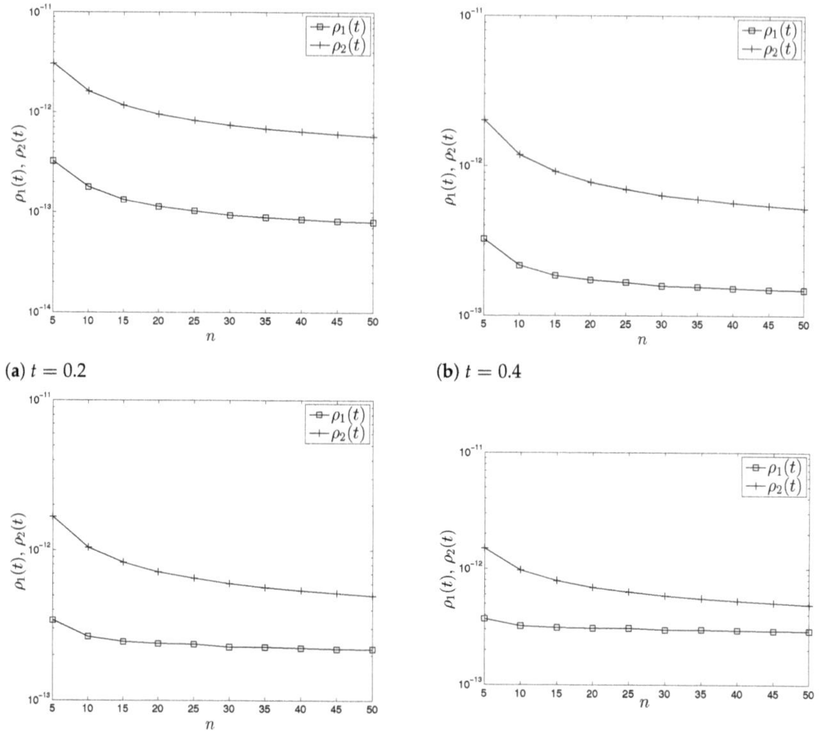

(a) $t = 0.2$ **(b)** $t = 0.4$

(c) $t = 0.6$ **(d)** $t = 0.8$

Figure 2. Example 2, experiment 2, bound $f(t) = f(\delta, t)$, (8)–(13) from Theorem 1, $\alpha = 5$, $j = 12$, $t = 0.2$ to 0.8, n from 5 to 50.

Example 2. *This example tests the effectiveness of the bound (9)–(13) in the case of large-scale NDRE. We consider a NDRE of order $n = 4000$, arising in neutron transport theory*

$$\dot{X}(t) = -(\Delta - eq^\top)X(t) - X(t)(\Gamma - qe^\top) + X(t)qq^\top X(t) + ee^\top,$$

on time interval $T = [\ 0,\ \ 2\ ]$, with matrices

$$\begin{aligned}
\Delta &= \operatorname{diag}(\delta_1, \ldots, \delta_n), \quad \delta_i = \frac{1}{c\omega_i(1+\alpha)}, \quad i = 1, \ldots, n \\
\Gamma &= \operatorname{diag}(\gamma_1, \ldots, \gamma_n), \quad \gamma_i = \frac{1}{c\omega_i(1-\alpha)}, \quad i = 1, \ldots, n, \\
& c = 0.5, \quad \alpha = 0.5 \\
& e = (1, \ldots, 1)^\top, \quad q = (q_1, \ldots, q_n)^\top, \text{ with } q_i = \frac{c_i}{2\omega_i}, \quad i = 1, \ldots, n,
\end{aligned}$$

where the sequences (c_i) and (ω_i), $i = 1, \ldots, n$ are the nodes and weights of the Gaussian-Legendre quadrature on $[\ 0,\ \ 1\ ]$, respectively:

$$c_i > 0, \ \sum_i^n c_i = 1, \text{ and } 0 < \omega_1 < \cdots < \omega_n, \ \ i = 1, \ldots, n.$$

The perturbation is chosen as:

$$\delta q = (rand(size(q))/\|q\|) * 10^{-j} \text{ for } j = 12.$$

The results, obtained for the relative perturbation $\rho_1(t) = \frac{\|\Delta X(t)\|}{\|X(t)\|}$ *and the nonlocal bound* $\rho_2(t) = \frac{f(t)}{\|X(t)\|}, f(t) = f(\delta, t)$, *(8)–(13) for* $t = 0.4, 0.8, 1.2, 1.6$ *and 2 are shown in Table 6.*

Table 6. Relative perturbations $\rho_1 = \frac{\|\Delta X(t)\|}{\|X(t)\|}$ and $\rho_2 = \frac{f(t)}{\|X(t)\|}$.

	$t = 0.4$	$t = 0.8$	$t = 1.2$	$t = 1.6$	$t = 2$
			$j = 10$		
$\rho_1(t)$	3.25×10^{-10}	4.09×10^{-10}	4.26×10^{-10}	4.29×10^{-10}	4.29×10^{-10}
$\rho_2(t)$	3.80×10^{-09}	4.09×10^{-09}	4.12×10^{-09}	4.13×10^{-09}	4.13×10^{-09}

Example 3. Results for size $n = 4000, j = 12$.

As is seen, over all the interval of integration $T \in [\ 0,\ \ 2\ ]$, *the perturbation bound* $f(\delta, t)$ *from (8)–(13) is valid, i.e., the condition (8) for existence of the bound* $f(\delta, t)$ *is not deteriorated. The bound* $f(\delta, t)$ *is a quite sharp upper bound—remains in the order of the estimated value. The perturbation bound* $f(\delta, t)$ *formulated in Theorem 1 is effective and could be used to estimate the sensitivity even of a large-scale NDRE.*

5. Conclusions

In this paper, a nonlocal sensitivity analysis of the nonsymmetric differential matrix Riccati equation is presented. Two computable perturbation bounds are derived using the techniques of Fréchet derivatives, Lyapunov majorants and fixed-point principles, developed in [14]. The first bound is based on the integral form of the solution. The second one exploits the statement of the classical Radon's theory of local equivalence of the solution to the differential matrix Riccati equation to the solution of the initial value problem of the associated differential system. It has the advantage of not being related with the solution of the NDRE and hence with problems of divergence of the numerical procedure. Numerical examples show that the estimates proposed are fairly sharp for both low-dimensional and large-scale NDRE. The perturbation bound is a crucial issue of the process of numerical solution of an equation as well as a tool to evaluate the stability of the computation process. The tight perturbation bounds, proposed in the paper, allow estimation of the accuracy of the solution to a numerically solved nonsymmetric differential matrix Riccati equation.

Author Contributions: Conceptualization, V.A. and K.J.; methodology, V.A. and K.J. ; software, M.H.; validation, V.A., M.H. and K.J.; writing—original draft preparation, V.A., M.H. and K.J.; writing—review and editing, V.A., M.H. and K.J.; visualization, V.A., M.H. and K.J.; supervision, K.J.; project administration, V.A., M.H. and K.J.; funding acquisition, V.A. All authors have read and agreed to the published version of the manuscript.

Funding: This work was partially supported by grant BG PLANTNET "Establishment of national information network genbank—Plant genetic resources".

Acknowledgments: Mustapha Hached acknowledges support from the Labex CEMPI (ANR-11-LABX-0007-01).

Conflicts of Interest: The authors declare no conflict of interest.

References

1. Fital, S.; Guo, C.H. Convergence of the solution of a nonsymmetric matrix Riccati differential equation to its stable equilibrium solution. *J. Math. Anal. Appl.* **2006**, *318*, 648–657. [CrossRef]
2. Juang, J. Global existence and stability of solutions of matrix Riccati equations. *J. Math. Analy. Appl.* **2001**, *258*, 1–12. [CrossRef]
3. Abou-Kandil, H.; Freiling, G.; Ionescu, V.; Jank, G. Matrix Riccati Equations in Control and Systems Theory. In *Systems & Control: Foundations & Applications*; Birkhäuser: Basel, Switzerland, 2003.
4. Freiling, G.; Jank, G.; Lee, S.R. Existence and uniqueness of open-loop Stackelberg equilibra in linear-quadratic differential games. *J. Opt. Theo. Appl.* **2001**, *110*, 515–544. [CrossRef]
5. Freiling, G. A survey of nonsymmetric Riccati equations. *Lin. Alg. Appl.* **2002**, *351*, 243–270. [CrossRef]
6. Jódar, L. A formula for the general solution of Riccati type matrix differential equations. *Systems Cont. Let.* **1989**, *12*, 39–43. [CrossRef]
7. Guldogan, Y.; Hached, M.; Jbilou, K.; Kurulay, M. Low rank approximate solutions to large-scale differential matrix Riccati equations. *App. Math.* **2018**, *45*, 233–254. [CrossRef]
8. Guo, C.-H.; Higham, N.J. Iterative solution of a nonsymmetric algebraic Riccati equation. *SIAM J. Matrix Anal. Appl.* **2007**, *29*, 396–412. [CrossRef]
9. Lin, Y.; Wei, Y. Normwise, mixed and componentwise condition numbers of nonsymmetric algebraic Riccati equation. *Appl. Math. Comput.* **2008**, *27*, 137–147. [CrossRef]
10. Liu, L. Mixed and componentwise condition numbers of nonsymmetric algebraic Riccati equation. *Appl. Math. Comput.* **2012**, *218*, 7595–7601. [CrossRef]
11. Liu, L.; Xu, A.-F. Condition number and backward errors of nonsymmetric algebraic Riccati equation. *Appl. Math. Comput.* **2014**, *242*, 716–728. [CrossRef]
12. Konstantinov, M.; Pelova, G. Sensitivity of the solutions to differential matrix Riccati equations. *IEEE Trans. Automat. Control* **1991**, *36*, 213–215. [CrossRef]
13. Konstantinov, M.; Angelova, V. Sensitivity analysis of the differential matrix Riccati equation based on the associated linear differential system. *Adv. Comp. Math.* **1997**, *7*, 295–301. [CrossRef]
14. Konstantinov, M.; Gu, D.; Mehrmann, V.; Petkov, P. *Perturbation Theory for Matrix Equations*; Elsevier: Amsterdam, The Netherlands, 2003.
15. Guo, C.-H. Nonsymmetric algebraic Riccati equation and Winner-Hopf factorization for M-matrices. *SIAM J. Matrix Anal. Appl.* **2001**, *23*, 225–242. [CrossRef]
16. Choi, C.; Laub, A.J. Constructing Riccati differential equations with known analytic solutions for numerical experiments. *IEEE Trans. Automat. Control* **1990**, *AC-35*, 437–439. [CrossRef]
17. Lancaster, P. *The Theory of Matrices*; Academic Press: New York, NY, USA, 1969.
18. Petkov, P.; Christov, N.; Konstantinov, M. *Computational Methods for Linear Control Systems*; Prentice-Hall: Hemel Hempstead, UK, 1991.
19. Angelova, V.; Hached, M.; Jbilou, K. Approximate solutions to large nonsymmetric differential Riccati problems with applications to transport theory. *Numer. Lin. Alg. Appl.* **2020**, *27*, e2272. [CrossRef]

mathematics

Article

An Inverse Mixed Impedance Scattering Problem in a Chiral Medium

Evagelia S. Athanasiadou

Department of Mathematics, National and Kapodistrian University of Athens, 157 84 Athens, Greece; eathan@math.uoa.gr

Abstract: An inverse scattering problem of time-harmonic chiral electromagnetic waves for a buried partially coated object was studied. The buried object was embedded in a piecewise isotropic homogeneous background chiral material. On the boundary of the scattering object, the total electromagnetic field satisfied perfect conductor and impedance boundary conditions. A modified linear sampling method, which originated from the chiral reciprocity gap functional, was employed for reconstruction of the shape of the buried object without requiring any a priori knowledge of the material properties of the scattering object. Furthermore, a characterization of the impedance of the object's surface was determined.

Keywords: inverse scattering; reciprocity gap functional; chiral media; mixed boundary conditions

MSC: 35Q60; 35R30; 78A46; 35P25

Citation: Athanasiadou, E.S. An Inverse Mixed Impedance Scattering Problem in a Chiral Medium. *Mathematics* **2021**, *9*, 104. https://doi.org/10.3390/math9010104

Received: 8 November 2020
Accepted: 31 December 2020
Published: 5 January 2021

1. Introduction

In this work, the inverse electromagnetic scattering problem of determining the surface impedance and the shape of a buried partially coated scattering object in chiral media is studied. In order to do this, we need information of the value of the electric and magnetic fields on the surface of the earth.

A chiral material is one that displays optical activity such that, when the plane of vibration of a linearly polarized light passes through an opticaly active medium is rotated. Over the last few years, chiral materials have been studied more intensely and there are more studies on the subject, covering both their applications and their theoretical background. Furthermore, various papers have been written on direct and inverse electromagnetic scattering problems for chiral media. Indicatively, we refer to Reference [1–4]. These materials are characterized by a set of two constitutive equations, in which electric and magnetic fields are connected via a physical variable or constant, known as chirality.

In this work, Drude-Born-Fedorov constitutive equations are used, as they are symmetric under time reversality and duality transformation [5]. In homogeneous and isotropic chiral media, the electric and magnetic fields are a combination of Left Circularly Polarized and Right Circularly Polarized components that have different phase speeds. So, in the applications, we can use the Bohren decomposition [6] of electric and magnetic fields into suitable Left and Right Circularly Beltrami fields. Such fields have been employed in Reference [2] for the definition of the chiral Herglotz wave functions and in Reference [6] for formulation of the electric dipole, which both play an important role in the present work. In Reference [7], the measure of chirality for a certain class of chiral scatterers has been calculated, while, in Reference [8], properties of chiral metamaterials are described. In addition, we note that Ammari and Nédélec in Reference [1] have proved that the well-known Silver-Müller radiation condition remains valid in chiral media. In Reference [4,9], the direct and the inverse electromagnetic scattering problems by a mixed impedance screen in a chiral environment are investigated, respectively. Beltrami fields have been used for the uniqueness and a variational method for the existence of the direct problem.

In the inverse problem, a modified linear sampling method, originated from a factorization of the chiral far field operator, has been employed.

In this work, the inverse scattering problem of specifying the shape and the surface impedance of a buried coated scattering object in a chiral environment is studied. A qualitative method [10], which is based on the chiral reciprocity gap operator, is used in Reference [11]. In fact, this procedure is a modified type of the linear sampling method (LSM). The classical LSM, which was first established by Colton and Kirsch [12], is simple, relatively quick and does not need any a priori information of the material parameters of the scattering object. However, in the electromagnetic imaging of a buried object via LSM, the computation of the Green's function of the background material is necessary. Sometimes, this computation is practically impossible. The reciprocity gap functional method helps us to overcome this difficulty. The combination of the LSM and the reciprocity gap functional method was established by Colton and Haddar in Reference [13] for acoustic waves and by Cakoni, Fares, and Haddar in Reference [14] for electromagnetic waves. In Reference [15], a reciprocity gap functional for elastic waves has been used for solving an inverse mixed impedance scattering problem. In Reference [11], a reciprocity gap functional for chiral media has been defined, in order for an inverse scattering problem for a perfect conductor to be solved.

The present paper extends this method to study inverse scattering problems for buried partially coated objects in a chiral environment. In Reference [16], the shape and the surface impedance of a buried coated scattering object have been determined. In Reference [17], the same method has been applied to solve an electromagnetic inverse scattering problem for a partially coated anisotropic dielectric, which is in the inner of the earth. Using this method in Reference [18], an inverse electromagnetic scattering problem for a perfectly conducting cavity, using measurements from the interior, has been solved. In Reference [19], an interior inverse acoustic scattering problem for a cavity with an inhomogeneous medium inside has been studied. The same method has been employed in Reference [20] in order for a sound field to be reconstructed in a spherical harmonic domain. In Reference [21], the reciprocity gap functional method is applied to calculate the boundary and the permittivity of the scattering object in radar imaging. Recently, the reciprocity gap functional method has been employed in order to study an inverse scattering problem in electrical tomography [22], in seismology [23] and in source identification [24]. For more details on the linear sampling and reciprocity gap functional method, we refer to Reference [12], while, for general aspect in scattering theory, we refer to Reference [25,26].

In Section 2 of this paper, the electromagnetic waves in chiral media are described and the chiral mixed impedance scattering problem is formulated. In Section 3, the chiral reciprocity gap operator is defined, proved that it is injective and it has a dense range. In Section 4, the main result of the paper is proved. In Section 5, the surface impedance is determined. Finally, a conclusion is given in Section 6.

2. Electromagnetic Waves in Chiral Media

We consider the scattering of a time-harmonic electromagnetic wave by an object embedded in a chiral medium. The Drude-Born-Fedorov constitutive relations [6] are employed:

$$\mathcal{D} = \varepsilon(\mathcal{E} + \beta \nabla \times \mathcal{E}) , \quad \mathcal{B} = \mu(\mathcal{H} + \beta \nabla \times \mathcal{H}) ,$$

where $\mathcal{E}$, $\mathcal{H}$ are the electric and magnetic fields, $\mathcal{D}$ the electric displacement, $\mathcal{B}$ the magnetic induction, β is the chirality measure, ε the electric permittivity, and μ the magnetic permeability. Then, applying the source-free Maxwell curl postulates:

$$\nabla \times \mathcal{E} - i\omega \mathcal{B} = 0 , \quad \nabla \times \mathcal{H} + i\omega \mathcal{D} = 0 ,$$

where ω is the angular frequency, we get the following relations:

$$\nabla \times \mathcal{E} = \beta\gamma^2\mathcal{E} + i\omega\mu\Big(\frac{\gamma}{k}\Big)^2\mathcal{H}\,, \tag{1}$$

$$\nabla \times \mathcal{H} = \beta\gamma^2\mathcal{H} - i\omega\varepsilon\Big(\frac{\gamma}{k}\Big)^2\mathcal{E}\,, \tag{2}$$

where $k^2 = \omega^2\varepsilon\mu$ and $\gamma^2 = k^2(1-\beta^2k^2)^{-1}$. We point out that k is not a wave number and does not have any particular physical significance. We assume that the physical parameters β, ε, μ are positive constants and $k\beta < 1$, (Reference [6] (p. 87)). The fields $\mathcal{E}$ and $\mathcal{H}$ satisfy:

$$\nabla \cdot \mathcal{E} = \nabla \cdot \mathcal{H} = 0\,.$$

We eliminate the magnetic field $\mathcal{H}$ in Equations (1) and (2) and obtain

$$\nabla \times \nabla \times \mathcal{E} - 2\beta\gamma^2\nabla \times \mathcal{E} - \gamma^2\mathcal{E} = 0\,. \tag{3}$$

In isotropic homogeneous chiral media, the electric and magnetic fields are composed of Left Circularly Polarized (LCP) and Right Circularly Polarized (RCP) waves with different phase speeds. So, for $\mathcal{E}$ and $\mathcal{H}$, we make use of the Bohren decomposition into Beltrami fields Q_L and Q_R [5], and we get

$$\mathcal{E} = Q_L + Q_R\,, \quad \mathcal{H} = -i\sqrt{\frac{\varepsilon}{\mu}}(Q_L - Q_R)$$

and hence

$$Q_L = \frac{1}{2}(\mathcal{E} + i\sqrt{\frac{\mu}{\varepsilon}}\mathcal{H})\,, \quad Q_R = \frac{1}{2}(\mathcal{E} - i\sqrt{\frac{\mu}{\varepsilon}}\mathcal{H})\,.$$

The Beltrami fields satisfy the differential equations:

$$\nabla \times Q_L = \gamma_L Q_L\,, \quad \nabla \times Q_R = -\gamma_R Q_R\,,$$

which show that the homogeneous isotropic chiral media are circularly birefringent. The wave numbers γ_L and γ_R for the LCP and RCP Beltrami fields, respectively, are given by:

$$\gamma_L = k(1-k\beta)^{-1}\,, \quad \gamma_R = k(1+k\beta)^{-1}$$

and satisfy:

$$\gamma_L + \gamma_R = \frac{2\gamma^2}{k}\,, \quad \gamma_L - \gamma_R = 2\beta\gamma^2\,, \quad \gamma_L\gamma_R = \gamma^2\,.$$

For further information on the physical background for chiral media, we refer to Reference [5,6,27].

We assume that a scatterer D with C^2-boundary, $\Gamma = \partial D$ is embedded in a piecewise isotropic homogeneous chiral material with $\mathbb{R}^3\setminus\overline{D}$ to be connected. It is assumed that Γ is divided into two open sets Γ_D and Γ_I, such that $\Gamma_D \cap \Gamma_I = \emptyset$ and $\overline{\Gamma}_D \cup \overline{\Gamma}_I = \Gamma$. On Γ_D (Dirichlet part), a perfectly conducting boundary condition is satisfied and Γ_I (impedance part) is covered from a very thin dielectric layer. We consider Ω to be a bounded domain, which contains $\overline{D}$, with C^2- boundary $\partial\Omega$. Let β_b, ε_b and μ_b be the chirality, the electric permittivity, and the magnetic permeability, respectively, that characterize the medium $\Omega\setminus\overline{D}$, which will be referred to as the background medium. In addition, let β_0, ε_0 and μ_0 be the corresponding parameters in the exterior $\mathbb{R}^3\setminus\overline{\Omega}$ of Ω. We suppose that the physical parameters are positive constants. Finally, ν denotes the outward normal unit vector on the corresponding surface.

The incident field is a chiral electric dipole with polarization $p \in \mathbb{R}^3$ located at x_0 in a chiral environment. We assume that x_0 lies on an auxiliary close surface Λ contained in $\mathbb{R}^3 \backslash \overline{\Omega}$. The electric incident field in a chiral medium is given by the formula [5,6]:

$$E_{x_0}(x, p, \gamma_0) = \frac{k_0}{2\gamma_0^2} p \cdot \left\{ \left(\gamma_{0L} \widetilde{I} + \frac{1}{\gamma_{0L}} \nabla\nabla + \nabla \times \widetilde{I} \right) \frac{e^{i\gamma_{0L}|x-x_0|}}{4\pi|x-x_0|} + \left(\gamma_{0R} \widetilde{I} + \frac{1}{\gamma_{0R}} \nabla\nabla - \nabla \times \widetilde{I} \right) \frac{e^{i\gamma_{0R}|x-x_0|}}{4\pi|x-x_0|} \right\},$$

where $\widetilde{I}$ is the identity dyadic in $\mathbb{R}^3$, and γ_{0L}, γ_{0R} are the wave numbers for the LCP and RCP Beltrami fields, respectively, in $\mathbb{R}^3 \backslash \overline{\Omega}$ with

$$\gamma_{0L} = k_0(1 - k_0\beta_0)^{-1}, \quad \gamma_{0R} = k_0(1 + k_0\beta_0)^{-1},$$

where $\gamma_0^2 = \gamma_{0L}\gamma_{0R}$, $k_0^2 \equiv k^2 = \omega^2 \varepsilon_0 \mu_0$.

The incident on the scatterer D electric wave E^i has the form:

$$E^i(x) \equiv E^i_{x_0}(x, p) = E_{x_0}(x, p, \gamma_0) + E^{s,b}_{x_0}(x, p), \tag{4}$$

where $E^{s,b}_{x_0}(x, p)$ is the scattered field due to the background material. In addition, the wave E^i in $\Omega \backslash \overline{D}$ is given by:

$$E^i(x) \equiv E^i_{x_0}(x, p) = p \cdot \widetilde{B}(x, x_0), \tag{5}$$

where $\widetilde{B}(x, x_0)$ is the dyadic Green's function of the chiral background material. If $\eta(x) = \eta_b = (\varepsilon_b\mu_b)(\varepsilon_0\mu_0)^{-1}$ for $x \in \Omega \backslash \overline{D}$, $\eta(x) = 1$ for $x \in \mathbb{R}^3 \backslash \overline{\Omega}$, $\beta(x) = \beta_b$ for $x \in \Omega \backslash \overline{D}$ and $\beta(x) = \beta_0$ for $x \in \mathbb{R}^3 \backslash \overline{\Omega}$, then $\widetilde{B}(x, x_0)$ satisfies the equation:

$$\left(k^{-2} - \eta(x)\beta^2(x)\right) \nabla \times \nabla \times \widetilde{B}(x, x_0) - 2\beta(x)\eta(x) \nabla \times \widetilde{B}(x, x_0) - \eta(x) \widetilde{B}(x, x_0) = \widetilde{I}\delta(x - x_0),$$

with respect to x. Let E^i be the incident on D electric field and $E^s \equiv E^{s,D}_{x_0}(\cdot, p)$ be the corresponding scattered field. Then, the total electric field E is given by $E = E^i + E^s$ and is the solution of the mixed impedance scattering problem:

$$(k^{-2} - \eta(x)\beta^2(x)) \nabla \times \nabla \times E - 2\beta(x)\eta(x) \nabla \times E - \eta(x)E = 0 \text{ in } \mathbb{R}^3 \setminus (\overline{D} \cup \{x_0\}), \tag{6}$$

$$\nu \times E = 0 \text{ on } \Gamma_D, \tag{7}$$

$$\nu \times \nabla \times E - i\frac{\gamma_b^2 \lambda}{k_b} (\nu \times E) \times \nu - \beta_b \gamma_b^2 \nu \times E = 0 \text{ on } \Gamma_I, \tag{8}$$

$$\hat{x} \times \nabla \times E^s - \beta_0 \gamma_0^2 \hat{x} \times E^s + i\frac{\gamma_0^2}{k_0} E^s = o\left(\frac{1}{|x|}\right), \ |x| \to \infty \tag{9}$$

$$\text{uniformly in all directions } \hat{x} = \frac{x}{|x|} \in S^2,$$

where S^2 is the unit sphere in $\mathbb{R}^3$, $k_b = \omega\sqrt{\varepsilon_b\mu_b}$, $\gamma_b^2 = \gamma_{b_L}\gamma_{b_R}$, with $\gamma_{b_L} = k_b(1 - k_b\gamma_b)^{-1}$ and $\gamma_{b_R} = k_b(1 + k_b\gamma_b)^{-1}$.

The direct scattering problem can be studied as in Reference [9]. The uniqueness of solution has been proved via the Beltrami fields, while, for the existence of solution, the variational method has been employed, using a Calderon type operator [28] for chiral media. The corresponding inverse scattering problem is the determination of the unknown boundary of D and the evaluation of surface impedance λ from the information of the tangential components $\nu \times E$ and $\nu \times H$ on the boundary $\partial\Omega$ for all points $x_0 \in \Lambda$. In chiral media, a Stratton-Chu type exterior integral representation for a radiating solution of Equation (3) is the following:

$$E^s(r) = -2\beta\gamma^2 \int_S \widetilde{B}(r,r') \cdot [\nu \times E^s(r')] ds(r')$$
$$+ \int_S \left\{ \widetilde{B}(r,r') \cdot [\nu \times \nabla \times E^s(r')] + \left[\nabla_r \times \widetilde{B}(r,r')\right] \cdot [\nu \times E^s(r')] \right\} ds(r') \,. \quad (10)$$

We define the function spaces:

$$H(curl, D) = \left\{ u \in \left(L^2(D)\right)^3 : \ \nabla \times u \in \left(L^2(D)\right)^3 \right\},$$
$$H_0(curl, B_R) = \{ u \in H(curl, B_R) : \ \nu \times u \,|_{\partial B_R} = 0 \},$$

where B_R is a ball of radius R containing D, as well as

$$\mathbb{H}(\Omega) = \{ u \in H(curl, \Omega) : \nabla \times \nabla \times u - 2\beta_b \gamma_b^2 \nabla \times u - \gamma_b^2 u = 0 \},$$
$$L_t^2(\partial D) = \left\{ u \in \left(L^2(\partial D)\right)^3 : \ \nu \cdot u = 0 \ on \ \partial D \right\},$$
$$L_t^2(\Gamma_I) = \{ u \,|_{\Gamma_I} : \ u \in L_t^2(\partial D) \},$$
$$X(D, \Gamma_I) = \{ u \in H(curl, D) \ : \ \nu \times u \,|_{\Gamma_I} \in L_t^2(\Gamma_I) \}.$$

The space $X(D, \Gamma_I)$ is equipped with the norm

$$||u||^2_{X(D,\Gamma_I)} = ||u||^2_{H(curl,D)} + ||\nu \times u||^2_{L_t^2(\Gamma_I)} .$$

For the trace $\nu \times u$ of $u \in H(curl, D)$, we have

$$H_{div}^{-\frac{1}{2}}(\partial D) = \left\{ u \in \left(H^{-\frac{1}{2}}(\partial D) \right)^3 : \ \nu \cdot u = 0 \,, \ div_{\partial D} u \in H^{-\frac{1}{2}}(\partial D) \right\},$$

and for $(\nu \times u) \times \nu$ of $u \in H(curl, D)$

$$H_{curl}^{-\frac{1}{2}}(\partial D) = \left\{ u \in \left(H^{-\frac{1}{2}}(\partial D) \right)^3 : \ \nu \cdot u = 0 \,, \ curl_{\partial D} u \in H^{-\frac{1}{2}}(\partial D) \right\}$$

The trace space of $X(D, \Gamma_I)$ on Γ_D is defined by:

$$Y(\Gamma_D) = \left\{ h \in \left(H^{-\frac{1}{2}}(\Gamma_D) \right)^3 : \ \exists u \in H_0(curl, B_R), \ \nu \times u \,|_{\Gamma_I} \in L_t^2(\Gamma_I), \ h = \nu \times u \,|_{\Gamma_D} \right\}.$$

Finally, for the exterior domain $\mathbb{R}^3 \backslash \overline{D}$, we define the spaces $H_{loc}(curl, \mathbb{R}^3 \backslash \overline{D})$ and $H_{loc}(\mathbb{R}^3 \backslash \overline{D}, \Gamma_I)$ considering the domain $(\mathbb{R}^3 \backslash \overline{D}) \bigcap B_R$.

The exterior mixed impedance boundary value problem in chiral media is the following problem: Let $f \in Y(\Gamma_D)$ and $h \in L_t^2(\Gamma_I)$, find $E \in X(D, \Gamma_I)$ such that:

$$(k^{-2} - \eta(x)\beta^2(x)) \nabla \times \nabla \times E - 2\beta(x)\eta(x) \nabla \times E - \eta(x) E = 0 \ \text{in} \ \mathbb{R}^3 \setminus \overline{D}, \quad (11)$$
$$\nu \times E = f \ \ \text{on} \ \Gamma_D \,, \quad (12)$$
$$\nu \times \nabla \times E - i \frac{\gamma_b^2 \lambda}{k_b} (\nu \times E) \times \nu - \beta_b \gamma_b^2 \nu \times E = h \ \text{on} \ \Gamma_I \,, \quad (13)$$
$$\hat{x} \times \nabla \times E - \beta_0 \gamma_0^2 \hat{x} \times E + i \frac{\gamma_0^2}{k_0} E = o\left(\frac{1}{|x|} \right), \ |x| \to \infty \quad (14)$$
$$\text{uniformly in all directions } \hat{x} = \frac{x}{|x|} \in S^2 \,,$$

If $f = -\nu \times E^i$ and $h = -\nu \times \nabla \times E^i + i \frac{\gamma_b^2 \lambda}{k_b} (\nu \times E^i) \times \nu + \beta_b \gamma_b^2 \nu \times E^i$, then the problem (11)–(14) is the mixed impedance scattering problem (6)–(9).

Let $z \in D$ and $E^z \in H(curl, D)$. We consider the following chiral interior mixed impedance boundary value problem corresponding to (6)–(9); given $f \in Y(\Gamma_D)$ and $h \in L_t^2(\Gamma_I)$, we find $E^z \in X(D, \Gamma_I)$ such that:

$$\nabla \times \nabla \times E^z - 2\beta_b \gamma_b^2 \nabla \times E^z - \gamma_b^2 E^z = 0 \text{ in } D\,, \tag{15}$$

$$\nu \times E^z = f \text{ on } \Gamma_D\,, \tag{16}$$

$$\nu \times \nabla \times E^z - i\frac{\gamma_b^2 \lambda}{k_b}(\nu \times E^z) \times \nu + \beta_b \gamma_b^2 \nu \times E^z = h \text{ on } \Gamma_I\,. \tag{17}$$

The values of parameter k for which the corresponding homogeneous interior mixed impedance scattering problem admits a nontrivial solution will be referred to as chiral Maxwell eigenvalues for D. This problem in the achiral case has been solved in Reference [29]. A similar scattering problem for a mixed impedance screen has been studied in Reference [9]. In particular, a Calderon type operator for chiral media and a variational method have been employed to prove uniqueness and existence of solution. The present scattering problem is to find the shape of D and the surface impedance λ from the knowledge of electric and magnetic fields on $\partial\Omega$. In what follows, a brief description of the solvability of the interior mixed impedance problem (15)–(17) is given.

For the uniqueness of (15)–(17), we consider the corresponding homogeneous problem ($f = h = 0$), and we multiply (15) with $\overline{E}$ (complex conjugate of E) and integrate over D. Taking into account the boundary conditions we get

$$\int_D \Big[|\nabla \times E|^2 - \gamma_b^2 |E|^2 - 2\beta_b \gamma_b^2 Re(E \cdot \nabla \times \overline{E})\Big] dv + i\frac{\gamma_b^2 \lambda}{k_b} \int_{\Gamma_I} |E_T|^2 ds = 0, \tag{18}$$

where $E_T = (\nu \times E) \times \nu$ is the tangential component of E. From (18), taking the imaginary part and using the unique continuation principle as in Reference [12,29], we conclude that $E = 0$ in D. For the existence, we consider the variational formulation for the problem (15)–(17). For all test functions $\phi \in \widetilde{X}$ with

$$\widetilde{X} = \Big\{u \in H(curl, D) : \nu \times u|_{\Gamma_D} = 0,\ \nu \times u|_{\Gamma_I} \in L_t^2(\Gamma_I)\Big\},$$

we have

$$\int_D \Big[\nabla \times E \cdot \nabla \times \overline{\phi} - \gamma^2 E \cdot \overline{\phi} - 2\beta\gamma^2 Re(\overline{\phi} \cdot \nabla \times E)\Big] dv + \frac{i\gamma^2 \lambda}{k} \int_{\Gamma_I} E_T \cdot \overline{\phi}_T\, ds$$
$$= -\int_{\Gamma_I} h \cdot \overline{\phi}_T\, ds\,. \tag{19}$$

We look for solution E of the form $E = W + U$, where $U \in X(D, \Gamma_I)$ with $\nu \times U|_{\Gamma_D} = f$, which there exists from the definition of $Y(\Gamma_D)$. Substituting in (19), we take:

$$a(W, \phi) = \langle h, \phi\rangle - a(U, \phi), \tag{20}$$

where

$$a(u, \psi) = (\nabla \times u, \nabla \times \psi) - \gamma^2(u, \phi) - 2\beta\gamma^2 Re(\nabla \times u, \phi) + \frac{i\gamma^2 \lambda}{k}\langle u_T, \psi_T\rangle\,. \tag{21}$$

In (21), $(\cdot,\cdot)$ denotes the $L^2(D)$ scalar product and $\langle\cdot,\cdot\rangle$ the $L_t^2(\Gamma_I)$ product. Equation (20) has been studied in Reference [28,29] for the achiral case. With a similar process for the chiral case, the following theorem is proved.

Theorem 1. *If $\Gamma_I \neq \emptyset$ then the chiral interior partially coated problem (15)–(17) has a unique solution.*

3. The Chiral Reciprocity Gap Operator

The reciprocity gap operator for electromagnetic scattering in chiral media has been defined in Reference [11], in order to study an inverse scattering problem for a perfectly conducting obstacle.

Let $E = E_{x_0}(\cdot, p)$ be the solution of the scattering problem (6)–(9). The chiral reciprocity gap functional is defined by

$$\mathcal{R}(E,W) = \int_{\partial\Omega}[(\nu \times E)\cdot \nabla \times W - (\nu \times W)\cdot \nabla \times E]ds - 2\beta_b\gamma_b^2 \int_{\partial\Omega}[(\nu \times E)\cdot W]ds\,, \quad (22)$$

where $W \in H(curl, \Omega)$ and the integrals are interpreted in the sense of the duality between $H_{div}^{-\frac{1}{2}}(\partial D)$, $H_{curl}^{-\frac{1}{2}}(\partial D)$. In particular, if $W \in \mathbb{H}(\Omega) \subset H(curl, \Omega)$, then the chiral reciprocity gap functional can be seen as an integral operator $R : \mathbb{H}(\Omega) \to L_t^2(\Lambda)$, given by:

$$R(W)(x_0) = \mathcal{R}(E_{x_0}(\cdot, p(x_0)), W)p(x_0)\,, \quad x_0 \in \Lambda\,. \quad (23)$$

The reciprocity gap functional method is based on the solvability of an integral equation for $\mathcal{R}$, which contains an appropriate family of solutions in $\mathbb{H}(\Omega)$. Usually, we use a set of either single layer potentials or Hergotz wave functions. Here, for the determination of the boundary of D, chiral Herglotz wave functions will be employed, because these functions satisfy density properties which will be used later. In Reference [2], the electric $\mathcal{E}_g$ and magnetic $\mathcal{H}_g$ chiral Herglotz wave functions have been defined and are given by

$$\mathcal{E}_g = \mathcal{E}_{g_L} + \mathcal{E}_{g_R}\,, \quad \mathcal{H}_g = -i\sqrt{\frac{\varepsilon}{\mu}}(\mathcal{E}_{g_L} - \mathcal{E}_{g_R})\,,$$

where

$$\mathcal{E}_{g_L}(x) = \int_{S^2} g_L(\hat{d}_L)e^{i\gamma_L \hat{d}_L\cdot x}\, ds(\hat{d}_L)\,, \quad (24)$$

$$\mathcal{E}_{g_R}(x) = \int_{S^2} g_R(\hat{d}_R)e^{i\gamma_R \hat{d}_R\cdot x}\, ds(\hat{d}_R)\,, \quad (25)$$

are the LCP and the RCP Beltrami Herglotz fields, with kernels g_L and g_R, respectively, and $\hat{d}_L, \hat{d}_R \in S^2$. In particular, for the kernels, we have $g_A : S^2 \to T_A^2(S^2)$, $A = L, R$, where

$$T_L^2(S^2) = \left\{b_L \in \left(L^2(S^2)\right)^3 : \nu\cdot b_L = 0\,,\ \nu \times b_L = -ib_L\right\},$$
$$T_R^2(S^2) = \left\{b_R \in \left(L^2(S^2)\right)^3 : \nu\cdot b_R = 0\,,\ \nu \times b_R = ib_R\right\}.$$

In addition, we define the following space:

$$T_{LR}^2(S^2) = \left\{b = b_L + b_R : b_L \in T_L^2(S^2)\,,\ b_R \in T_R^2(S^2)\right\},$$

with the inner product:

$$< b,h >_{T_{LR}^2(S^2)} = (b_L, h_L)_{T_L^2(S^2)} + (b_R, h_R)_{T_R^2(S^2)}\,,$$

where b_A, h_A, $A = L, R$, are the Beltrami fields of b and h, respectively, and $(b_A, h_A)_{T_A^2(S^2)} = \int_{S^2} b_A \cdot \overline{h}_A ds$ [2]. Let

$$E_z(x,q,\gamma_b) = \frac{k_b}{2\gamma_b^2}q\cdot\left\{\left(\gamma_{bL}\widetilde{I} + \frac{1}{\gamma_{bL}}\nabla\nabla + \nabla\times\widetilde{I}\right)\frac{e^{i\gamma_{bL}|x-z|}}{4\pi|x-z|}\right.$$
$$\left. + \left(\gamma_{bR}\widetilde{I} + \frac{1}{\gamma_{bR}}\nabla\nabla - \nabla\times\widetilde{I}\right)\frac{e^{i\gamma_{bR}|x-z|}}{4\pi|x-z|}\right\},$$

be the electric dipole with polarization $q \in \mathbb{R}^3$ located at z in a chiral medium. We study the solvability of the integral equation:

$$\mathcal{R}(E, \mathcal{E}_g) = \mathcal{R}(E, E_z(\cdot, q, \gamma_b)) , \tag{26}$$

with respect to g in $T^2_{LR}(S^2)$.

We will prove that the operator R, under appropriate conditions, is injective and has dense range.

Lemma 1. *If Γ_I is not empty then the operator $R : \mathbb{H}(\Omega) \to L^2_t(\Lambda)$, defined by (23) is injective.*

Proof. We assume that $RW = 0$. Then, $\mathcal{R}(E_{x_0}(\cdot, p), W) = 0$ for all $x_0 \in \Lambda$ and $p \in \mathbb{R}^3$. On (22), we apply the second vector Green's theorem for the first integral, Gauss' theorem for the second integral for E, W in $\Omega \backslash \overline{D}$, which are both solutions of (15), we use the boundary conditions on ∂D to take

$$\begin{aligned}
0 &= \int_{\partial D} [(\nu \times E) \cdot \nabla \times W - (\nu \times W) \cdot \nabla \times E] ds - 2\beta_b \gamma_b^2 \int_{\partial D} (\nu \times E) \cdot W ds \\
&= - \int_{\Gamma_D} (\nu \times W) \cdot \nabla \times E \, ds \\
&\quad - \int_{\Gamma_I} E \cdot \left[\nu \times \nabla \times W - i \frac{\gamma_b^2 \lambda}{k_b} (\nu \times W) \times \nu - \beta_b \gamma_b^2 (\nu \times W) \right] ds .
\end{aligned} \tag{27}$$

Let $\breve{E}$ be the unique solution of the boundary value problem:

$$(k^{-2} - \beta(x)^2 \eta(x)) \nabla \times \nabla \times \breve{E} - 2\beta(x)\eta(x) \nabla \times \breve{E} - \eta(x) \breve{E} = 0 \text{ in } \mathbb{R}^3 \setminus \overline{D} , \tag{28}$$

$$\nu \times (\breve{E} - W) = 0 \text{ on } \Gamma_D , \tag{29}$$

$$\nu \times \nabla \times (\breve{E} - W) = i \frac{\gamma_b^2 \lambda}{k_b} [\nu \times (\breve{E} - W)] \times \nu + \beta_b \gamma_b^2 \nu \times (\breve{E} - W) \text{ on } \Gamma_I , \tag{30}$$

$$\frac{x}{|x|} \times \nabla \times \breve{E} - \beta_0 \gamma_0^2 \frac{x}{|x|} \times \breve{E} + \frac{i \gamma_0^2}{k_0} \breve{E} = o\left(\frac{1}{|x|} \right) , \ |x| \to \infty , \tag{31}$$

$$\text{uniformly in all directions of } \frac{x}{|x|} \in S^2 .$$

Substituting $\nu \times W$ and $\nu \times \nabla \times W$, from (29) and (30) into (27), we take

$$\begin{aligned}
0 &= - \int_{\Gamma_D} (\nu \times \breve{E}) \cdot \nabla \times E \, ds \\
&\quad - \int_{\Gamma_I} E \cdot \left[\nu \times \nabla \times \breve{E} - i \frac{\gamma_b^2 \lambda}{k_b} (\nu \times \breve{E}) \times \nu - \beta_b \gamma_b^2 (\nu \times \breve{E}) \right] ds .
\end{aligned} \tag{32}$$

The total electric field E is given by:

$$E = p \cdot \widetilde{B}(\cdot, x_0) + E^s .$$

Hence, using (32) and the boundary conditions (7) and (8), we get

$$\begin{aligned}
0 = &\int_{\partial D} \left[\left(\nu \times \left(p \cdot \widetilde{B}(\cdot, x_0) + E^s \right) \right) \cdot \nabla \times \breve{E} - (\nu \times \breve{E}) \cdot \nabla \times \left(p \cdot \widetilde{B}(\cdot, x_0) + E^s \right) \right] ds \\
&- 2\beta_b \gamma_b^2 \int_{\partial D} \left[\left(\nu \times \left(p \cdot \widetilde{B}(\cdot, x_0) + E^s \right) \right) \cdot \breve{E} \right] ds
\end{aligned}$$

and taking into account that the fields $\check{E}$ and E^s are both radiating solutions of (28), we have:

$$-p\cdot\left\{\int_{\partial D}\left[\widetilde{B}(\cdot,x_0)\cdot(\nu\times\nabla\times\check{E})+(\nabla\times\widetilde{B}(\cdot,x_0))\cdot(\nu\times\check{E})\right]ds\right.$$
$$\left.-2\beta_b\gamma_b^2\int_{\partial D}\widetilde{B}(\cdot,x_0)\cdot(\nu\times\check{E})ds\right\}=0\,.$$

From the Stratton-Chu type formula (10) for chiral media, we take

$$p\cdot\check{E}(x_0)=0\,,$$

for arbitrary polarization p, and therefore $\nu\times\check{E}(x_0)=0$ for $x_0\in\Lambda$. Then, by the uniqueness of the electromagnetic scattering in a chiral environment for a perfect conductor [1,3], we conclude that $\check{E}=0$ outside the surface Λ. Applying unique continuation, we have $\check{E}=0$ in the domain between the boundary ∂D and the surface Λ. Therefore,

$$\nu\times W=0 \text{ on } \Gamma_D\,,$$
$$\nu\times\nabla\times W-i\frac{\gamma_b^2\lambda}{k_b}(\nu\times W)\times\nu-\beta_b\gamma_b^2\nu\times W=0 \text{ on } \Gamma_I$$

and using the uniqueness of the interior partially coated chiral electromagnetic problem for W, implying $W=0$. □

Lemma 2. *If Γ_I is not empty then the operator $R:\mathbb{H}(\Omega)\to L_t^2(\Lambda)$ defined by (23) has dense range.*

Proof. Let $q\in L_t^2(\Lambda)$, such that $(RW,q)_{L_t^2(\Lambda)}=0$ for all $W\in\mathbb{H}(\Omega)$. We will prove that $q=0$. In view of the bilinearity of functional $\mathcal{R}$ and the definition of operator R, we get

$$(RW,q)_{L_t^2(\Lambda)}=\int_\Lambda\mathcal{R}(E_{x_0}(\cdot,\alpha(x_0)),W)ds\,,$$

where $\alpha=(p\cdot q)p$. If we define

$$\mathcal{E}(x)=\int_\Lambda E_{x_0}(x,\alpha(x_0))ds(x_0)\,,$$

then, from (22) and the assumption for q, we have that

$$\mathcal{R}(\mathcal{E},W)=0\,.$$

Using Green's and Gauss' theorems for W, $\mathcal{E}$ in $\Omega\backslash\overline{D}$ as in Lemma 1 and taking into account the boundary conditions on ∂D, we conclude that

$$\mathcal{R}(\mathcal{E},W)=-\int_{\Gamma_D}(\nu\times W)\cdot\nabla\times\mathcal{E}ds$$
$$-\int_{\Gamma_I}\mathcal{E}\cdot\left[\nu\times\nabla\times W-i\frac{\gamma_b^2\lambda}{k_b}(\nu\times W)\times\nu-\beta_b\gamma_b^2(\nu\times W)\right]ds=0\,,$$

for all $W\in\mathbb{H}(\Omega)$. The density of the chiral Herglotz wave functions has been used in order to prove that the set $\{\nu\times W|_{\Gamma_D},\ \nu\times\nabla\times W-i\frac{\gamma_b^2\lambda}{k_b}(\nu\times W)\times\nu-\beta_b\gamma_b^2(\nu\times W)\ |_{\Gamma_I}\}$ is dense in $Y(\Gamma_D)\times L_t^2(\Gamma_I)$. This follows from the fact that $\mathbb{H}(\Omega)$ contains the chiral Herglotz wave functions, given by (24) and (25) (see [2,29]), which satisfy the Equation (3) and $\nabla\times\nabla\times Q_A-\gamma_A^2Q_A=0$, $A=L,R$. In addition, we have taken into account that the interior mixed impedance boundary value problem (15)–(17) is well-posed. Therefore, $\nu\times\nabla\times\mathcal{E}=0$ and $\nu\times\mathcal{E}=0$ on ∂D. Hence, $\mathcal{E}$ has zero Cauchy data on ∂D and therefore

$\mathcal{E} = 0$ in the domain between Λ and ∂D. Finally, taking into account the jump relations [3] of $\nabla \times \mathcal{E}$ across Λ, we arrive at $\alpha = 0$ on Λ. Therefore, $(p \cdot q)p = 0$ for all $p \in L_t^2(\Lambda)$, hence $q = 0$. □

4. The Reconstruction of the Shape

These properties of the chiral reciprocity gap operator are used for the determination of the boundary of the scatterer D. The main result of this paper is the following theorem.

Theorem 2. *Assume that Γ_I is not empty.*
(i) Let $z \in D$. Then, for a given $\epsilon > 0$ there exists a $g_z^\epsilon \in T_{LR}^2(S^2)$ such that

$$||\mathcal{R}(E, \mathcal{E}_{g_z^\epsilon}) - \mathcal{R}(E, E_z(\cdot, q, \gamma_b))||_{L^2(\Lambda)} < \epsilon$$

and the chiral Herglotz wave function $\mathcal{E}_{g_z^\epsilon}$ converges to the solution of interior boundary value problem in $X(D, \Gamma_I)$ as $\epsilon \to 0$.
(ii) For a fixed $\epsilon > 0$, we get

$$\lim_{dist(z,\partial D) \to 0} ||\mathcal{E}_{g_z^\epsilon}||_{X(D,\Gamma_I)} = \infty\,, \quad \lim_{dist(z,\partial D) \to 0} ||g_z^\epsilon||_{T_{LR}^2(S^2)} = \infty\,.$$

(iii) For $z \in \mathbb{R}^3 \backslash \overline{D}$ and $\epsilon > 0$, if $g_z^\epsilon \in T_{LR}^2(S^2)$ satisfies

$$||\mathcal{R}(E, \mathcal{E}_{g_z^\epsilon}) - \mathcal{R}(E, E_z(\cdot, q, \gamma_b))||_{L^2(\Lambda)} < \epsilon\,,$$

then we have that

$$\lim_{\epsilon \to 0} ||\mathcal{E}_{g_z^\epsilon}||_{X(D,\Gamma_I)} = \infty\,, \quad \lim_{\epsilon \to 0} ||g_z^\epsilon||_{T_{LR}^2(S^2)} = \infty\,.$$

Proof. (i) Suppose $z \in D$. Taking into account that E is the total field and W and $E_z(\cdot, q, \gamma_b)$ are solutions to Equation (11) in $\Omega \backslash \overline{D}$ and using the mixed boundary conditions on D, we have that

$$\mathcal{R}(E, W) - \mathcal{R}(E, E_z(\cdot, q, \gamma_b)) = -\int_{\partial D} [\nu \times W - \nu \times E_z(\cdot, q, \gamma_b)] \cdot \nabla \times E\, ds\,.$$

Taking into account that the set of chiral Herglotz functions is dense in $\mathbb{H}(\Omega)$ with respect to the $H(curl, D)$ norm and using the trace theorem it follows that for every $\epsilon > 0$ there exists a chiral electric Herglotz function $\mathcal{E}_{g_z^\epsilon}$ such that: $\nu \times \mathcal{E}_{g_z^\epsilon}$ approximates $\nu \times E_z(\cdot, q, \gamma_b)$ with respect to $Y(\Gamma_D)$ norm, and $\nu \times \nabla \times \mathcal{E}_{g_z^\epsilon} - i\frac{\gamma_b^2 \lambda}{k_b}(\nu \times \mathcal{E}_{g_z^\epsilon}) \times \nu - \beta_b \gamma_b^2 (\nu \times \mathcal{E}_{g_z^\epsilon})$ approximates $\nu \times \nabla \times E_z(\cdot, q, \gamma_b) - i\frac{\gamma_b^2 \lambda}{k_b}(\nu \times E_z(\cdot, q, \gamma_b)) \times \nu - \beta_b \gamma_b^2 (\nu \times E_z(\cdot, q, \gamma_b))$ with respect to $L_t^2(\Gamma_I)$ norm. In addition, g_z^ϵ solves by approximation the Equation (26) and $\mathcal{E}_{g_z^\epsilon}$ converges to the solution of the mixed chiral interior boundary value problem (15)–(17).
(ii) Taking into account that $E_z(\cdot, q, \gamma_b)$ blows up as z approaches the boundary ∂D from inside, with respect to the $X(D, \Gamma_I)$ norm, we conclude: $\lim_{dist(z,\partial D) \to 0} ||\mathcal{E}_{g_z^\epsilon}||_{X(D,\Gamma_I)} = \infty$ and $\lim_{dist(z,\partial D) \to 0} ||g_z^\epsilon||_{T_{LR}^2(S^2)} = \infty$, with fixed $\epsilon > 0$.
(iii) Let $z \in \Omega \backslash \overline{D}$. The total electric field $E(x) \equiv E_{x_0}(x, p)$, due to the incident point-source $E_{x_0}^i(x, p)$, is given by:

$$E(x) \equiv E_{x_0}(x, p) = p \cdot \widetilde{B}(x, x_0) + E_{x_0}^s(x, p)\,, \tag{33}$$

where $E_{x_0}^s(x, p)$ is the corresponding scattered field. From (33) and the definition (22) we obtain

$$\mathcal{R}(E, E_z(\cdot, q, \gamma_b)) = I_1 + I_2\,,$$

where

$$I_1 = \int_{\partial\Omega}\Big[\Big(\nu \times \Big(p \cdot \widetilde{B}(x,x_0)\Big)\Big) \cdot \nabla \times E_z(x,q,\gamma_b) - (\nu \times E_z(x,q,\gamma_b)) \cdot \nabla \times \Big(p \cdot \widetilde{B}(x,x_0)\Big)\Big]\, ds(x)$$
$$- 2\beta_b\gamma_b^2 \int_{\partial\Omega}\Big(\nu \times \Big(p \cdot \widetilde{B}(x,x_0)\Big)\Big) \cdot E_z(x,q,\gamma_b)\, ds(x)\,,$$

$$I_2 = \int_{\partial\Omega}\big[(\nu \times E^s_{x_0}(x,p)) \cdot \nabla \times E_z(x,q,\gamma_b) - (\nu \times E_z(x,q,\gamma_b)) \cdot \nabla \times E^s_{x_0}(x,p)\big]\, ds(x)$$
$$- 2\beta_b\gamma_b^2 \int_{\partial\Omega}(\nu \times E^s_{x_0}(x,p)) \cdot E_z(x,q,\gamma_b)\, ds(x)\,,$$

For $z \in \Omega\backslash\overline{D}$, the function $E_z(x,q,\gamma_b)$ is the fundamental solution of

$$\nabla \times \nabla \times E - 2\beta_b\gamma_b^2 \nabla \times E - \gamma_b^2 E = 0 \tag{34}$$

and $p \cdot \widetilde{B}(x,x_0)$, $x \in \Omega\backslash\overline{D}$, is a a solution of (34). Hence, I_1 is an integral representation Stratton-Chu type in chiral media (10) for $-p \cdot \widetilde{B}(z,x_0)$, $z \in \Omega\backslash\overline{D}$. By making use of the reciprocity properties [6]

$$\widetilde{B}(x,x_0) = \Big[\widetilde{B}(x_0,x)\Big]^{\top},\ \nabla_x \times \widetilde{B}(x,x_0) = \Big[\nabla_{x_0} \times \widetilde{B}(x_0,x)\Big]^{\top},$$

where $\top$ denotes transposition, we conclude that the background dyadic Green's function solves (34) with respect to x_0. Hence, $E^s_{x_0}(x,p)$ satisfies the same equation with respect to x_0. Therefore, the integral I_2 gives a solution $W(x_0)$ of (34). Let $\mathcal{E}_{g_z^\epsilon}$ be a chiral electric Herglotz functions such that

$$||\mathcal{R}(E,\mathcal{E}_{g_z^\epsilon}) - \mathcal{R}(E,E_z(\cdot,q,\gamma_b))||_{L^2(\Lambda)} < \epsilon\,.$$

From the definition (22) and the boundary conditions (7) and (8), we obtain

$$\mathcal{R}(E,\mathcal{E}_{g_z^\epsilon}) = -\int_{\Gamma_D}(\nu \times \mathcal{E}_{g_z^\epsilon}) \cdot \nabla \times E\, ds$$
$$- \int_{\Gamma_I} E \cdot \left[\nu \times \nabla \times \mathcal{E}_{g_z^\epsilon} - i\frac{\gamma_b^2\lambda}{k_b}(\nu \times \mathcal{E}_{g_z^\epsilon}) \times \nu - \beta_b\gamma_b^2(\nu \times \mathcal{E}_{g_z^\epsilon})\right] ds\,.$$

Therefore

$$\mathcal{R}(E,\mathcal{E}_{g_z^\epsilon}) - \mathcal{R}(E,E_z(\cdot,q,\gamma_b)) = -\int_{\Gamma_D}(\nu \times \mathcal{E}_{g_z^\epsilon}) \cdot \nabla \times E\, ds$$
$$- \int_{\Gamma_I} E \cdot \left[\nu \times \nabla \times \mathcal{E}_{g_z^\epsilon} - i\frac{\gamma_b^2\lambda}{k_b}(\nu \times \mathcal{E}_{g_z^\epsilon}) \times \nu - \beta_b\gamma_b^2(\nu \times \mathcal{E}_{g_z^\epsilon})\right] ds - W(x_0) + p \cdot \widetilde{B}(x,x_0)\,. \tag{35}$$

We assume that $||\mathcal{E}_{g_z^\epsilon}||_{X(D,\Gamma_I)} < c$, with c constant, positive and independent of ϵ. Applying the trace theorem, we take the trace of $\mathcal{E}_{g_z^\epsilon}$ also bounded, with respect to the corresponding norms. Therefore, there exists a weakly convergent subfamily converging to a function $V \in X(D,\Gamma_I)$ as $\epsilon \to 0$. For $x_0 \in \Lambda$, we set:

$$U(x_0) = -\int_{\Gamma_D}(\nu \times V) \cdot \nabla \times E_{x_0}(\cdot,p)\, ds$$
$$- \int_{\Gamma_I} E \cdot \left[\nu \times \nabla \times V - i\frac{\gamma_b^2\lambda}{k_b}(\nu \times V) \times \nu - \beta\gamma_b^2(\nu \times V)\right] ds\,. \tag{36}$$

From (35) and (36), we obtain:

$$U(x_0) = W(x_0) + p \cdot \widetilde{B}(z,x_0),\ x_0 \in \Lambda\,. \tag{37}$$

Taking into account that the functions $U(x_0)$ and $W(x_0)$ are radiating solutions of (34) and using the unique continuation principle, we conclude that (37) holds true in $\mathbb{R}^3\backslash(\overline{D}\cup\{z\})$. If we now let $x_0 \to z$, then we arrive at a contradiction. □

Remark 1. *The determination of the boundary ∂D of the scatterer is based on the integral Equation (26), which contains chiral Herglotz functions in $\mathbb{H}(\Omega)$. In particular, if $\mathcal{E}_{g_z^\epsilon}$ is a solution of (26), then the boundary ∂D of the scatterer is reconstructed from points z, with $\lim_{\epsilon\to 0}||g_z^\epsilon||_{T^2_{LR}(S^2)} = \infty$. It is obvious that the boundary ∂D cannot be found from the $\lim_{\epsilon\to 0}||\mathcal{E}_{g_z^\epsilon}||_{X(D,\Gamma_I)} = \infty$ since the corresponding norm is defined on the unknown scatterer D. Alternatively, one can use instead of the chiral Herglotz functions appropriate potentials [3,10].*

5. The Determination of the Surface Impedance

Finally, after determining D, we will establish an expression for the surface impedance λ. In particular, we prove the following theorem.

Theorem 3. *Let E^z be the solution of (15)–(17) for a fix point $z \in D$. Then, the surface impedance λ is given by*

$$\lambda = \frac{k_b}{2\gamma_b^2}\,\frac{Im(q\cdot E^z(z)) + I_z(\Omega,q,\gamma_b)}{\int_{\partial D}|\nu\times(E^z - E_z(\cdot,q,\gamma_b))|^2 ds}, \tag{38}$$

where the integral

$$I_z(\Omega,q,\gamma_b) = -i\int_{\partial\Omega}\Big[(\nu\times E_z(\cdot,q,\gamma_b))\cdot\nabla\times\overline{E_z(\cdot,q,\gamma_b)} - (\nu\times\overline{E_z(\cdot,q,\gamma_b)})\cdot\nabla\times E_z(\cdot,q,\gamma_b)\Big]ds$$
$$+\,2i\beta_b\gamma_b^2\int_{\partial\Omega}(\nu\times E_z(\cdot,q,\gamma_b))\cdot\overline{E_z(\cdot,q,\gamma_b)}\,ds$$

is depended on z,Ω and q.

Proof. For a fix point $z \in D$, we consider the unique solution E^z of the interior mixed boundary value problem (15)–(17). We define the function:

$$U^z(x) = E^z(x) - E_z(x,q,\gamma_b),\ x\in D$$

and we evaluate the integral:

$$I = \int_{\partial D}[(\nu\times U^z)\cdot\nabla\times\overline{U^z} - (\nu\times\overline{U^z})\cdot\nabla\times U^z]ds - 2\beta_b\gamma_b^2\int_{\partial D}(\nu\times U^z)\cdot\overline{U^z}ds\,.$$

Taking into account the boundary conditions

$$\nu\times U^z = 0 \text{ on } \Gamma_D\,,$$
$$\nu\times\nabla\times U^z = i\frac{\gamma_b^2}{k_b}\lambda(\nu\times U^z)\times\nu + \beta_b\gamma_b^2\nu\times U^z \text{ on } \Gamma_I\,,$$

we have that

$$I = 2i\frac{\gamma_b^2\lambda}{k_b}\int_{\Gamma_I}|\nu\times U^z|^2 ds\,.$$

Furthermore, in view of the bilinearity of the integral I, we have

$$I = I_1 + I_2 + I_3 + I_4\,, \tag{39}$$

where

$$I_1 = \int_{\partial D} \left[(\nu \times E^z) \cdot \nabla \times \overline{E^z} - (\nu \times \overline{E^z}) \cdot \nabla \times E^z \right] ds$$
$$- 2\beta_b \gamma_b^2 \int_{\partial D} (\nu \times E^z) \cdot \overline{E^z}\, ds$$
$$I_2 = - \int_{\partial D} \left[(\nu \times E^z) \cdot \nabla \times \overline{E_z(\cdot, q, \gamma_b)} - (\nu \times \overline{E_z(\cdot, q, \gamma_b)}) \cdot \nabla \times E^z \right] ds$$
$$+ 2\beta_b \gamma_b^2 \int_{\partial D} (\nu \times E^z) \cdot \overline{E_z(\cdot, q, \gamma_b)}\, ds$$
$$I_3 = - \int_{\partial D} \left[(\nu \times E_z(\cdot, q, \gamma_b)) \cdot \nabla \times \overline{E^z} - (\nu \times \overline{E^z}) \cdot \nabla \times E_z(\cdot, q, \gamma_b) \right] ds$$
$$+ 2\beta_b \gamma_b^2 \int_{\partial D} (\nu \times E_z(\cdot, q, \gamma_b)) \cdot \overline{E^z}\, ds$$
$$I_4 = \int_{\partial D} \left[(\nu \times E_z(\cdot, q, \gamma_b)) \cdot \nabla \times \overline{E_z(\cdot, q, \gamma_b)} - (\nu \times \overline{E_z(\cdot, q, \gamma_b)}) \cdot \nabla \times E_z(\cdot, q, \gamma_b) \right] ds$$
$$- 2\beta_b \gamma_b^2 \int_{\partial D} (\nu \times E_z(\cdot, q, \gamma_b)) \cdot \overline{E_z(\cdot, q, \gamma_b)}\, ds$$

For the evaluation of I_1, we apply the second vector Green's theorem for the first integral and Gauss' theorem for the second integral for the functions E^z and $\overline{E^z}$ in D and taking into account that $E^z, \overline{E^z}$ are solutions of (15) we get $I_1 = 0$. A similar application in $\Omega \backslash \overline{D}$ for $E_z(\cdot, q, \gamma_b)$ and $\overline{E_z(\cdot, q, \gamma_b)}$ gives

$$I_4 = \int_{\partial \Omega} \left[(\nu \times E_z(\cdot, q, \gamma_b)) \cdot \nabla \times \overline{E_z(\cdot, q, \gamma_b)} - (\nu \times \overline{E_z(\cdot, q, \gamma_b)}) \cdot \nabla \times E_z(\cdot, q, \gamma_b) \right] ds$$
$$- 2\beta_b \gamma_b^2 \int_{\partial \Omega} (\nu \times E_z(\cdot, q, \gamma_b)) \cdot \overline{E_z(\cdot, q, \gamma_b)}\, ds\,.$$

Finally, using the representation (10) with $E_z = q \cdot \widetilde{B}(\cdot, z)$ we have that $I_2 = -q \cdot E^z$ and $I_3 = q \cdot \overline{E^z}$. Substituting the values of the integrals I_1 to I_4 in (39), we obtain (38). □

6. Conclusions

In this paper, the reciprocity gap functional method has been employed to reconstruct scatterers with mixed boundary conditions, embedded in a piecewise chiral medium. The importance of this method lies in the fact that we avoid the need to compute Green's function of the background medium. In the basic integral Equation (26) of the method, we have used the chiral Herglotz wave functions, which form a dense set of solutions of (3). The solution g of this equation has been employed to determine the surface impedance. If the chirality measures β_0 and β_1 become zero, then the chirality reciprocity gap functional coincides with the corresponding functional in achiral media. In the future, the present method should be extended to solve inverse transmission problems in chiral media.

Funding: This research received no external funding.

Conflicts of Interest: The author declares no conflict of interest.

Dedication: This paper is dedicated to the inspired mathematician Constantin M. Petridi, who has devoted his life to Mathematics.

References

1. Ammari, H.; Nédélec, J.C. Time-harmonic electromagnetic fields in thin chiral surved layeres. *SIAM J. Math. Anal.* **1998**, *29*, 395–423. [CrossRef]
2. Athanasiadis, C.; Kardasi, E. Beltrami Herglotz functions for electromagnetic scattering theory in chiral media. *Appl. Anal.* **2005**, *84*, 145–163. [CrossRef]
3. Athanasiadis, C.; Costakis, G.; Stratis, I.G. Electromagnetic scattering by a homogeneous chiral obstacle in a chiral environment. *IMA J. Appl. Math.* **2000**, *64*, 245–258. [CrossRef]

4. Athanasiadis, C.E.; Sevroglou, V.I.; Skourogiannis, K.I. The inverse electromagnetic scattering problem by a mixed impedance screen in chiral media. *Inverse Probl. Imaging* **2015**, *9*, 951–970. [CrossRef]
5. Lakhtakia, A.; Varadan, V.K.; Varadan, V.V. Time-harmonic electromagnetic fields in chiral media. In *Lecture Notes in Physics*; No 335; Springer: Berlin, Germany,1989.
6. Lakhtakia, A. *Beltrami Fields in Chiral Media*; World Scientific: Singapore, 1994.
7. Arens, T.; Hagemann, F.; Hettlich, F.; Kirsch, A. The definition and measurement of electromagnetic chirality. *Math. Methods Appl. Sci.* **2018**, *41*, 559–572. [CrossRef]
8. Wang, Z.; Cheng, F.; Winsor, T.; Liu, Y. Optical Chiral Metamaterials: a Review of the Fundamentals, Fabrication Methods and Applications. *Nanotechnology* **2016**, *27*, 20. [CrossRef]
9. Athanasiadis, C.E.; Sevroglou, V.I.; Skourogiannis, K.I. The direct electromagnetic scattering problem by a mixed impedance screen in chiral media. *Appl. Anal.* **2012**, *91*, 2083–2093. [CrossRef]
10. Cakoni, F.; Colton, D. *Qualitative Methods in Inverse Elctromagnetic Scattering Theory*; Springer: Berlin, Germany, 2005.
11. Athanasiadis, C.; Athanasiadou, E.; Kikeri, E. The reciprocity gap operator for electromagnetic scattering in chiral media. Submitted.
12. Cakoni, F.; Colton, D.; Monk, P. *The Linear Sampling Method in Inverse Electromagnetic Scattering*; SIAM Society for Industrial and Applied Mathematics: Philadelphia, PA, USA, 2011.
13. Colton, D.; Haddar, H. An application of the reciprocity gap functional to inverse scattering theory. *Inverse Probl.* **2005**, *21*, 383–398. [CrossRef]
14. Cakoni, F.; Fares, M.; Haddar, H. Analysis of two linear sampling methods applied to electromagnetic imaging of buried objects. *Inverse Probl.* **2006**, *22*, 845–867. [CrossRef]
15. Athanasiadis, C.E.; Natroshvili, D.; Sevroglou, V.; Stratis, I.G. An application of the reciprocity gap functional to inverse mixed impedance problems in elasticity. *Inverse Probl.* **2010**, *26*, 085011. [CrossRef]
16. Cakoni, F.; Colton, D. Target identification of buried coated objects. *Comput. Appl. Math.* **2006**, *25*, 269–288.
17. Cakoni, F.; Haddar, H. Identification of partially coated anisotropic buried objects using electromagnetic Cauchy data. *J. Integral Equ. Appl.* **2007**, *19*, 359–389. [CrossRef]
18. Sun, Y.; Guo, Y.; Ma, F. The reciprocity gap functional method for the inverse scattering problem for cavities. *Appl. Anal.* **2016**, *95*, 1327–1346. [CrossRef]
19. Zeng, F.; Liu, X.; Sun, J.; Xu, L. Reciprocity gap method for an interior inverse scattering problem. *J. Inverse Ill-Posed Probl.* **2017**, *25*, 57–68. [CrossRef]
20. Takida, Y.; Koyama, S.; Ueno, N.; Saruwatari, H. Reciprocity gap functional in spherical harmonic domain for gridless sound field decomposition. *Signal Process.* **2020**, *169*, 107383 . [CrossRef]
21. Charnley, M.; Wood, A. Object identification in Radar imaging via the reciprocity gap method. *Radio Sci.* **2020**, *55*, e2019RS006946. [CrossRef]
22. Di Cristo, M.; Milan, G. Reconstruction of inclusions in electrical conductors. *IMA J. Appl. Math.* **2020**, *85*, 933–950. [CrossRef]
23. Faucher, F.; Alessandrini, G.; Barucq, H.; de Hoop, M.V.; Gaburro, R.; Sincich, E. Full reciprocity-gap waveform inversion enabling sparse-source acquisition. *Geophysics* **2020**, 85, R461–R476. [CrossRef]
24. Ghanmi, A.; Mdimagh, R.; Saad, I.B. Identification of points sources via time fractional diffusion equation. *Filomat* **2018**, *32*, 6189–6201. [CrossRef]
25. Colton, D.; Kress, R. *Inverse Acoustic and Electromagnetic Scattering Theory*; Springer: New York, NY, USA, 1998.
26. Dassios, G.; Kleinman, R. *Low Frequency Scattering*; Oxford University Press, Clarenton Press: Oxford, UK, 2000.
27. Lindell, I.V.; Sihvola, A.H.; Tretyakov, S.A.; Viitanen, A.J. *Electromagnetic Waves in Chiral and Bi-isotropic Media*; Artech House: Boston, MA, USA, 1994.
28. Monk, F. *Finite Element Methods for Maxwell's Equations*; Oxford University Press: Oxford, UK, 2003.
29. Cakoni, F.; Colton, D.; Monk, P. The electromagnetic inverse scattering problem for partially coated Lipschitz domains. *Proc. R. Soc. Edinb.* **2004**, 134, 845–867. [CrossRef]

MDPI
St. Alban-Anlage 66
4052 Basel
Switzerland
Tel. +41 61 683 77 34
Fax +41 61 302 89 18
www.mdpi.com

Mathematics Editorial Office
E-mail: mathematics@mdpi.com
www.mdpi.com/journal/mathematics

www.ingramcontent.com/pod-product-compliance
Lightning Source LLC
LaVergne TN
LVHW070553100526
838202LV00012B/450
* 9 7 8 3 0 3 6 5 2 1 6 5 7 *